# INSIGHT GUIDES

*Created and Directed by Hans Höfer*

# MIAMI

Edited by Joann Biondi
Photography by Tony Arruza
Managing Editor: Martha Ellen Zenfell

Editorial Director: Brian Bell

*Houghton Mifflin*

APA PUBLICATIONS

*Höfer*

*Biondi*

**B**roached in a blind letter and conceived during a phone call halfway around the world, *IG: Miami* is a progeny of many born out of a labor of love. It is just one of the nearly 200 titles covered in the award-winning *Insight Guide* series, a unique collection of guidebooks founded in 1970 by **Hans Höfer**. The first title, covering the exotic island of Bali, was hailed as a breakthrough in the field of travel publishing.

For this book, the project editor, **Joann Biondi**, a former flight attendant turned professor of geography, wrote to the headquarters of Apa Publications in Singapore asking to become a part of the Insight team. She was attracted, she said, by the idea of provocatively written travel guides that successfully combine sharp, insightful writing with eye-catching photojournalism. Soon, the words were in the works.

Having lived in South Florida since 1975, Biondi began her journalism career at the *Miami Herald* and is now a freelance writer who specializes in people and places. After years of feeling guilty about admitting that she actually enjoyed living in such a hedonistic and crime-ridden place, she now argues that Miami is, in fact, the most interesting of American cities in which to live. In addition to the Miami Mystique chapter, she wrote several essays and short features that describe the city's idiosyncracies. Her savvy on the city aided her search for the best editorial talent in town to round out the rest. Biondi is now Insight's woman in South Florida, the sole author of a number of *Insight Pocket Guides*.

*Zenfell*

**T**o help guide her through this project on Miami was Apa's editor-in-chief of North American titles, **Martha Ellen Zenfell**. Hailing from the American South but now based in Apa's London office, Zenfell produced the Insight Guides to the Greek Islands, New York City and Bermuda as well as overseeing a series of American city guides. After a warm winter week in Miami, she was convinced it would make a "terrific book." Zenfell has had warm thoughts about the city ever since that first visit, putting them into practice by getting married in Miami Beach City Hall.

The bold, beautiful and sometimes brazen photos were taken by veteran Insight photographer **Tony Arruza**. Born in Cuba and now based in West Palm Beach, Arruza shot the Insight Guides to Barbados, Portugal and Lisbon. Although slightly hesitant at first about tackling another demanding Apa project, Arruza couldn't resist the chance to hit the streets of the city. From a joyous Easter mass in Little Haiti to a sultry *salsa* on Calle Ocho, he captured it all.

Bringing the personal and poignant story about his own long-term love affair with Miami Beach was the late **Isaac Bashevis Singer**. Born in Poland, Singer moved to the United States in 1935. He won the Nobel Prize for Literature in 1978 and was often quoted as saying that he loved living in Miami Beach because it is paradise, and paradise should have drugstores.

The history section of the book was written by the respected historian and Miami native **Arva Moore Parks**, author of *Miami: The Magic City* and *The Forgotten Frontier*.

The chapter on Miami's ethnic mix came from **Lisandro Perez**, Associate Professor of Anthropology and Sociology at Florida International University. Havana-born Perez has gained international acclaim for his writing on the Cuban population in the US.

A colleague at FIU, **Alex Stepick**, Associate Professor of Anthropology and Sociology, wrote the Places piece

*Arruza*

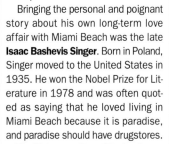

*Singer*

on Little Haiti. Stepick, recipient of a Margaret Mead Award, is recognized as one of the foremost scholars on the Haitian community in the United States. He and his family lived in Miami's Little Haiti for six years.

From the *Miami Herald*, Biondi recruited three solid journalists. **Geoffrey Tomb** has reported on South Florida for the *Herald* since 1978, along with contributing to several magazines and travel guides. He wrote the sections on the deep south and food. He is deeply devoted to South Florida strawberries. Writing the chapters on Miami's vice as virtue, the body culture and downtown Miami was **Patrick May**. He spent years traveling around the world with extended stays in Turkey, France, and Iran before starting his career in journalism; he now lives in Coral Gables with his wife and two daughters.

*May*

**Sandra Dibble**, who wrote the section on Little Havana, was a member of the *Herald*'s team that won a Pulitzer Prize for national reporting. For several years she has written extensively about Miami's Cuban, Nicaraguan and Haitian communities.

*Glass*

For the chapters on Coral Gables and Coconut Grove, Biondi called in former newspaper travel editor and guidebook author **Ian Glass**. A long-time Miamian who has lived through several of the city's metamorphoses, Glass says he has lived off and on in Coconut Grove for many years, but has yet to be able to afford to live in Coral Gables. "I came to Miami from London many years ago," he says, "and the contrast in lifestyles was overwhelming. Here was a boisterous, brash, unsophisticated city kicking up its heels, and I fell in love with its exuberance. After all this time, it still never gives me a dull moment."

**Alice Klement**, an ex-journalist, ex-

*Klement*

lawyer and ex-university professor, brought no fewer than 20 years of ex's to use in her sections on Miami festivals and Key Biscayne. Klement currently works as a writing coach and consultant. Her personal travel library, a legend at 650 volumes, includes dozens of dog-eared, well-read *Insight Guides*. Klement has also joined the Insight team, the author of two *Insight Pocket Guides*.

**Henry Green**, director of the Judaic Studies Program at the University of Miami, contributed the chapter on the Jewish community. Green has written numerous books and articles on contemporary Jewry and directs "Mosaic", a traveling cultural exhibit that traces the history of Jews in Florida.

Writing about Miami Beach was **Christina Cheakalos**, a former staff writer for both the *Miami Herald* and *New Times*, Miami's alternative weekly newspaper. For the chapter on the three sister cities, Biondi asked **Ivan A. Rodriguez**, architectural author and former director of the Dade County Historic Preservation Board.

*Hiller*

The creation of the daytrips section called for **Herb Hiller,** author of the *Guide to the Small and Historic Lodgings of Florida*. He serves on the national board of American Youth Hostels and loves to write about backroads travel, preferably by bicycle. Hiller is a strong advocate of the belief that "Florida, a state that is significantly dependent on tourism, should become more involved in preserving and promoting its historic districts and natural environment rather than relying on make-believe attractions that promote fantasy lifestyles."

Thanks, too, to the **Historical Museum of Southern Florida**; to **Jill Anderson** for flowing the book through various Macintosh computers, and to **Christopher Catling** and **Kate Owen** for the indexing and proof-reading.

# CONTENTS

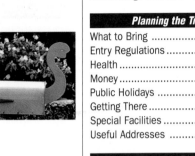

# THE MIAMI MYSTIQUE

It is young and vibrant, uninhibited, unafraid. It is sensual and warm, spicy and seductive – chock-full of forbidden fruits just ripe for the picking. Prim and proper Miami is not; the city abhors convention. Images of exotic women, fancy cars, illegal drugs and the threat of danger define its persona; and somewhere between their myth and reality lies the intriguing and inviting mystique of the city itself.

Deluged in recent years by journalists looking for and often finding something to write home about, Miami has been called the capital of Latin America, city of the future, paradise lost, paradise found – and, of course, the new Casablanca.

Situated just two degrees above the Tropic of Cancer, which slides across to the Sahara Desert, Miami is a subtropical city full of harsh white light and soft salty air. Umbrellas come in handy, but mostly for the sun. Late in the evenings, night-blooming jasmine and orange blossom petals fill the air with their sweet, sultry smells.

"Greater Miami," as it is often called, sits inside of Dade County and consists of 28 different municipalities. Its population is about two million – nearly half of whom speak Spanish as their native tongue. It sprawls over 2,000 sq. miles, including a 15-mile stretch of soft, sandy beaches where nudity is illegal, but rear-end revealing tongas and topless sun-bathing are tolerated by the older locals and enjoyed by some of the younger. Topographically, it is a one-dimensional experience; there are no hills.

The average yearly temperature is a mild 75°F. Although the National Weather Service insists the mercury has never hit 100°F in Miami "proper," the summers can sometimes get so steamy that the entire city feels afire. Hurricane season – the most easily identifiable "season" of the year except for the tourist months – brings an occasional threat. But more than likely it means a bathtub filled with beer, candles just in case, and a *cause célèbre* for a party.

Punctuated with pink houses and aquamarine waters, Miami is casual and clean, cosmopolitan and chic. In winter, women flaunt their tanned bare legs atop high-heeled shoes from underneath their crisp linen dresses. The look is of a ripe mango: heavy on the makeup with cleavage in full bloom. For men, a $5,000 gold watch and "Guayabera" shirt are more in vogue than a suit and tie.

If it were an automobile, Miami would be a sleek, white convertible cruising to catch a sunrise at the beach after a night on the town. If it were a drink, it would be 100-proof dark rum with a squeeze of lime and a spoonful of sugar. Travelers, who swarm to the city by the millions each year, often become addicted to its pacifying ways.

Residents from around the state refer to it as that dreadful place "down there." Not like the good-old-boys to the north or the Waspy snowbirds to the west. The town is too hot-tempered and pretentious, flamboyant and fast.

For America, Miami means more than just a bustling Sun Belt baby; it is the new Ellis Island, an immigrant's dream. It hosts a ragtag collection of characters – Cubans, Colombians, Nicaraguans, Venezuelans, Peruvians, Bahamians, Jamaicans, Haitians. Young Turks and old Jews.

The "newest" of immigrants hawk bags of limes to motorists in traffic and in a few months can "move up" to selling carnations from a push-cart. It is a wide-open land of endless possibilities where a Cuban who rafted to its shores can, in 10 years, own a cafeteria, car lot and Cadillac. In Miami, "old money" means a mere generation.

It has become the most "foreign" of US cities, full of dark eyes and heavy accents. It feels like a first cousin to the Caribbean, a total stranger to the state of Montana. It sounds like *merengue*, conga, reggae and calypso. *Salsa* seems an integral part of the collective local unconscious.

Billboards talk to passers-by in Spanish, as do radio stations, newspapers and many restaurant menus. Across America, Hispanics represent less than 10 percent of the total population; in Miami, the figure is almost 50. Its multi-cultural identity is evident in everyday life. When an invitation to a party says dinner at 8pm, sensitive to their city's ethnic possibilities, guests phone ahead to ask: Latin time (two hours later) or American time (promptly at 8 o'clock).

While in recent years Miami has undergone a renaissance that has included a generous sprinkling of big-city sophistication, some of its old tourist-town mentality still remains. Not far from the chi-chi fashion boutiques, tawdry souvenir shops sell rubber alligators, canned sunshine and orange perfume. Throughout the city, this contrast is constant.

Inside pastel-painted apartments, yuppies indulge in Art Deco decadence by turning up the air-conditioning to light their fireplaces. On the streets, bag ladies scrounge for food as down-and-out young men do a window-washing dance while begging for a dollar. A juxtaposition of affluence and survival, hedonism and hardships – the stuff this city is made of. Welcome to the Miami mystique.

**Right**, pastel-painted Deco detail.

Of Florida.

For 10,000 years people have been coming to South Florida. The early Indians, who may have migrated from Alaska and Siberia seeking the sun, lived along the river banks in a tropical Garden of Eden. Lacking metal, they fashioned their tools from sea shells. A Spanish adventurer was the first to intrude on their simple way of life.

Juan Ponce de Leon traveled the world in search of glory. What he hoped to discover, as he sailed north from Puerto Rico on March 3, 1513, was an island called Bimini and its fabled spring that gave eternal youth. What he found instead was the tip of a huge new continent, which he named "Pascua florida." Three months after he landed somewhere between today's St Augustine and Jacksonville, Ponce de Leon sailed into Biscayne Bay, noting in his journal that he had reached Tequesta.

For the next half-century, Spaniards tried unsuccessfully to conquer this unruly peninsula. They were no match for the native people – or for an even fiercer enemy, the ubiquitous mosquito. Challenged by the French, who in 1562 established an outpost near present-day Jacksonville named Ft Caroline, Spain's King Philip II sent Pedro Menendez de Aviles as governor to secure Florida. By 1565, Menendez had routed the French and founded St Augustine, the first permanent settlement in what is now the United States.

A Jesuit mission at Tequesta flourished briefly, then failed. It was reopened, and failed again. However, the Spaniards and the native Indians had formed an alliance that, over the years, resulted in friendly treatment for Spanish ships and shipwrecked sailors who landed there.

Slowly, Spain began to cede to England its claim to supremacy in the New World. As the English took over Creek Indian land, renegade Creeks crossed over the border into Spanish Florida, plundering and burning as

they came. The native Indians, who were now Spanish allies, fled before them. The Spanish, unhappy about the possibility of a Florida populated by hostile Creeks, decided to make another attempt to settle in South Florida, sending Father Joseph Maria Monaco and Father Joseph Xavier de Alana to Tequesta in the summer of 1743. They established a settlement, which consisted of a triangular fort with mortared corners, and called it "Pueblo de Santa Maria de Loreto"

– Miami's second name. By this time the Indians had grown unfriendly, however, and the settlement did not flourish; the king ultimately ordered the mission to be abandoned.

**A British colony:** In 1763 the Treaty of Paris, which ended the Seven Years' War (the "French and Indian War" to Americans), made Florida a British colony after two centuries of Spanish rule. When the Spanish left South Florida, the remaining Indians followed them to Cuba. Britain thus became the proud owner of a new land with very few inhabitants. The British were quick to map the area (the entire east coast of Florida was surveyed between 1765 and 1771) and to change the Spanish names to English ones. With the stroke of a pen, Biscayne Bay became "Sandwich Gulf."

During the 20 years of the British period there were several grand plans to settle South Florida, "the most precious jewel of His Majesty's American dominion," but none of them succeeded. Britain shocked the Tories, who had poured into Florida during the American Revolution, with the announcement that it would swap Florida for the Bahamas, which Spain had captured during the war. Many Loyalists fled again, this time to the Bahamas, as Spain took control and the

– just one point of contention between the US and Spain. By 1819, the Spanish were ready to cut their losses on their unsuccessful Florida adventure. By 1821, the Stars and Stripes fluttered over America's most tropical territory.

The US confirmed the Egan family's land claim, with additional grants, plus land for Polly and Jonathan Lewis along the banks of the bay and the river that from this time on was called the "Miami." Mary Ann Davis received title to 175 acres on Key Biscayne which she had bought from Pedro Fornells. In all, just a little over 3,000 acres in all of South Florida was privately owned. A light-

Photo. only, Copyright 1904 by the Rotograph Co.
G 15230  Old Fort Dallas, Miami, Fla.

second Spanish period (1784–1821) began.

Miami's first two landowners date from this time, when Pedro Fornells was granted 175 acres on "Cayo Biscaino" (today's Key Biscayne) and John Egan received 100 acres on the north bank of the *Rio nombrado de aqua dulze*" (now the Miami River). People called the small oasis of "civilization" in South Florida the "Cape Florida Settlement." Although it was officially Spanish, South Florida was in reality almost part of the Bahama Islands, linked through trade and sentiment.

Florida became a haven for runaway slaves

house at Cape Florida, erected by Boston builder Samuel Lincoln, began operating in December, 1825. Its light was so ineffective that sailors complained that they'd "go ashore looking for it."

Richard Fitzpatrick, who dreamed of re-creating his South Carolina plantation here, bought, in the 1830s, all the mainland land grants. Fitzpatrick was the first to campaign for the developing of the Miami area. But Indian troubles interfered.

**Seminole wars:** In Florida, as in the rest of the country, the history of settlers and Indians was one of shattered promises and broken treaties. Land-hungry white men planned to send the Indians to reservations in the West, but a steadfast group of Seminoles refused to go.

What began with the "Dade Massacre" in December 1835, when Major Francis Langhorne Dade (for whom the newly formed Dade County was named) and 109 of his men died during a bloody Seminole attack, did not end until 1857. The US responded by sending in the troops, who erected Fort Dallas as a defensive outpost on the north bank of the Miami River.

Among the many who died during the years of the three Seminole Wars was the

Indian problems took their toll, and by 1860 Miami, with its handful of inhabitants, had disappeared from public records.

The Civil War that tore the nation apart barely touched Miami. Florida joined the Confederacy, but Key West remained in Federal control. The monthly mailboat, Miami's link with the outside world, was suspended and South Florida sat out the war in complete isolation.

William H. Gleason was a carpetbagger who came to Miami in 1866, liked what he saw, and decided to keep it for himself. He was responsible for foiling a plan to settle former slaves in South Florida under the

noted New York horticulturalist Henry Perrine, who managed to save his wife and children before he was killed by Seminoles attacking Indian Key in August, 1840. Fitzpatrick sold his land for $16,000 to his nephew, William H. English. Within a year of his arrival in 1842, English had settled the village of Miami on the river's south bank. He was the first to call the area "Miami."

The US Coastal Survey made the first map of the new town in 1849. But continuing

**Left**, Fort Dallas near the Miami River. **Above**, early settlers at Kirk Munroe's home.

1862 Homestead Act (which granted 160 acres of land free to any citizen who would live on it for five years and improve it). Gleason maintained almost total control of the area for many years, to the point that when a land dispute forced him to leave the Miami River area he took Miami with him – that is, the Miami post office, whose name he changed to "Biscayne."

**Early snowbirds:** Settlers were beginning to come into the area. Long-time resident Edmund Beasley filed a claim for 160 acres of what is now Coconut Grove in 1868. Two years later William B. Brickell and Ephraim

T. Sturtevant arrived from Cleveland, Ohio. Brickell bought land and built a home and trading post on the bank of the Miami River. Sturtevant acquired land in Biscayne, where his daughter, Julia Tuttle, visited him as early as 1875.

In 1873 settlers opened a post office in the bayfront community called "Coconut Grove." Government engineers completed Fowey Rock lighthouse in 1878, and the old Cape Florida Light was darkened.

As would be the case for years to come, Miami's mild winters attracted northern visitors, the first of the tourists. Among them was Ralph M. Munroe of Staten Island, who

stayed with his friends Charles and Isabella Peacock at the Bay View House (which overlooked the bay from the bluff in what is today Peacock Park), the first lodging place in the area.

**Club for women:** Coconut Grove became a community of "firsts" as civilized institutions began to pop up on the Florida frontier. Ralph and Kirk Munroe (no relation) founded the Biscayne Bay Yacht Club in 1887. A school was opened the next year, and in 1891 Ralph Munroe donated a parcel of his land so that the Union Chapel (later to become Plymouth Congregational Church) could be built.

That same year schoolteacher Flora McFarlane, the area's first woman homesteader, organized the Housekeepers Club for women, out of which the Pine Needles Club for young girls would come, and the area's first library on the second floor of Charles Peacock's store.

The future city of Miami, however, was still only an idea – an idea in the mind of a recently widowed Cleveland matron named Julia Sturtevant Tuttle. She decided to start a new life for herself in Florida, not on her late father's homestead, but on the "best" piece of property available, on the north bank of the Miami River. She arrived with her 23-year-old daughter and 21-year-old son on November 13, 1891, and immediately began to plan her city.

She had hoped that Henry Plant, the railroad magnate whose line had reached as far south as Tampa in 1893, would extend his train to tiny Miami. In this she was disappointed. But another railroad man, Henry M. Flagler, who made his first millions in Standard Oil with John D. Rockefeller, had recently begun to fall in love with Florida. His railroad inched southward from St Augustine, reaching Palm Beach by 1893. Still, he proclaimed that he wasn't interested in bringing it the last 66 miles to Mrs Tuttle's doorstep. That, however, was before the winter of 1894–95.

A killer freeze hit Florida that winter, destroying most of the area's valuable citrus crops. But in semi-tropical Miami, orange blossoms still bloomed. Mrs Tuttle invited James Ingraham, Flagler's lieutenant, to come and see for himself. He did, and was impressed. When Mrs. Tuttle offered Flagler half of her land (300 acres), plus some of Brickell's, the deal was made. The railroad was coming.

The new era, pulled by a locomotive and greeted wildly by the whole populace (all 300 residents), arrived on April 15, 1896. The clanging of the engine's bell decisively marked the end of Miami's days as a sleepy frontier town.

**Left**, Julia Sturtevant Tuttle, one of Miami's most aggressive pioneers. **Right**, Flagler's famous railroad finally clamors into town.

34

Important events followed each other with dizzying speed after Flagler's famous railroad came to town. Within a month the first newspaper, the *Miami Metropolis,* rolled off the press. Local citizens voted to incorporate the city (which was never, officially, a town) on July 28 and elected Flagler's man, John B. Reilly, as mayor. The city fathers laid out streets (rather badly) and founded churches and schools. Then, on Christmas morning, a fire started in Brady's grocery store at what is today Miami Avenue and S.W. Second Street and destroyed 28 buildings, wiping out almost the entire business district.

Miami citizens, undaunted by this first crisis, set about the task of rebuilding their downtown district. Just three weeks later they had a reason to celebrate when Flagler's enormous, elegant Royal Palm Hotel opened with a gala dinner.

The city, which had already begun to proclaim itself "America's sun porch" to potential tourists, hosted far different visitors during the scorching summer of 1898. They were American troops on their way to Cuba to fight the Spanish after the sinking of the battleship *Maine* in the harbor of Havana. But 7,000 bored soldiers plus humidity plus swarms of mosquitoes do not equal peace, quiet, and happiness. As one frustrated soldier put it: "If I owned both Miami and Hell, I'd rent out Miami and live in Hell." Fortunately, the war was brief and the troops were soon on their way.

**Early growth:** In the early years of the 20th century Miami began a modest boom. The Tatum brothers built a toll bridge across the river at Flagler Street and began developing the Riverside subdivision. A new business district, which was growing rapidly, included Seybold's ice-cream parlor, two rival Burdines department stores, banks, saloons, moving picture theaters and a new newspaper, the *Miami Evening Record,* edited by Frank M. Stoneman.

**Left**, an early promotional map. **Right**, first of the many Miami bathing beauties.

Until 1909 what there was of Miami's downtown area and outlying communities such as Coconut Grove and Larkins (today's South Miami) was built on the narrow, 4-mile-wide coastal ridge sandwiched between the Atlantic Ocean to the east and the Everglades to the west which began at today's N.W. 27th Avenue. Governor Napoleon Bonaparte Broward campaigned on a promise of draining Florida's vast wetlands to create an "Empire of the swampy Ever-

Waiting for you in Miami, Fla.

glades." As part of the plan, government engineers dug the Miami Canal to facilitate drainage in the Everglades .

They also dug "Government Cut," which would later become the Port of Miami, across the lower end of the future Miami Beach, improving the access to Miami's harbor and in the process creating Fisher Island. Florida began its infamous tradition of selling wetlands and, as developers dreamed of profits from land where there was none before, dredges began to hum in the wilderness west of Miami. (It was not until 1916 that the Florida Federation of Women's Clubs, concerned about preserving the Everglades, acquired 4,000 acres, which they called Royal Palm State Park. It would become the nucleus of the wildlife-rich Everglades National Park.)

Meanwhile, Flagler's goal of extending his railroad to Key West (which some called "Flagler's Folly") was nearing fruition. When the work began in 1905 the railroad extended to Detroit (Florida City), where it opened up lucrative northern markets for South Dade farmers. Within three years the construction crews reached the half-way point of the project and embarked on their greatest challenge yet: building "the great one," the 7-

Miami had a way of attracting visionaries. One was John Collins, a New Jersey Quaker who became sole owner of Ocean Beach in 1909. He borrowed money and began building a bridge (called, not surprisingly, "Collins' Folly") that would connect Miami with the beach. But half-way through, his money ran out. Fortunately, this man with land and a grand dream met up with a man with hard cash: Carl Graham Fisher, who had made his mint with Prest-O-Lite, the first really bright automobile headlight. Fisher loaned Collins $50,000 to finish his bridge; in return, Collins gave Fisher a piece of his land on the island that would become Miami Beach.

mile-long bridge which would begin just below Knight's Key.

William J. Krome, who was in command of the latter part of the construction, aimed for the impossible: to have the railroad completed a full year ahead of schedule, in time for Flagler's 82nd birthday. He succeeded. The *Extension Special* train, filled with notables, politicians, and pulling Flagler's own car, the *Rambler*, arrived in Key West on January 22, 1912. The old man, greeted by 10,000 cheering people, declared: "We did it. Now I can die in peace." Sixteen months later he did just that.

On June 12, 1913, a long line of motor cars rattled over the wooden planks of Collins' bridge. When they got to Bull Island (now Belle Isle), where the bridge temporarily ended, the drivers hopped out, lifted their lightweight automobiles, turned them around, and headed back to the mainland. That same summer workmen leveled the beach's native mangroves which allowed Fisher's dredge to go to work, throwing up sand and shells from the bay bottom night and day to create his island.

**Miami Beach:** In 1915 the citizens of Miami Beach voted to incorporate and elected J.N.

Lummus their first mayor. Ocean Beach, on the south end of the island, became a "people's playground." It boasted several casinos (swimming pool and cabana complexes) as well as a restaurant that Joe and Jennie Weiss ran out of their home, which would later become Joe's Stone Crab. Farther north, Fisher envisioned an exclusive playground for the wealthy, complete with golf, tennis and polo.

Back in Miami, Ev Sewell, a pioneer merchant, had become the city's first great promoter. His nationwide advertising campaign lured thousands, including the rich and famous, many of whom built homes on Brick-

aviation school. In October 1917 the American government purchased land in Coconut Grove and began building Dinner Key Naval Air Station. By the war's end, 128 seaplanes were based there, filling Miami's once peaceful skies with noise.

**Roaring Twenties:** Nowhere did the roaring 1920s roar louder than in Miami. The war was barely over when developers began to carve up orange groves and tomato patches into subdivisions. The city, faced with a nightmarish jumble of street names and numbers, adopted a new naming system, the Chaille Plan, in 1921. Avenue D became Miami Avenue, 12th Street turned into Flagler

Girls Fishing in Biscayne Bay, Bayfront Park, Miami, Florida

ell Avenue or Coconut Grove's "Millionaires' Row." The most lavish of these was Vizcaya, a European-style palace surrounded by formal gardens constructed by James Deering of International Harvester, which was finished in 1916.

Sewell had convinced Glenn Curtiss, a pioneer in the aviation industry and a pilot himself, to open a flying school in Miami. After Congress declared war in April 1917, Sewell began promoting the idea of a naval

**Left**, Miami Flying School instructors. **Above**, postcards from paradise – come on down.

Street, and streets and avenues were renumbered outward from their intersection. The post office was temporarily happy.

Between 1920 and 1923 the population doubled. City fathers moved forward with a grand plan for "modernization," which included a large new bayfront park and a skyscraper courthouse. Downtown parking became a disaster; downtown land became a gold mine.

But the real boom was yet to come. By 1925 the frenzy, fueled by Miami's superb climate and huge amount of available land, was well out of control. The list of new subdivisions grew long: Hialeah, Biltmore, Melrose Gardens, Flagler Manor, Miami Shores, Miami Beach, plus Central Miami and dozens of others.

One stands out: George Merrick's "Coral Gables, Miami's Master Suburb," a totally planned community of Mediterranean homes, graceful plazas and wide boulevards. Unlike many developers, Merrick delivered on his promises. He made enormous profits and poured them back into his suburb. He spent millions on advertising, increasing the nation's interest in booming Miami. He hired silver-tongued orator William Jennings Bryan for $100,000 to make promotional

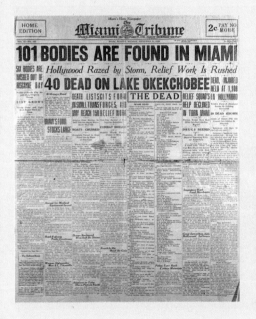

speeches at Coral Gables' Venetian Pool on DeSoto Boulevard. Few structures exemplified the flamboyance of the period better than this architectural bit of whimsy. Once a rock pit, the pool featured extravagant waterfalls, caves made of coral and landscaping on a grand scale.

The talk of the town – indeed all over Florida – was real estate. It seemed like everyone was making a bundle as land changed hands once, twice, many times a day at spiraling prices. "Binder boys," real estate salesmen who sold "binders" (10 percent deposits) on land, then resold them,

flocked to the state. But most of the profits were on paper.

With three replicas of Spain's Giralda Tower under construction (the Biltmore Hotel, the *Miami News* Tower and Miami Beach's Roney Plaza Hotel) and the University of Miami on the drawing board, the bottom began to fall out of the boom. In August 1925 the Florida East Coast Railway announced an embargo of all but essential freight so that it could repair its tracks, cutting off the supply of building materials via land. So developers turned to the sea, using anything that would float to transport their lumber and supplies. The flotilla was interrupted in January 1926 when the *Prinz Valdemar* overturned in the middle of Miami's shipping canal, closing the port for more than three weeks.

Anti-Florida campaigns in northern states hurt, too. Still, the Biltmore Hotel opened on January 16, 1926, and in February workmen began construction of the University of Miami. But the boom was clearly over. By midsummer even Coral Gables' previously excellent sales were slipping.

**The big one:** Few people paid much attention to the newspaper headlines on September 17, 1926, that warned of an impending tropical storm. They should have. They awoke in the middle of the night in a city without electricity and storm winds (measured at 128 miles an hour before the wind gauge blew away) screaming past their windows. At dawn the torrents seemed to have stopped and many people ran from their homes to survey the terrible destruction, not realizing that they were in the eye of the storm. The hurricane resumed, this time from the opposite direction, stranding thousands. More than 100 people died.

By the afternoon of September 18, when the brutal storm at last blew past, Miami was in chaos. The hurricane left houses smashed to pieces and business destroyed. Boats had been lifted out of the water and thrown on to dry land. Miami had been reeling before the hurricane. Afterwards, it was ruined.

**Left**, newspaper headlines tell the deadly story. **Right**, the city wiped out by a hurricane tries to recover amid the floods, destruction and debris.

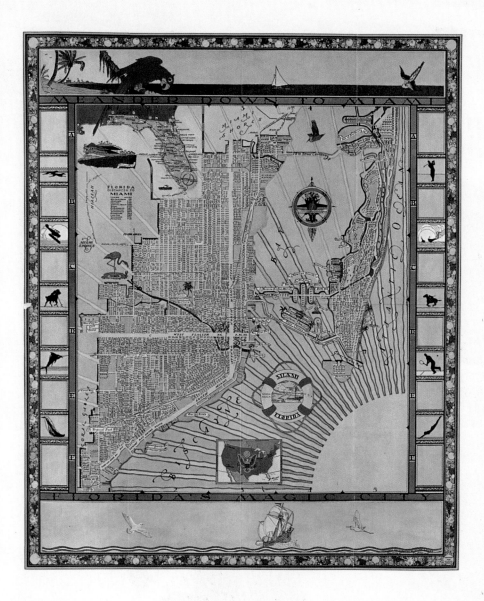

40

The national headlines that proclaimed "Miami is Wiped Out!" were correct – but only temporarily. The damage was great, but so was the spirit of the stricken city. Within a week Mayor Ed Romfh was already talking about Miami's comeback. University of Miami officials gave South Florida hope for the future when they opened their "cardboard college" on October 15, 1926. They had converted a bankrupt apartment hotel into classrooms with thin cardboard partitions. It was a start.

The next couple of years brought a few bright spots, such as the opening of the Everglades and Robert Clay Hotels and the completion of the Tamiami Trail in 1928. But for the first time the majority of traffic was flowing north, out of Miami, away from the abandoned skeletons of buildings rising stark against the sky – ruined by the winds of the storm.

With the passage of the 18th Amendment in 1920, the US had become officially dry. Miami hardly noticed. Rumrunners loved the canals and coves of South Florida and soon the area had acquired yet another nickname: "the leakiest spot in America." Miami's reputation for winking at both the liquor and the gambling laws attracted some new, far-from-desirable residents, including the infamous gangster Al "Scarface" Capone, who moved to a mansion on Palm Island in 1928.

**Aviation history:** Most of the local leaders, including the Sewell brothers and George Merrick, were bankrupt. Much-needed cash flowed into Miami from outsiders like Joseph Widner, who purchased Hialeah race track in 1932, and the Phipps family, who completed Biscayne Boulevard in 1927. At this time Miami's aviation industry was born. What began as Florida Airways Corporation, founded by the air ace Eddie Rickenbacker in 1926, became Eastern Airlines by 1930; Pan Am began its Key West–Havana

service in 1927. Airports were built and in 1929 Miami hosted both Charles Lindbergh and Amelia Earhart at the "Olympics of Aviation."

In 1932 America elected Franklin D. Roosevelt as president with hopes that he would lead the country out of hard times. He almost died before his inauguration. Roosevelt, who had been vacationing in South Florida, agreed to make an appearance at the Bayfront Park bandshell on February 15,

1933. Among the 18,000 people there that night was an unemployed Italian bricklayer named Guiseppe Zangara. Zangara, who resented people with wealth and authority, fired his $8 pawn-shop pistol five times. He wounded four people before hitting Chicago Mayor Anton Cermak, who was standing only inches from Roosevelt. Cermak died on March 6; Zangara went to the electric chair soon afterwards.

Once President Roosevelt was in office, his New Deal programs launched an "alphabet soup" of agencies. Among them was the CCC (Civilian Conservation Corps), which

**Left**, a map of Greater Miami in its youth. **Right**, Hialeah Race Track, an early tourist attraction.

employed young men to work in the nation's parks. In Miami they worked on Matheson Hammock and built Greynolds Park. The PWA (Public Works Administration) constructed many new public buildings, including the Coral Gables Fire Station, Miami Shores Golf Club and Liberty Square, which was Florida's first public housing project.

The government also hired unemployed World War I veterans to work on an overseas highway to Key West. Many of them met a tragic fate when a monster hurricane struck on Labor Day in 1935, killing more than 400 people and wrecking both the uncompleted highway (which in the end did not open until

ments sprang up along Collins Avenue. Unhappily, anti-Semitism also began to flourish. Carl Fisher and John Collins had originally developed the north part of the beach as a "restricted" area, and now "Gentiles Only" signs began to appear in hotels and apartments. Across the ocean, an Austrian paperhanger named Adolf Hitler came to power in Germany. A second world war was on the horizon.

**World War II:** Tourism, already the mainstay of Miami's economy, dropped dramatically after the Japanese bombed Pearl Harbor and the US declared war. German submarines torpedoing a tanker in full view of

1938) and Flagler's Overseas Railroad.

Tourists, including many from Latin America, were starting to flock to Miami. In 1922 the Palm Fete, which had been sporadically celebrated in the past, put on a New Year's Day football game featuring the University of Miami versus Manhattan College. The next year the game was played at the site of the future Orange Bowl. The newly named "Orange Festival" held its first New Year's Eve parade in 1936. Instantly, a Miami tradition was born.

The economy was looking up in Miami Beach, too. New "modern" hotel and apart-

Florida's coast in February 1942 didn't help. Suddenly the city's hotels were empty – but not for long.

The solution was American soldiers – lots of them. The city's fathers convinced the government that warm and deserted South Florida would make a good place to train soldiers. By the end of 1942, the military had turned 147 Miami hotels into barracks. GIs drilled on golf courses and exercised on wide sandy beaches. Miami became a war camp. Even the country's ultimate matinée idol, Clark Gable, came to Miami Beach in uniform. Before the war was over, one-fourth of the officers and one-fifth of the enlisted men in the US Army Air Corps had trained in Miami Beach.

The Navy took command of Miami's only post-boom skyscraper, the Alfred I. duPont Building, which people promptly nicknamed the "USS Neversink." Still, since most US ships were in the Pacific Ocean, German submarines roamed the Florida Straits practically at will. Germans torpedoed four tankers in full view of Miami, and 25 between Key West and Cape Canaveral during 1942.

Many hotels were turned into temporary hospitals for wounded soldiers. (After the war the Biltmore Hotel continued to be an

ian use. People sensed that a major change was in the air. As early as 1942 the *Miami Herald* predicted that "political, economic and geographical factors slowly are swinging Miami into a position that will make the Indian wars, coming of the railroad, the land boom and even the present military caldron look like a quiet Sunday afternoon on a Swiss Alp."

The talk across America that started as far back as 1896 about Miami being the "coming metropolis" was coming true. After the war, thousands of soldiers returned to the place where they'd gotten "sand in their shoes." Rows of pastel-painted boxy GI

Army hospital, Pratt General, until 1968.) The government held German prisoners of war at camps in Kendall (across from what is now Dadeland Mall) and in Homestead. Rationing, blackouts, dimouts, thousands of servicemen around town, and, above all, the ever-present submarine threat just offshore, made Miami feel very close to war.

War-born prosperity made tourists return to Miami and hoteliers clamor to get their facilities back from the government for civil-

**Left**, soldiers training on Miami Beach. **Above**, beginnings of the Orange Bowl Parade tradition.

houses sprang up in isolated, outlying areas. GIs swarmed to the University of Miami, breathing new life into a moribund institution. By 1947 the main campus, so long vacant, was the site of the Memorial Classroom Building. The skeleton of the university's planned adminstration building, abandoned after the boom, became the Merrick Building in 1949.

A record eight hurricanes hit Miami between 1945 and 1950. The two that hit a month apart in the fall of 1947 were minimal but very wet. After the storm on October 11, 1947, more than four-fifths of Dade and

Broward counties was under water. Two feet of water lay in the Orange Bowl and areas west of Red Road resembled lakes full of houseboats instead of subdivisions. People clamored for action that would prevent future floods. The government obliged, sending the Army Corps of Engineers to build new canals, locks and levees that would dry up much of the eastern Everglades. The legacy of these projects, in addition to large tracts of new land for development, was an ongoing threat to the Everglades and to South Florida's water supply.

Crime again became a problem in the late 1940s, as gangsters took over casinos and

public officials looked the other way. Influential citizens formed the "Secret Six," a group dedicated to stopping illegal gambling. Their efforts exposed corruption in high places (including the governor's office) and culminated in 1950 in an investigation by Senate crime fighter Estes Kefauver. Miami's door was no longer wide open to criminals.

A new era arrived in 1949 when WTVJ, Florida's first television station, began to broadcast. Although at first few homes boasted TVs, it wouldn't be long before tuning in to watch Miami newsman Ralph

Renick would become a nightly ritual. Arthur Godfrey, whose show was one of the most popular on television, broadcast from the Kennilworth Hotel in Bal Harbour for many years. To express the city's appreciation for this wonderful coast-to-coast publicity, Miami Beach renamed 41st Street "Arthur Godfrey Road."

Florida had its share of unpleasantness during the communist scares of the early 1950s. The 1950 Senate campaign between Miamian George Smathers and incumbent Senator Claude Pepper turned nasty when Smathers said his opponent was soft on communism and called him "Red Pepper." (Smathers won that election. Pepper, who had moved to Miami, ran for the House of Representatives in 1962 and served there till his death in 1989.)

In 1951 racial violence erupted in Carver Village, a black housing project. The first Dade County Council for Human Relations was organized in response and by the late 1950s several area schools had been desegregated. In 1952 the contralto Marian Anderson sang to an integrated audience in the Dade County auditorium.

**Tourism grows:** Newcomers continued to arrive in the Miami area in record numbers. Farmland became suburbs as the town turned into a metropolis. The voters approved a metropolitan government for Dade County in a highly debated decision in 1957. By the end of the decade the population was nearing 1 million people.

Air-conditioning and glamorous grand-scale hotels like the Fontainebleau, which boasted 1,206 rooms, crystal chandeliers and marble staircases, and the equally plush Eden Roc encouraged tourism. Movie stars and business moguls arrived in droves, eager to be seen in such lavish surroundings. The "Gentiles Only" and "Whites Only" signs that had haunted hotel entrances for years disappeared. The future looked upbeat and promising.

But fate had a surprise waiting for Miami. His name was Fidel Castro.

**Left, mobster Al Capone called Miami home. Right, tourism takes hold as the glamorous, air-conditioned hotels attract many to their doors.**

The celebration of the new year in 1959 continued well beyond the traditional "morning after." Crowds were cheering about events in Cuba, where a 32-year-old rebel in rumpled fatigues named Fidel Castro had deposed dictator Fulgencio Batista. But most Miamians paid little attention. It seemed like just another upheaval in the nearby island's power structure.

It proved to be more than that. As disillusionment with the "conquering hero" set in, and Castro revealed his communist leanings, more and more Cubans fled their homeland. By the summer of 1960, six planes a day departed Havana carrying destitute exiles, most of whom left with $5 and the clothes they stood up in.

Initially, Miamians welcomed these refugees, taking pity on their plight and admiring their hard-working ways and strong family structure. Some resentment and hostility followed, however, as almost overnight schools and neighborhoods filled with people speaking only Spanish.

**Bay of Pigs:** The Cubans weren't happy either; most of them wanted to go home. Until 1961 they believed they would – and soon. The CIA organized and trained a small exile brigade of 1,300 to invade Cuba and depose Castro. On April 17, 1961, "Brigade 2506," as it was called, landed on Cuba's southern coast near the Bay of Pigs. The men were counting on US air support. It was not forthcoming, and the mission was doomed from the start. Almost 100 men died and about 1,000 were taken prisoner. Exile leaders in Miami believed their valiant fighters had been betrayed by the United States.

In the fall of 1962, US planes discovered signs of a military build-up in Cuba. Once more soldiers swarmed into Miami. President John F. Kennedy addressed the nation on October 22 to explain the crisis. War loomed. In the end, Soviet leader Nikita

**Preceding pages: first waves of Cuban refugees. Left, President John F. Kennedy salutes Bay of Pigs veterans. Right, refugee vaccinations.**

Khrushchev backed down and agreed to remove Russian missiles from Cuba. In return, the US promised not to invade – or allow anyone else to invade – Cuba. The exile community, now at about 100,000, had to face the realization that Miami was to be more than just a temporary home.

Kennedy honored the Bay of Pigs prisoners (freed in late 1962 in exchange for $62 million) at an emotional ceremony in the Orange Bowl. The young president visited

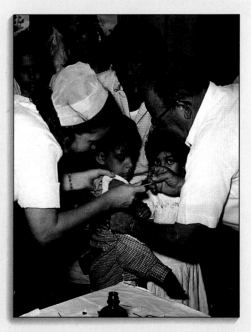

Miami once more, in November 1963, en route to his fatal stop in Dallas.

Beginning in December 1965, twice-daily flights took off from Havana to bring refugees to Miami. By the end of the 1960s, a Cuban refugee was arriving every seven minutes. Miami's Cuban population doubled, reaching 300,000 by the time the "Freedom Flights" ended in 1973. In order to process this wave of immigrants, the government took over the old *Miami News* tower, which was renamed the "Freedom Tower."

**Illegal drugs:** As the era of "Camelot" faded into the Vietnam protest years, Coconut

Grove attracted flower children and hippies, who congregated in Peacock Park and made long-time residents feel as if their town was under siege. The hard-to-patrol coastline that made South Florida so inviting to rumrunners in the 1920s proved equally attractive to smugglers eager to supply America's growing appetite for illegal drugs. Huge amounts of drugs, and drug-tainted money, poured into Miami.

"Great Society" urban renewal brought bulldozers to Overtown as new housing projects and expressways took shape. Displaced residents poured into Liberty City, once a model black community. Substan-

broadcast weekly television shows from Miami Beach. A new, long-haired singing group, the Beatles, crossed the Atlantic in 1964. When they arrived in Miami for their landmark appearance on the *Ed Sullivan Show* (broadcast live from Miami Beach), thousands of teenage girls went wild. It was the shape of things to come.

While the city continued to grow (the population reached 1 million in February 1962), people began to express concern about the environment. Their efforts led to the saving of the old Cape Florida Lighthouse and the establishment of John Pennekamp State Park (which contains the last living

dard housing became horribly overcrowded. A time bomb began to tick.

Liberty City exploded in August 1968, just as Richard Nixon, who had vacationed for years on Key Biscayne, was giving his acceptance speech to the Republican National Convention on Miami Beach. It was Miami's first race riot.

The 1960s had their good moments, too. Miami-Dade Junior (later Community) College opened, as well as a new seaport at Dodge Island. A professional football team called the Dolphins came to town and Jackie Gleason, America's favorite "bus driver,"

Florida reef) and Biscayne National Park in the upper Keys.

**The Seventies:** At the beginning of the 1970s Miami seemed poised on the brink of a new boom. Community pride ran high as President Nixon's "vacation White House" on Key Biscayne and the Dolphins' "perfect season" and Superbowl sports victories kept Miami in the news. Florida International University, Miami's long-awaited state university, opened in 1972. Cubans, no longer refugees, were running successful businesses; "Calle Ocho" was thriving.

Then a recession, the worst since the 1930s,

hit. Construction projects were abandoned and once again half-finished buildings marred the skyline. Unemployment was as high as 13 percent by 1975.

In spite of hard times and Watergate (perpetrated by four Miamians), the nation paused to celebrate its Bicentennial. During the celebration in Miami, which was one of the three official bicentennial cities, 7,300 people, mainly Cuban refugees, became American citizens in a huge ceremony.

City leaders formed the Downtown Action Committee and began to help Miami revitalize its downtown and make energetic plans for the future. Miami became an inter-

erty City and other areas erupted in riots. The city despaired.

Meanwhile, "Haitian boat people" were landing on South Florida's beaches daily, fleeing dictatorship but bringing with them few skills with which to make a new life.

**Mariel:** Events in Cuba once again rewrote Miami's history. Fidel Castro announced that anyone who wished to leave the island could do so, and thousands did. Miami Cubans sailed to Mariel harbor to help their countrymen escape. Castro's government forced them to bring back to Miami unwanted passengers as well: the refuse from Cuba's jails and mental institutions. Miami

national banking center; it seemed like a bank was going up on practically every corner. By the late 1970s a rapid transit system was under construction and new government and cultural centers were growing up.

But the new decade got off to a bad start. The popular black Superintendant of Schools was charged (and later convicted) of theft of school property. In May 1980, after a Tampa jury acquitted a white policeman in the slaying of a black man, Arthur McDuffie, Lib-

struggled under the weight of 125,000 "Marielito" refugees, many of them criminals. Tent cities sprang up to house them and the prison population swelled.

Things looked bleak; in the early 1980s there was not much magic in the Magic City. Residents who were tired of crime and upheaval and of listening to Spanish and Creole and "Spanglish" moved to quieter, calmer places. Cars sported bumper stickers that read: "Will the last American leaving Miami please bring the flag?"

But Miami had been down before and it never lasted long. This time was no excep-

**Left**, an early visit by the Beatles. **Above**, Haitian "boat people."

tion. The city began to make headlines other than the frequent drug stories on the nightly news. In 1982 the *Wall Street Journal* referred to its business as "bustling." The next year *House and Garden* magazine called Miami "magical." A $3 billion building boom was underway downtown. Offices and shopping centers, apartment blocks and marinas were under construction. But none of this captured the nation's imagination as quickly as what happened on September 16, 1984, with the TV debut of *Miami Vice*.

The city passed a political milestone in 1985 when its citizens elected Xavier Suarez as its first Cuban-born mayor. The new open-

and every spring downtown reverberated with noise and excitement as Grand Prix race cars roared through the streets. The University of Miami basked in the limelight as its football team claimed the number one ranking three times: 1983, 1987 and 1989. Joe Robbie Stadium opened in the fall of 1987 and hosted the Superbowl in January 1989.

**Future promise:** Miami entered the 1990s with a new sense of self. The skyline had suddenly become beautiful. People were coming back to downtown – for sports, culture and fun. Horatio Alger was alive and well and living in Miami. But most of all, for the first time in years – if ever – Miami had

air Bayside Marketplace attracted tourists and shoppers. Metrorail and Metromover facilitated transportation to, from and around downtown. Even the Pope came to town, visiting for two days in September 1987 as part of his US tour. During his short stay John Paul II strolled with President Reagan in Vizcaya's peaceful gardens and met with American Jewish leaders.

Miami became a sports fan's paradise, as the new Miami Arena welcomed a professional basketball team, the "Miami Heat," with sell-out crowds. Key Biscayne hosted tennis luminaries at the Lipton Tournament,

a feeling that it was coming into its own.

No longer just sun and fun, people were beginning to take Miami seriously. As the world became smaller and political changes that were unthinkable a short time earlier unfolded daily, Miami's rather rapid transformation into a diverse, international metropolis gave the rest of the nation a preview of what to expect in the 21st century. And, in the midst of the chaos, Miami not only survived, it thrived.

<u>Above</u>, Mariel refugees on their way to Miami.
<u>Right</u>, Cuba's president, Fidel Castro.

# FIDEL CASTRO

He is the most hated man in Miami. Spanish radio commentators refer to him as "the tyrant." Others curl their lips and spit his name in disdain. Even his sister Juanita, owner of a Little Havana pharmacy, despises her bully of a brother.

The longest reigning military leader in Latin America, Fidel Castro is still the controversial and charismatic leader that he was when he first captured Cuba in 1959. But, in the political arena, his hardline, purist stance has earned him the title "Fossil Communist."

As much of the communist world crumbles around him, Castro remains faithful to his "socialism or death" philosophy and continues to condemn Yankee imperialism. His country, an economic disaster, is mockingly called the Albania of the Caribbean.

But Castro, through his miraculous perseverance, has maintained much of his mystique.

Soon after the Cuban Revolution, American mobster Meyer Lansky, who lost a fortune in the communist take-over, offered a million-dollar bounty to anyone who could bring him Castro's head. Later, several CIA plots, including an outright invasion, exploding cigars and drops of poison, were also thwarted by the bearded boy wonder. And amid it all, in a country severely short of food, clothing and medicine, Castro has kept a chokehold on his island's own dissidents.

Ironically, Castro has had as great an influence on Miami as any individual in the city's history and many say much of what is good about modern Miami could not have happened if it were not for the impetus of Fidel Castro.

But for the more than 600,000 Cubans in Dade County, this influence has reared its head in the form of a powerful anti-Castro feeling that is as much a personal vendetta against the man as it is a political statement against communism. For exiles who still pine for the "good life" of their homeland, and for their children who feel deprived of their roots, Castro-bashing is one of Miami's most passionate pastimes.

Sometimes, the city seems awash in the Honk-If-You-Hate-Fidel sentiment. Bumper stickers touting "Cuba Si, Castro No," dartboards with Castro's face on them, and posters with the infamous bearded head hung in a noose are as common as the American flag.

On one occasion, thousands of people joined hands in a 160-mile Miami to Key West human chain to display publicly their anti-Castro camaraderie and then sent 1,500 balloons aloft towards Cuba with a strong message urging the islanders to revolt.

Several exile groups in the city constantly dream of toppling Castro. During the 1970s and early 1980s, the anti-Castro crusade took a violent course. Local "freedom fighters" turned into bomb-tossing terrorists who targeted Miami businesses and individuals whom they thought were "soft on Fidel" because they advocated peaceful dialogue with the Cuban government. Many Miamians were injured and several killed.

The city has also been the center for the heated airwave wars that caught the nation's attention. Radio Marti and TV Marti – two US broadcasts designed to transmit American programs and anti-communist propaganda to Cuba – have had the support of much of the Cuban community. Both programs have brought pleasure to Miami's Cubans, who see them making the "dirty little worm squirm."

When Panamanian General Manuel Noriega was captured by the US government, a billboard 40-ft wide was set up with the slogan: "Now Manuel, Next Fidel." Motorists honked in approval. When the communist governments in East Germany and Nicaragua were given their last rites, Miami's anti-Castro enthusiasm turned into euphoria. So much so that police began a strategic plan for the possibility of Castro's fall from power and what they speculated would be the wildest street party in the world.

But, after more than three decades of Castro's despotic rule on his isolated tropical island, political scientists began to feel that the "Maximum Leader" would probably not fall so easily. And if – or when – he does, they said, it would take Miami many years to recover from the most passionate hate affair it has ever had. ■

# MIAMI'S ETHNIC MIX

What is perhaps most distinctive about Miami among American cities is the peculiar role ethnicity has played in shaping, and even dominating, the social, economic and political landscape of the city. Delving into Miami's ethnic dynamics is not an excursion into the world of quaint foreign customs and interesting immigrant subcultures at the margins of the city's mainstream. Rather, it is to reach into what has become the soul of Miami. Ethnicity is at the core of Miami's uniqueness.

For those familiar with the long history of immigration and ethnicity in the United States, a visit to Miami may well prove unsettling, or at least puzzling. Many of the expected patterns do not materialize. The rules of the game appear – and indeed are – different. What is supposed to be a marginal and struggling minority is a dominant and successful majority. What is "foreign" is commonplace, what is "native" is hard to find. The newcomer feels at home, while the established resident feels alienated. Miami's actors do not play their expected roles. Some regard it as the world of immigrant America turned upside down. Others view it as a preview of the United States in the 21st century. It might be both.

**Cuban presence:** There are few who would argue with the premise that it is the Cubans who are primarily responsible for Miami's unique ethnic character. The "Cubanness" of contemporary Miami is evident not only in demonstrable terms, such as economic activities and cultural events, but also in a more intangible manner, an "ambience." David Rieff, a New Yorker who has written on Miami, observed that Cubans have largely taken control of the "atmosphere" of the city.

There is a demographic basis for the role of the exiles from Castro's Cuba. Persons born in Cuba or of Cuban descent represent Miami's largest ethnic group by far, larger

**Preceding pages:** lounging in the sun; the many shades of Miami; spectacles of youth. **Left**, Bahamian beauty. **Right**, Haitian boy.

than the white native-born English-speaking population. Those born in Cuba account for 56 percent of metropolitan Miami's foreign-born population, and persons of Cuban origin constitute the bulk – nearly 70 percent – of all Latin Americans in the area. Nearly a third of the population of Greater Miami is of Cuban birth or descent. The Cuban community of South Florida exceeds 600,000.

Its growth has been fueled not only by migration from the island, but also by the

increasing concentration of Cubans from other parts of the United States. Miami is the capital and mecca for US Cubans, to the point now where more than half of the Cuban immigrant population lives in South Florida.

But the importance of the Cuban community for Miami is not just a question of numbers. It also has to do with the very nature of that community.

At the heart of Cuban Miami is entrepreneurship, plenty of it and of many different types. Of all US cities, Miami has by far the largest number, per capita, of Hispanic-owned businesses. Many of those businesses are small family-run operations while others are large corporations. They range from the typical ethnic businesses – such as restaurants and grocery stores – to professional and financial services. The basis of such a community was established largely by the wave of Cuban exiles that arrived in the early 1960s, those who were among the first to feel alienated by the island's rapid transformation from a capitalist to a socialist system. First in the exodus were the entrepreneurial, managerial and professional sectors; those who possessed skills and attitudes that would ease their entry into self-employment in the United States. To put it simply, as one soci-

not confined to the retail store. It also extends to wholesale trade, financial and professional services, manufacturing, construction and commerce. Cubans are very present in the public sector, too, so that even contact with government bureaucracies may take place within the ethnic network.

The wide variety of self-employment that flourishes in the ethnic community has led to the creation of a true enclave, an institutionally complete ethnic community. Such a community makes it possible for the immigrant to live out his or her entire life, if desired, entirely with like-minded people. Unlike most ethnic neighborhoods whose

ologist once did, they had experience in the "art of buying and selling."

The importance of entrepreneurship among Cubans in Miami is evident driving along S.W. Eighth Street, Flagler Street, or some of the principal thoroughfares in the Hispanic neighborhoods. Countless small businesses line the streets, many concentrated within small shopping centers. Restaurants and cafeterias, grocery stores and fruit stalls, flower shops, drugstores, clothing boutiques, barbershops and beauty salons, and even jewelry stores abound.

But business ownership among Cubans is

residents must go outside of it, to satisfy many of their needs, Miami's Cubans can literally go from birth to grave existing entirely within the confines of their community. There is no shortage in Miami of Cuban pediatricians and funeral directors, and everything in between.

This, of course, is not typical and has a unique set of implications for Miami's social climate. A strong ethnic enclave is largely responsible for the "Cubanization" of Miami's "atmosphere." It also has a number of consequences for the relationship between Cubans and other ethnic groups.

**Bilingual blues:** The characteristics of the Cuban enclave largely shape what is the most evident ethnic issue – or perhaps battle-field – in Miami: language. Because of the institutional completeness of the Cuban community, Spanish is a very public language. It is heard everywhere, and is literally in Miami's air – on radio and television waves. There are myriad Spanish-language radio stations on both the AM and FM dials, and two television stations transmit exclusively in Spanish.

In most immigrant communities, the language of the country of origin is the language of intimacy, spoken only among family and

that the movement to make English the official language in the United States was born in Miami. In 1980, after the Dade County Commission passed an ordinance officially declaring the county bilingual, a grassroots citizens' movement succeeded in passing a referendum to abrogate the ordinance and require that the county's public documents and publicly supported events be in English. Years later, in 1988, the voters of the State of Florida overwhelmingly approved a constitutional initiative to declare English the official language of the state.

For most Cubans in Miami, the anti-bilingualism movement is of little relevance or

friends. But in Miami one can conduct the entire spectrum of one's affairs in Spanish, from shopping, banking, working and recreational activities to obtaining specialized professional services.

It is precisely this widespread and public use of Spanish that has raised the issue of bilingualism. No other issue related to ethnicity provokes as much controversy – and acrimony – in Miami. It is no coincidence

**Left**, Puerto Rican woman shops in Little Havana. **Above**, salty sea captain; Cuban grandmother.

consequence. The enclave is built on self-employment and private enterprise. It is a community that works primarily in the private sector, beyond the reach of the ambiguous language requirements imposed on government business. The tendency of the immigrants to speak Spanish, the *lingua franca* of the enclave, has not been affected. Consequently, the use of Spanish in public has not been officially curtailed and continues to be a major irritant to many English speakers in the city. Complaints are frequently aired by those who do not speak Spanish that they cannot understand what is being said in stores, offices and crowded elevators. Those complaints transcend linguistics and have more to do with the broader question of feeling at home in one's city and one's country. Those who are supposed to be the natives, the established residents, feel as if they are outsiders, while the newcomers feel at home. And so one common response has been "Anglo flight." The white non-Latin population of Dade County has declined dramatically in the past two decades.

But the Cubans do feel at home. With the exception of the elderly and the new arrivals from the island, Cubans in Miami are fully bilingual. There is a sense that this is "their

ent from the experience of other immigrants in the United States, for whom their native language was expendable in the process of adjustment.

**Hispanic advantage:** In Miami, there is an economic advantage to being Cuban and speaking Spanish. Within the community, an ethnic network helps in the search for employment, the establishment of business and professional contacts and the creation of opportunities for self-employment.

It has been argued that the enclave is as much a cause as it is a consequence of the much-touted "Cuban success story." The economic vitality of the community was a

city." There are, as one would expect, dramatic inter-generational differences within the Cuban community in the use of language. The younger generation shows a marked preference for English, a phenomenon that parents have largely encouraged because it remains the language that must be mastered if one is ambitious and planning to enter the professional and managerial worlds. But the retention of Spanish, even as a second language, is also useful in getting ahead in Miami. Its retention is based not so much on immigrant nostalgia as it is on the economic realities of a bilingual Miami. This is differ-

major factor in the eventual economic integration of the large influx that arrived from Cuba in 1980 during the famous Mariel boatlift. Many of the new arrivals were able to get their first jobs in the US largely through the ethnic network and within a familiar language and culture.

To a large extent, the economic benefits of the enclave extend to those immigrants who are not Cuban but speak Spanish. The community established by the Cubans has served as the entry into the US labor market for many Central and South Americans who represent a growing segment of Miami's

Hispanic population. Since no large-scale migration from Cuba has occurred since 1980, many of the entry-level jobs in the enclave are now largely being filled by non-Cuban Latins. It is typical, for example, to find that the waitresses in a Cuban restaurant are Nicaraguan, Salvadoran or Colombian.

The increasing mixture in the national origins of Miami's Latin American community is becoming more and more evident in the proliferation of retail businesses that cater for specific national clienteles: restaurants, cafeterias, bakery shops, and so on. Entrepreneurship is no longer limited to the Cubans. The Colombian pastry shops and

of the population of Greater Miami, African-Americans live in one of the most racially segregated cities in the US. Miami's black neighborhoods are not "predominantly black"; they are black. And there is considerable physical distance between them and almost every other ethnic group.

The physical segregation is compounded by an undeniable social distance. In many US cities, especially in the Northeast and the Midwest, there is an evident solidarity between Latins and African-Americans. They usually share a political agenda and have been successful in combining their strengths at the polls to elect sympathetic candidates.

the Nicaraguan restaurants are found primarily in Little Havana, Sweetwater, West Dade and Hialeah, the same areas where Cubans are concentrated.

**Native blacks:** If it can be said that Cubans and other Latin Americans are fairly well integrated, economically and spatially, with each other, the same cannot be said about the relationship between Miami's Latin Americans (including Cubans) and native African-Americans. Accounting for about 18 percent

**Left**, University of Miami's Hurricane cheerleaders. **Above**, corn-row coiffure.

This is not the case in Miami. There is little political and social integration between Latins and African-Americans, no shared sense that they have overlapping concerns. The explanation probably rests on the immigrant character of Miami's Latins. In other US cities, where Mexican-Americans and/or Puerto Ricans comprise the bulk of the Latin population, there is an emphasis on issues that are typical of a "minority" agenda: public housing, access to education and public services, employment, etc.

The "minority" worldview predominates – that is, the view that the dominant society discriminates against members of the minority and that there are entrenched barriers to the advancement of racial and ethnic groups. These are concerns and views shared with African-Americans and are an expected response to many decades and generations of discrimination.

Miami's Latins, however, are recent immigrants. They have not accumulated the experiences that would lead them to think like members of minority groups. They came here because they believe this place is a better place than where they came from. Their view of US society is a positive one: a land of opportunity and political freedoms.

Although Haitians, as blacks, have been subjected to much prejudice and discrimination, especially from negative treatment by the US Immigration and Naturalization Service, they still share many patterns with immigrants in Miami that are distinct from African-Americans. The most evident is the importance given to self-employment and entrepreneurship. The business district of Little Haiti is growing fairly rapidly and reflects a uniquely immigrant adaptation that is similar to the Latins. The immigrant black Jamaican community, another sizable group in the city, also shows more similarities to Latins than to the African-Americans.

There is little basis for embracing a minority agenda and identifying with the plight of African-Americans. This, of course, serves to further isolate Miami's African-Americans and to make even more acute their sense of powerlessness.

An immigrant orientation is one of the factors that differentiates foreign blacks in Miami from native African-Americans. The Haitians are the most numerous of the foreign blacks, numbering in excess of 70,000. Little Haiti is perched on the southeastern territorial limits of the large African-American neighborhood of Liberty City.

The absence of a minority-group orientation is, of course, especially acute among Cubans who perceive themselves as political exiles and who disproportionately represent Cuba's pre-revolutionary elite. Their agenda has been characterized by a concern with affairs of the homeland, with only secondary interest in "immigrant" issues, and much less in "minority" issues.

There is little basis for the perception of a common ground between Cubans and African-Americans. This was painfully evident when the results came in for a special election to select a successor to deceased US

Congressman Claude Pepper, a longtime Miami Democrat. More than 90 percent of the Cubans voted for one of their own, a conservative Republican who won the election, while more than 90 percent of the Black voting precincts went for the Democratic candidate.

**Exile politics:** The distinctly "exile" political culture of the Cubans is yet another wrinkle in the ethnic fabric of Miami. The staunchly anti-Castro and anti-communist views of Miami's Cubans represent their most visible trademark. It is this political militancy that frequently attracts national attention to the Cuban community. It is re-

been characterized by strong liberal and civil libertarian traditions that contrast with the conservatism of the Cubans.

Miami is a new city, one that developed entirely in the 20th century. Appropriately, its immigrant groups are also new. The Cubans, who largely set the tone for the ethnic character of the city, started arriving, in massive numbers, only within the past three decades, and the same can be said of virtually every other ethnic group. Yet, for a young city that was once a winter resort for wealthy transients, three decades is a long time. Cubans and other immigrants have come to form part of the city's "establishment" and to

garded as a conservative and right-wing community with deeply felt opinions about the political status of the homeland and an intolerance of opposing viewpoints.

The decidedly conservative bent of the political culture of Cuban Miami is frequently a source of distancing and tension with another, older, ethnic group in the area. The elderly and predominantly Jewish community that has long settled in South Florida after retirement in the Northeast has usually

**Left**, Little Haiti herb and grocery vendors. **Above**, a traditional wedding vow.

define the core of what Miami has become as it approaches the 21st century.

While Miami's multi-ethnic character is at times conflictive and gives the appearance of a city divided along racial and ethnic lines, it also imbues the city with a unique and varied dynamism. Miami's ethnic groups have yet to demonstrate that they have been mixed into a salad, and much less a stew. Rather, Miami offers a wide selection of separate and distinct dishes. To visit Miami and its distinctive neighborhoods without becoming aware of its ethnic diversity is virtually impossible. Ethnicity permeates Miami.

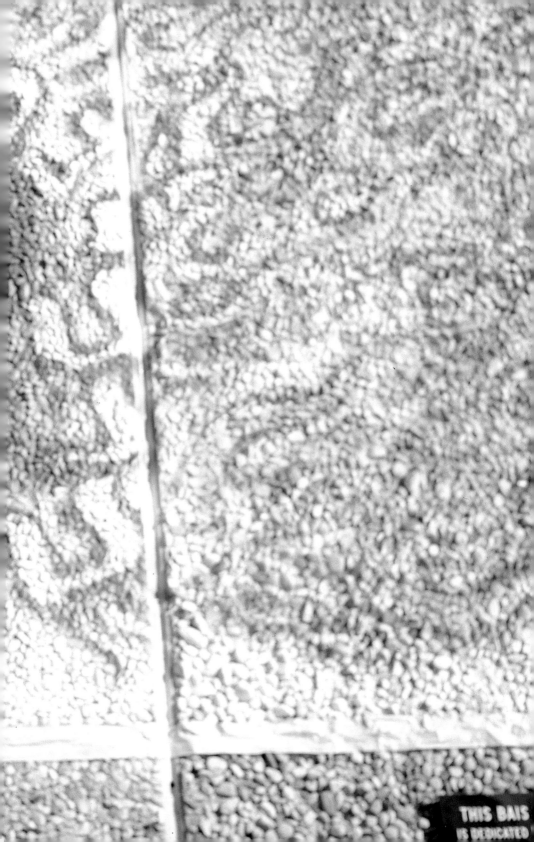

THIS BAIS
IS DEDICATED

# THE JEWISH COMMUNITY

During an episode of the popular American television show *All in the Family*, Archie Bunker, the lead character, was asked where a Jewish acquaintance had moved. Bunker replied, "The Hebe left for the Promised Land – Miami Beach!"

By the 1960s Miami Beach had become a national monument for elderly Jews, a place where condo commandos (politically active retirees) and earlybird specials (restaurant meals offered at a discount to the elderly) became commonplace. In 1975, nearly 300,000 Jews lived in the Greater Miami area. Of those living in Miami Beach, 75 percent were aged 60 or over. Ironically, Miami Beach only a generation earlier was guilty of rampant discrimination boldly apparent in posted signs that read: "No Dogs, No Blacks, No Jews."

Considering the fact that, as late as 1949, Miami developers encouraged this discrimination by placing restrictive covenants in the deeds to their properties that forbade Jews from renting hotel rooms, Miami's metamorphosis has been described as miraculous. Today, the Jewish community of the Miami area represents the second largest concentration of Jews in America after New York City and serves as a powerful voice in the area's politics.

**Early merchants:** The Jewish question surfaced from the early days of Flagler's railroad. Jewish merchants such as Jake Schneidman, Sam Singer, Morris Kanner and Isidor Cohen joined in to help develop the new southern outpost.

In his autobiography, Cohen described negotiating a real estate deal with pioneer Julia Tuttle. During the late 1800s Tuttle offered him not a mortgage, but a laborer's job. Cohen retorted: "The last labor of this character my race had performed was in the land of Egypt, and it would be a violation of my religious convictions to resume that condition of servitude." Nevertheless, Cohen,

**Preceding pages:** going to temple. **Left**, Orthodox Jewish women enjoy a day at the beach.

who owned a Miami department store, prospered and was instrumental in the formation of the Miami Chamber of Commerce.

The handful of early Jewish settlers tended to be Key Westers in pursuit of employment and Northerners in search of better health. One such pioneer family was that of Joe and Jennie Weiss who moved to Miami Beach in 1913 and would soon after open the landmark Joe's Stone Crab restaurant. But it was not until the inter-war years that Miami's Jewish community developed a prominent profile. The promise of land booms, natural beauty and employment drew many to the city. A number came in order to escape the

mold the Jewish community and spawn the growth of other Jewish organizations and periodicals like the *Jewish Floridian*, which was published from 1928 to 1990.

In addition to these historic temples, the old Miami City Cemetery has a Jewish section full of ornate tombstones that date back to the early 1900s.

**Community acceptance:** Just as World War II changed the contours of Europe, so it changed the map of Miami. With the US Supreme Court outlawing restrictive covenants and promulgating a series of rulings promoting the rights of minorities, Miami Beach began to attract Jewish property de-

horrors that were about to strike Europe.

Others came to salvage the wreckage left over from the 1926 real estate bust and the hurricanes that followed. And still others were galvanized by the idealism and romanticism of being a part of something new.

Many of Miami's early Jewish institutions still stand: Beth David, Miami's first synagogue (originally B'nai Zion), founded in 1912; Temple Israel, one of the most beautifully designed Reform temples in America, erected in 1927; and Beth Jacob, Miami Beach's first synagogue, which opened in 1929. The birth of these synagogues helped

velopers. The building of the Fontainebleau Hotel in 1954 by Ben Novak and his architect Morris Lapidus appeared to many to crown Miami Beach's reputation as the winter playground for American Jews. Soon after, Yiddish became a Beach staple along with Kosher butchers and Hebrew classes.

In the late 1950s Jews began to move out of Miami Beach and into other areas of the city and further up the Florida coast. More comfortable with themselves and with their integration in Miami, a new generation emerged. Communities were formed and leaders weaned. Shepard Broad was a leader of this generation. Broad, a migrant from New York, built Bay Harbor Village and at the same time was instrumental in the purchasing of ships locally which would eventually be donated to the state of Israel when it was in need of a navy. He also helped build a synagogue on the former site of the Nautilus Club's polo grounds from which Jews had been excluded in earlier years.

The 1960s brought more of the same. Meyer Lansky, reputedly the Mafia's Jewish *consigliore*, walked his dog along Collins Avenue unrecognized. Miami's Jewish population exploded with Jews from the Northeast seeking vacations in the South and Cu-

raeli events. Well-known Jewish entertainers are often seen wandering down Collins Avenue. Comedians regularly fly down from the North to visit their moms. Teenagers come to visit their grandparents. After their much ado in Washington, Israeli politicians relax and gather support in Miami. Local radio stations offer Israeli/Hebrew programs featuring Yiddish music, and cable television stations broadcast a choice of Jewish cultural shows.

Two recent events have brought a closing link to the karmic circle of Miami's Jewish community. The dedication of the Holocaust Memorial on Miami Beach in early 1990

ban Jews fleeing Fidel Castro's take-over. Miami's 10,000-strong Jewish Cubans remain an enigma. Locked in a subculture that exhibits their most recent experience, they remain loyal Cubans to the point of voting Cuban over Jewish in local elections. Although they have built several congregations, they remain apart from the Miami Jewish community.

Today, in the winter season, Miami is the capital for Jewish-American as well as Is-

**Left**, morning talks of days gone by. **Above**, the somber Holocaust Memorial on Miami Beach.

served as a much-needed catharsis for Holocaust survivors. So too did the emotional ceremony that accompanied the joint commemoration linking the 1989 anniversary of the *SS St Louis* and the symbolic sinking of Adolf Hitler's 85-ft yacht, the *Ostwind*, off the coast of Miami Beach.

Unlike the state of Israel, Miami Beach was never promised to the Jews. It became a promised land through America's progression from a melting-pot mentality to one that accepts cultural pluralism and the success of those Jews who came to it as immigrants, snowbirds and exiles.

# THE BODY CULTURE

Miami has always been a city in love with itself. It rests not on bedrock, but on a shallow sand spit of fantasy and flamboyance. Like the convertibles whisking tourists from Miami International Airport to the closest beach, this is a top-down, look-at-me, full-tilt metropolis. Look at the ice-blue glass towers along Brickell Avenue, each bank with its own sky-high logo as corporate ego. Look at the "Longest Conga Line In The World" bumping 23 blocks up and down Little Havana's Calle Ocho. It's spelled out right there in the tan lines: Miami is stalled in a perpetual Me Generation.

"It's Miami," went one recent, catchy booster jingle. "It's my Miami. And Miami's for me."

It figures. Like the great seasonal storms that whip through the Caribbean each summer, Miami has always been the eye of its own hurricane. Its winds suck in the curious from all points of the compass. To dreamers in New York and Bogota alike, the city sends out its drum beat of self-promotion. And who gets seduced? A red-hot mix of Cubans and Haitians, Jewish immigrants and American blacks, Central American refugees and retirees from Cleveland.

It doesn't take them long to see that the place is as much a parade as it is a working city. In fact, it hits them right in the face. Which is precisely where the town's vanity first pops up.

**Looking good:** Miami is the land of the 120-minute nose job. At the film festival benefit one year, they auctioned off a complimentary face lift. Fat recycling and tummy tucks are big business, too. For a quarter-century, the annual Cosmetic Surgery Symposium has drawn the *crème de la crème* of the world's plastic surgeons to Miami. And a place called Futureshape advertises "skin toning," or smearing aloe gel on wrinkles – then working it in with an electrical current.

**Preceding pages**: indulgence at the Doral Saturnia Spa. **Left** and **right**, Miami attracts the young and the beautiful.

Of course, all that toned skin would be useless sitting at home alone. Fortunately, Miami shares with California the North American copyright on the fine art of Flaunting It. It's not uncommon to find people at six different tables working cellular phones over lunch at downtown delis. Calling attention to oneself is Miami's favorite pastime; teenagers install 150-watt speakers in their car trunks, then blast music so loud it sets off school alarms. Then there's that ill-fated

poster proposed for the tourist bureau, featuring a photo of a female snorkeler, taken from behind, *sans* bathing suit top. "Miami," it proclaimed. "See It Like A Native."

This love of self carries over into love of wealth. Status symbols – racing boats, self-cleaning backyard pools, fine Cuban cigars – are practically a cottage industry in South Florida. By the beginning of the 1990s, Miami had become BMW's top growth market in the United States. Forever in capitalistic heat, every Miamian is a bit of a gold-toothed pimp. Some of the Miami "River Cops," on trial a few years back for ripping off drug dealers while on duty, appeared in court decked out in their finest gold neckware. Key Biscayne lifeguards, valets outside Joe's Stone Crab restaurant and steakhouse busboys in Little Managua drip with those same 10-carat icons of contemporary Miami. Miami is driven by a sort of underground economy of vanity. People go out Saturday night to Coconut Grove to see and be seen; grabbing a bite to eat is almost an afterthought. They schmooze in the skyboxes at Joe Robbie Stadium and loiter for hours at Little Havana's Domino Park for the same reason. Even the architecture here is pretentious and corny. There are minarets rising

ami Beach, this end of the Florida peninsula has made a cash crop of dreams, many of them too good to be true.

People have always come to Miami to shortcircuit the aging process, and to pretend they'll never die. It's small wonder that narcissism, a fine anesthesia for mortality, comes so naturally to Miamians. Maybe it's in the water. Then again, the town does sit on the youngest piece of land mass in all of America. Fisher may have had that in mind when he called Miami Beach a place "where the old could grow young and the young never grow old."

Fisher arrived in South Florida with deep

from Opa-locka's City Hall; there's Coral Gables' grandiose hole in the ground, the Venetian Pool, and there's the famous Atlantis, a condominium with a gaping hole in the side.

What gives? How on earth can a town where 5,000 people attend an annual festival dedicated to nothing less than addiction to chocolate ever survive without suffocating on its own hedonistic excess?

**History of hedonism:** Just watch. Today, as in 1913 when Carl Fisher arrived to suck up enough muck from Biscayne Bay and create that perfect symbol of self-promotion, Mi-

pockets and the prototype of the modern Miami man: part visionary, part exile, part huckster. By dredging his dreamland in a place eternally suspended between ocean and land, he set the tone that things here would never be what they seemed, always a little too superficial, somehow suspect.

From the beginning, appeals to the ego were shameless. And the train was only leaving the station. Over the years, to a steady rattle of boom-bust, boom-bust, Miami has clung to its eternal present, a picture-perfect postcard of itself. "The whole creation of the Beach was to appeal to escape," publicist Hank Meyer once said. "You were dealing with subliminal suggestion – moods, desires, dreams, fantasies."

Miami's founders had plenty to work with, not the least of which was its weather. For nearly a century, that average yearly temperature of 75°F has coaxed Americans into moving as far south as they could go and starting over. It's easy to do: Miami's a flat, timeless place where seasons blur and the imagination soars. It's moist, warm, womblike. The search for the fountain of youth is still stuck in overdrive. Miamians of the 1990s are forever chasing that perfect tan, that body beautiful, that fast buck.

estimate there are as many skin cancers in the state as all the other 60,000 cancers combined), and joking about Miami Beach becoming the "Sun and Shade Capital of the World," people keep going for the bronze.

A national panel of experts recently warned Floridians to apply sunscreen every day, even just going to work and back. Few comply. "I don't believe in skin cancer," a teen bather told a reporter. "It doesn't worry me to get burned, and you'll be wrinkled when you get old anyway."

Since so few clothes are necessary, skin here is also quite the status symbol. People even come here just to talk about it: Miami

**Bronze is beautiful:** Here's a classic image: 20 elderly apartment dwellers, lined up in lounge chairs across the front deck of a 1930s hotel, eyes closed, faces skyward, each holding a reflecting fan just below the chin to catch the rays. Day in, day out, year after year, retirees and seasonal tourists spend hours at these altars practicing Miami's official religion: Sun Worship. Largely ignoring Florida's status as the state with the highest cancer rate in the United States (researchers

**Left**, disco darlings stay out all night. **Above**, the beautiful people posing pretty.

recently hosted the first International Congress of Esthetics, a meeting of beauticians who specialize in skin care. And the first thing visitors to Miami see, either driving in along Interstate 95 or leaving the airport, is that legendary, decades-old advertisement for suntan lotion: a billboard featuring a puppy tugging at the swimsuit bottom of a cocoa-skinned toddler. "Tan. Don't Burn," the billboard says. "Get a Coppertone Tan."

**The perfect body:** Assuming one's tan is suitable for framing, a firm body is in order. Miami comes through: it's hard to jog along a city block without passing a tennis court, health-food store, golf course, martial arts school, yoga club, diet center, dance studio or workout gym. Bicycle and jogging paths line grand winding routes like Old Cutler Road and the causeway to Key Biscayne.

Rollerskaters by land, windsurfers by sea. They are members all of Miami's Sweat Set. But it's the almighty spa that bottles this *esprit de corps*. These cathedrals of callisthenics have mushroomed in the subtropical heat. There are even spas on the cruise ships that sail from the Port of Miami. The spa at the Fontainebleau Hilton boasts 30,000 sq. ft. The spa at the Doral Country Club flies in plankton-rich mud from Italian hot springs

to soften its guests' hides. And the spa in the $60-million Miracle Center features a row of stationary bikes in a glassed-in mezzanine.

**Flaunting it:** Once tanned and taut, Miamians take to the streets. And beaches. And clubs. Evening bras are *de rigueur*. Topless bathing on Miami Beach, if not officially sanctioned, has become *la mode*. Dressed to kill, party-goers descend 5,000-strong on some South Beach and Grove nightclubs. One spot changes its decor every four or five months; owners say club-goers are easily bored. They dance all night in old Art Deco dance palaces, where intermission includes lingerie and swimsuit shows. At other nightspots, huge video screens project images of 2,000 people cramming the dance floor.

Men wear bobtails and earrings. One club owner is renowned for his collection of 60 pairs of shorts, often worn with tuxedo jacket and no socks. The women stick orchids in their hair. It's ego-dressing: low-cut blouses, silk nightgowns, skirts slit up to the thigh. Heavy on floral patterns, leopard skin and leather, worn tighter by mini-skirted women than by the cows who made it possible.

By day, fashion models stalk the town, posing along Miracle Mile; at Main Highway cafés; beside Calle Ocho in the Cuban district; at dawn's early light in the Art Deco District. This rich natural light, at all hours, has made South Florida a hot spot for fashion photography. Even non-fashion models are always posing. It's not uncommon to see Miamians carrying parrots on their shoulders, or even boa constrictors.

It's that kind of place. *Maître d's* are cult personalities. Fantastic arched bridges lead to luxurious residential islands. It was on one such island that one Arab sheik, His Royal Highness Prince Mohammed al-Fassi, threw up a garish mansion. With mosque. And bowling alley. Not only are streets here named for the famous – Arthur Godfrey, Jackie Gleason, Ed Sullivan – but also for the people who helped construct their fame. In 1984, even publicist Hank Meyer – assembly line foreman in this factory of dreams – got his name up there on a street sign.

They should have called it Me-ami. On one tiny stretch of the Grove, 18 sidewalk cafés give people 721 seats from where they watch everyone else. "We thought about getting entertainment," says one owner. "But we don't need it. People have people."

So it goes. Non-stop entertainment. Over a stage backdropped by fruit salad sunsets and palm tree props, the curtain for 100 years has risen faithfully each dawn. And there it stands, tongue firmly in cheek, hogging the spotlight. The show-off of American cities admiring itself in a full-length mirror.

Me-ami, indeed.

<u>Left</u>, **happy hour cocktails to top off a long day.**
<u>Right</u>, **the perfect piña colada.**

Crime defines Miami. It packs its punch. It's the fertilizer for what someone once called "the Garden of America." That someone was the notorious mobster Al Capone. He sure knew what he was talking about. With Miami Beach his base in the 1930s, Capone and his chums milked a wide-open Miami for all it was worth. They muscled in on the illegal casinos and nightclubs. They scooped up politicians into their pockets like car keys. They ran the joint.

The town was risky then, rotten to its core. The underworld flourished above ground. Everyone looked the other way. No sweat. This was Miami. This was a kick.

Things haven't changed much. Today, as they did back then, people love living on the edge. Miami is America's edge, geographically and morally. And crime, in all its ghoulish glamour, keeps it there. There's a certain *laissez-faire* to living in these subtropics. That's not to say Miamians weren't embarrassed in 1981 when their city became Murder Capital USA and 621 people died violent deaths in Dade County.

Still, as major American cities go, Miami's as safe as the next, assuming one's not involved in drugs or looking for trouble – synonymous endeavors in this modern frontier town. In any given year, other cities may even be statistically more dangerous. It's just that Miami wears its crime like a cheap perfume. It's hard to ignore. But it's also a driving city, so Miamians and their visitors are often hermetically sealed inside cars; unlike pedestrian cities around the world, one can pretty much motor around most of Miami's crime.

**Nonchalance:** The good citizens of Miami, despite living in a place where there's a sort of one-upmanship to bizarre criminal acts, have learned to carry on.

Or maybe they're just jaded. In 1986, when 12 corpses were recovered from the

rear of abandoned automobiles, you could almost hear Dade medical examiner Dr Joe Davis's patience wearing thin: "There seems to be no let-up in people found in trunks. We've become used to it," the doctor mused.

As it careers into the next millennium like a runaway bulletproof Mercedes 550 (available for $160,000 at one local dealer), Miami has already seen it all:

• A cocaine ring at Eastern Airlines that ran more than one ton of coke a week through the airport – a quarter of all the cocaine

smuggled into the United States in 1985.

• A proliferation of handguns – 220,000 sold between 1977 and 1981 alone – and the bloodiest shoot-out in FBI history.

• A drug-smuggling industry churning as much as $12 billion a year, rivaling even the volume of the region's enormous real estate industry.

• A crush of immigrants, first in the 1980 Mariel boatlift that landed 120,000 Cubans in Miami practically overnight, and later with 150,000 Haitians and 75,000 Nicaraguans fleeing their respective rulers. That, added to what had long been not so much a

**Preceding pages:** drug-sniffing police hound. **Left**, TV's *Miami Vice's* slick, streetwise image. **Right**, motorcade en route to an officer's funeral.

"melting pot" as a "boiling pot" of bad vibes, spawning several major racial disturbances over two decades.

Those are just the broad strokes. Woven into this tapestry of social ills are a million telling tales from Sin City: one motorist fatally shooting another for making a left turn too slowly. A naked man arrested after he threw the severed head of his girlfriend at a police officer. A bar patron who was shot five times in the head – and survived. Body parts awash in Biscayne Bay. A health-spa prostitution ring. People robbed on the freeways. In their driveways. In their living rooms. Sometimes by intruders masquerad-

Reserve. The Internal Revenue Service estimates the average coke deal in Miami nets at least around $300,000.

Toss in crooked politicians and pot bales washing up on the beach and drug couriers ingesting and then smuggling condoms full of cocaine into the country and self-proscribed freedom fighters shooting bazookas off at Polish freighters and, suddenly, Miami's reputation as America's Casablanca makes perfect sense. Bad news, right? Wrong. Just when things were getting really low down and dirty, just when the murder rate popped the national crime barometer in 1980 at no fewer than 70 homicides per 100,000

ing as cops. Even gory stories of people being fed to alligators.

Forget yellow journalism. This town's stories call for an entire rainbow.

Tying them all together are jaw-dropping statistics that could raise the dead: agents estimated in the late 1980s that there were 700 "free-base" houses in Dade and neighboring Broward counties. In 1987, police seized 69,000 pounds of cocaine in the Miami area, worth $464 million, even at Miami's then relatively low wholesale price. In 1985, some $6 billion more in cash came in than left the Miami branch of the Federal

population, a funny thing happened.

Miami got hot. And not just weatherwise. In a curious and collective about-face, the national critics were suddenly documenting a veritable renaissance unfolding at the foot of Florida. Just as they had loved kicking the city when it was down and out, the nation's journalists, now cheering on the underdog they had helped breed, rejoiced. Miami, they said, was "bouncing back."

Aided and abetted by the MTV-ish soundtrack and slick pastels of *Miami Vice* every Friday night, a new national consensus about Murder Capital USA was forged. The hype was hip, but it was only skin-deep. After all, the city was still located at that convenient crossroads for Caribbean and South American misadventures; and the city was still fermenting its unusual mix of dumb rednecks, macho Latins, scam artists and hotheads who couldn't hack it in the rest of the United States. People who bailed out for balmier climates and the curious heritage Miami offered: anonymity and glistening acres of white sand.

The city's murder rate may have slipped from the Top of the Charts, but Miami remained every bit as feloniously funky as it ever was. In the latter part of 1984, for instance, the hallmarks of drug killings – multiple murders, victims handcuffed, bodies in car trunks – began to reappear. There were 17 double murders, five triple slayings and a quintuple killing (five men and women in a drug house).

The mere mention of a quintuple slaying begs the question: is Miami any place to spend a summer vacation?

**A "safe" city:** Go to the experts. Edna Buchanan, *Miami Herald* reporter turned crime novelist, has said that "solid citizens who stay alert are usually safe. There are no tail-gunners on bread trucks. Life in Miami is simply life in the big city… nowhere near as bad as some people think." Buchanan should know. She won the coveted Pulitzer Prize in 1986 for documenting more than 5,000 violent deaths over 16 years.

Fact is, most deadly violence is either the result of domestic strife or a soured drug deal. Fact is, a handful of neighborhoods are notorious for their street crime. By steering clear of them, visitors to Miami can leave safely on the same airplane they came in on.

A few years ago, the *Miami Herald* looked at each of the city's 438 homicides. The investigation revealed that most murder suspects were accused of killing someone they knew. Forty percent of the cases remained unsolved a year later, and police figured a third of them were drug-related.

__Left__, over $22 million in cash seized in Miami during a US Customs drug-smuggling bust. __Right__, Pulitzer Prize-winning crime reporter Edna Buchanan.

There are experts, too, who say that not only are innocent bystanders safe in Miami – but that they have never been safer. One local historian points out that the town's crime rate per capita in 1925 was three times greater than it was during the tumultuous 1980–81 era when Miami came unglued.

Such authorities, though, do have a point. In 1926, one in every 908 residents was murdered. Sixty years later, it was a mere one in every 2,600. At this rate, Miami may well become the safest vacation bet in the world. Until then, the weirdness marches on.

It always has. This corner of the country has a legacy of violence. Long before Miami

was legally incorporated in 1896, American forces waged a terrorist campaign to "liberate" Florida from the Indians and the independent souls who had settled in the peninsula. To win Florida for the United States, Andrew Jackson massacred American blacks who had sought freedom here, then burned and destroyed Indian villages, strung up chiefs and brutally slaughtered Indian women and children.

Crimewise, it was downhill from then on. In the 1930s and 1940s, thanks to such bootlegging bad boys from the Midwest as Capone, Miami really got a taste of what was to come over the next half-century. Mafia bosses, far from the bridle of those who knew their tricks, went on a feeding frenzy on the Beach. They bought up nightclubs and hotels and took over the gambling industry already in place.

**Cocaine cowboys:** Like the Mafiosi of the 1930s, the cocaine warriors of the 1970s received at least a *de facto* open-armed welcome in Miami. They were, like their predecessors, good for the bottom line. Yacht dealers took cash for $250,000 Cigarette boats, sleek vessels equipped with radar scanners and infra-red night-vision scopes that were perfect for bringing in coke from

"mother ships" offshore. Real estate experts bemoaned the fact that rich drug smugglers were buying up the land, especially prime waterfront lots, thus jacking up the cost of home-ownership for the law-abiding set. But they sold, nevertheless.

And car dealers willingly traded wheels for cocaine cash. In the early 1990s, in some parts of South Florida, as much as 20 percent of automobile transactions were in cash. Even with new laws that require banks to report cash deposits of $10,000 or more, Miami was still awash with dirty dollars.

With them has come dirty deeds. In one period during the 1980s, an average 13 cocaine-processing labs a year were discovered in South Florida. Some were stocked with enough highly flammable ether, a key ingredient to refining the white powder, to flatten three city blocks. Some were found in suburban homes and next to elementary schools; at least eight exploded in flames. During the so-called "cocaine wars" in the late 1970s, some 35 drug killings were recorded in a single six-month stretch.

But it was the infamous Dadeland Mall shoot-out in 1979 that made people take notice. In the heart of one of the county's most popular shopping centers, a bastion of suburban safety, drug war assassins sprayed 60 bullets into a liquor store, killing two and wounding another two bystanders. The getaway vehicle was nothing less than a war wagon, equipped with reinforced steel, gun portholes and bulletproof vests. Now *that* was a bit too much.

**Vigilantes fight back:** Soon, anti-crime groups became the rage. The tidal wave of crime washing over Miami, most of it drug-related, has also inspired countless solo acts of heroism and, its awkward bedfellow, vigilantism.

Perhaps the most famous to hit the front page was in 1986 when shopkeeper Prentice Rasheed jerry-rigged a booby trap to discourage burglars at his inner-city store. Sure enough, a would-be thief was electrocuted in Rasheed's steel grill as the man tried to shimmy through a hole in the roof. Here was a classic, albeit distasteful, example of Miami fighting back. The grand jury was shocked, but refused to indict Rasheed, who went on to become a local hero.

Just like that burglar trying to squeeze through Rasheed's roof, the crime that has dogged this town for the better part of five decades has never been able to douse its spirit. Neither voodoo curses, baseball bats nor Uzi machine guns can stop this city from pulling through. In fact, the ever mysterious Miami mystique seems to thrive on chaos.

Miami, Florida. Heck of a place to buy a bulletproof Mercedes.

**Above, officer accepts a snack. Right, stylish "gangster car" parked on Ocean Drive.**

In a recent year, with compelling drum beats, 119,986 people in Miami's Little Havana squeezed, shoved and sweated into the longest Conga line on record. Why? Because, in Miami, especially in high season, it's a civic duty to party.

Year-round, unlike cities of chill, Miami hosts its parties in the street – with sunshine and sensuality guaranteed. Visitors have always come for "fun in the sun" – tourists believing the sales pitch, college kids starting a break, senior citizens outlasting winter's wrath. And if weather is no concern, why not party outdoors?

This street-party tradition started years ago as revelers gathered for sport, art and business. As early as 1915, cars bedecked with comptie plants rolled through the Magic Knight of Dade's Mid-Winter Festival parade, advertising arrow root starch as the locally supplied ingredient.

**Lots of noise:** With verve from Cuban immigrants, Miami has pumped these festivals over the past decade with ethnic flair. Now, with lots of noise and no subtlety whatsoever, Miami tells the world: "We're here. Come celebrate with us!"

Carnaval Miami/Calle Ocho, a week-long festival in mid-March, typifies this boast. When Miamians conga-ed into the *Guinness Book of World Records*, they turned a neighborhood block party into an *event*. Touted as America's biggest Hispanic bash, the celebration reveals the Hispanic soul – its pride and hospitality – through scents and sounds, color and chaos.

From the start in 1978, the festival outstripped expectations, spilling over 15 blocks. And, by the mid-1980s, with a million visitors due, planners added five more. At last count filling 23 blocks, the all-day party offers "dance 'til you die" on Calle Ocho or S.W. Eighth Street between Fourth and 27th Avenues. Other Carnaval *salsa* overflows to stadiums and sites throughout the city. Fame

spawned size: a beauty pageant, masquerade ball, big-name performers like the Miami Sound Machine and José Feliciano. And hypo: a huge foot race, bike race, and supposedly the world's largest chicken and rice dinner to feed the winners.

Growth has not always been graceful. The Calle Ocho organizers, the civic-minded Kiwanis Club, exposed provincial roots in the late 1980s. They twice banned entertainers who performed in Cuba, claiming insult

to Miami's staunchly anti-Castro exile community. Protests and lawsuits followed. But the music lingered, on *Calle Ocho* albums that – surprise! – included blacklisted stars.

The Hispanic hullabaloo spurred challengers. Rivaling it for national prominence at the moment is the Miami/Bahamas Goombay Festival. Dubbed the largest black heritage festival in the United States, this summer street party in Coconut Grove celebrates Bahamian slaves' independence and 100-year ties between Miami and the Bahamas.

The weekend romp in early June, dating from 1977, captures the joy of *junkanoo* –

**Preceding pages:** Goombay Festival in the June heat. **Left,** cowbells ring. **Right,** drums beat.

dancers, costumed in gaudy crêpe-paper concoctions, swaying to the clamor of cowbells, whistles and washboards. On street and on stage, rappers' words compete with steel band sounds from "The Islands." In noon-time parades, the Royal Bahamian Police Marching Band conducts precision drills, in uniforms, starched bright white.

More than 400 vendors of arts, crafts and food line Grand Avenue – with conch fritters and Bahama Mama's salads already legendary. In just a few short blocks, thousands of would-be Bahamians or real Bahamians (who make up the largest national group of tourists to Miami), are near to home.

family," it's a parade where bands playing spirited John Phillip Sousa marches and school fight songs stir onlookers.

The mythical King Jamboree often takes physical shape as a 20-ft smiling balloon face – sometimes buoyed by helium or cold air, sometimes anchored by stick or human legs. The Orange Bowl queen is also regal, but definitely human.

With behemoth floats elaborately lit inside and out, the parade claims to be the largest night-time fanfare in the world. Paced for a half-hour's local television coverage and an hour on a national network, it moves slowly and deliberately along a 2.2-mile

Miami's oldest festivals are linked to sport and art traditions, not ethnic roots, especially the largest, oldest and arguably most traditional: the Orange Bowl, the college football classic that frequently decides national championships. Since 1935, the annual King Orange Jamboree Parade on New Year's Eve has mated with the Orange Bowl on New Year's Day, to send football fans into ecstasy for the year.

The jamboree regularly tallies 80,000 fans in bleachers along the downtown route, plus 20 million viewers on television. Promoted by organizers as "G-rated for the whole

route on Biscayne Boulevard, and back.

Planning extends year-round for the Orange Bowl December-to-January hoopla: sailing regatta, international tennis tournament, fashion show, and offspring, like the Junior Orange Bowl Parade, which holds its own celebrations in Coral Gables.

Engine blasts in late winter – the end of February – signal the Grand Prix of Miami, perhaps the only city street sport where competitors make more noise than the usually rowdy spectators.

At straight-away speeds of more than 160 miles an hour, the world's best drivers compete in a race that dominates the international Camel GT circuit – *and* the streets of Homestead, about 20 miles south of Miami. Since 1983, when an unseasonal downpour doused a promoter's dream, top racers and cars have revved up in a demanding three-hour, 1.87-mile circuit.

Shielded by concrete barricades, partygoers with precious tickets climb grandstands while others hover above in helicopters and blimps.

When Miamians leave the streets, they head to special alternatives – water parties, such as the Columbus Day Regatta, which flows in mid-October from Coconut Grove

It is also the time of year said to be the best for smuggling drugs in via boats. The Coast Guard is so busy monitoring the safety of the regatta's participants, that they have no manpower or time to be on the look-out for smugglers bringing drugs into the city.

Docked overnight at around the half-way point, sailors turn into swimmers with sociable skinny dips into the water. Exploding fireworks and bellowing conch shells keep crews alert.

For many years, the bustling Miami River had a festival in its honor each October, complete with antique marine exhibits, fish fries, boat tours and alligator wrestling. One

to Elliott Key and back. Early on Saturday, boats lurch to a start through Biscayne Bay, and television and radio stations record the quantity of beer drunk and the number of topless bathers spotted.

The cruising regatta regularly logs up to 650 participant and 2,000 spectator boats, with, admittedly, some doubts about who's who. A mainstay from the early 1950s, the weekend is a non-stop event, more camaraderie than competition.

**Left**, good times. <u>**Above**</u>, once held downtown, the Grand Prix has now moved to Homestead.

unfortunate year a pipe line broke beneath the river, spewing raw sewage along the banks. Later, festival organizers created a peace-pipe ceremony advertised by a logo of an Indian in full head-dress. Angry river tribes – Seminoles and Miccosukees – pointed out how their ancestors, supposedly honored by the fest, instead wore turbans with a single feather. These days, the Miami Riverfest is on shaky ground.

Apart from sport, Miamians look for art in their streets, with the mid-February open-air Coconut Grove Arts Festival cited as the largest, oldest and most diverse in the entire state. In 1963, at its start-up, a few dozen local artists casually chatted with a few thousand neighbors. Now, art exhibitors and art lovers still talk, one on one, but over the din of a crowd guesstimated between 200,000 and 1 million people.

Saturday through Monday, the Grove hyperventilates to accommodate festivalgoers. With nationwide competition for 300 display spots, familiar sites disappear. The Bad Portrait booth got ousted. But, wielding six brushes, and in less than four minutes, Denny still created 8-ft high portraits of music personalities (Beethoven, Stevie Wonder) with a Two-Fisted Art Attack. And

up next to Art Deco T-shirts, sometimes even found on the very same body.

An afternoon parade winds from Miami Beach City Hall through the mile-square, pastel-painted architectural district. Rhythm and blues, reggae and *lambada* merge with poolside chatter. Crowds top a half million and increase about 100,000 each year.

It's here that Deco dominates. Street theater sets scenes at 1930s beach resorts or 1940s railway stations. Auctions offer stylized doors salvaged from modern renovations. While promoting Deco throughout the world, the Miami Design Preservation League does not neglect the neighborhood. Activists chide

Haagen-Dazs donated glue and a million ice cream sticks. Corporate support for Art by the Passer-by?

Art lovers also head to Miami Beach, where Art Deco Weekend in mid-January tints South Beach pastel colors. Café-hopping on the promenade, strollers drift with the breezes, eyeing booths along Ocean Drive from Fifth to 15th Streets.

Even the elite "Moon Over Miami" fundraiser for Art Deco preservationists tumbles into the street, closing Collins Avenue between 10th and 11th Streets. Amid Big Band revivals, conservative black tuxedos brush

owners of dilapidated buildings, suggesting a coat of whitewash "for the image." And the League sells plastic sandpails with "I dig Deco" in appropriate hues: pale blue, pink or even white.

Even events normally indoors, like book and film festivals, take to the streets in Miami. Plus they offer a cultural, even – gasp! – intellectual twist, just enough to confuse those who think Miami is all beach and bare bottoms and little or no brain.

At the Miami Film Festival in February, film buffs and directors from around the world congregate at the downtown Gusman

Center and small art theaters across the city for this start-studded local event. Lining up outdoors, onlookers wait for hours for a glimpse of celebrities – Sylvester Stallone, Melanie Griffith, Madonna – and then scream out loud like teenage fans.

Between shows, *mariachis* circulate indoors and out, afloat on "Cielito Lindo" refrains. At fund-raising events, black ties and sequins mix with loafers and jeans at Bayside Marketplace, or move on to the leather-and-lace party at the stately Vizcaya Museum where the champagne flows to the early morning hours.

In 1984, local booksellers, a community

and buyers, shoulder to shoulder, on to the downtown Wolfson Campus of Miami-Dade Community College.

In just a decade, partying has become serious business in Miami. Promoters supply street antics, security, and assurances that thousands will get invited and actually attend. Competition now forces organizers to fix dates early.

Beaux Arts, an arts-and-crafts show on the University of Miami's Coral Gables campus, clamored for "first festival" status in 1990, moving to an early-January slot after almost four decades of being held in March. Also in January the Miami Beach Festival of

college and the public library invented an international book fair, which has blossomed to eight days of show-and-tell about books. A November annual, the fair attracts more than 300 exhibitors and 500,000 browsers.

A week-long conference features prominent writers like Alice Walker or Norman Mailer, sometimes hawking a book, sometimes a heritage, such as the Latin or Caribbean traditions appropriate to Miami. Over the closing weekend, books spill, with sellers

the Arts monopolizes Collins Avenue between 50th and 54th Avenues, aiming at peak Beach tourism. And, A Taste of the Grove, an outdoor food fest hosted by dozens of Miami's finest restaurants, takes place in Coconut Grove.

Not everyone loves a party. Local residents complain that out-of-towners and traffic tangles bar them from their own streets. And cutbacks may be inevitable. Miami commissioners are now obliged to consider citizens' petitions to limit the number and size of festivals.

With 17-page agreements to handle de-

**Left**, Calle Ocho draws an evening crowd for jazz.
**Above**, crêpe-paper costumes for grown-ups.

tails like disposing of trash and providing toilets, planning spontaneity in Miami gets more challenging.

But this is irrelevant niggling for those bound for the streets. Parking is *always* impossible, but homeowners rent the front lawn and radio disc jockeys provide tips on available car space. Public transport like Metrorail just adapts, and festival shuttles and trains move crowds from their stops.

Party-goers just arrive early, bring patience, and hunker. When partying or planning gets too exhausting, they consider lying down – at the Coconut Grove Bed Race, for instance, where one Sunday each May four-member teams push and pull beds to raise money for local charities.

Attendance estimates, bulging from corporate sponsors who think big-is-better, may discourage those who like intimacy. Indeed, those people phobic of large crowds should stick to the side streets, where Miami's other ethnic communities – the Haitians and the Jamaicans, among others – have their own special days.

Or be philosophical, like King Mango Strut paraders who each December offer a fresh perspective on a year of nonsense. Half party, half parody, the Strut evolved when the Mango Marching Band, playing kazoos and conch shells, was rejected by Orange Bowl organizers in 1981.

The following year, band members started a tradition, instantly, Miami-style. Committed to wackiness and a late start, their colorful half-hour parade in Coconut Grove struts two blocks from Commodore Plaza to Peacock Park.

En route, it abandons all propriety. Such "irregulars" as the Synchronized Briefcase Drill Team, Flamingo Freedom Band, and Marching Freds highlight festival foibles. As Strut founder Glenn Terry explains: "We like to show that Miami has a sense of humor. We like to make people happy. And we like to have fun and enjoy ourselves."

Look for the Tomatoland Trot in Kendall in early April. As Miamians know, allow people into the streets to eat, drink, gawk – and there's no reason to go home.

**Right**, shoulder to shoulder for the show.

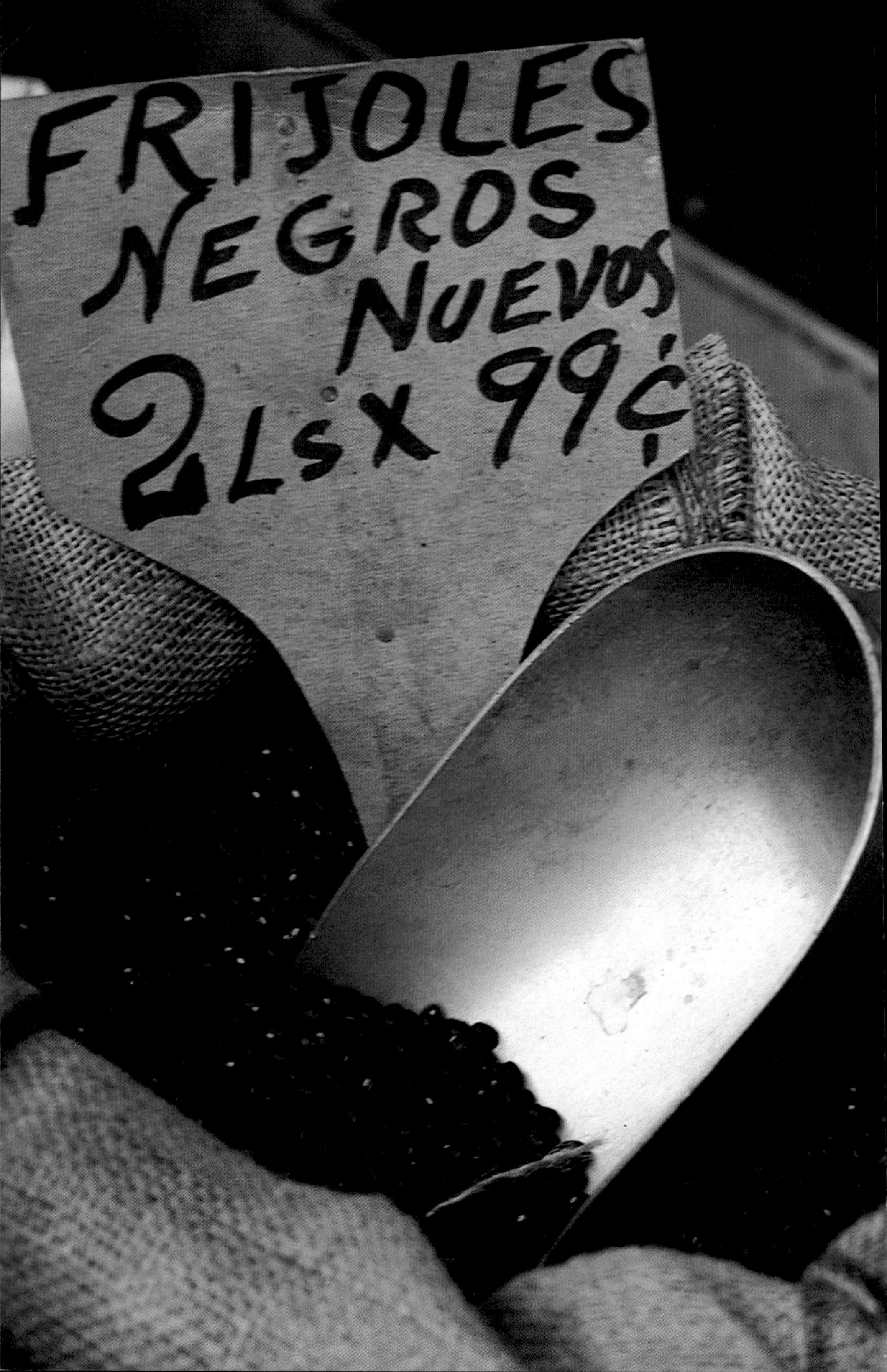
FRIJOLES
NEGROS
NUEVOS
2Ls X 99¢

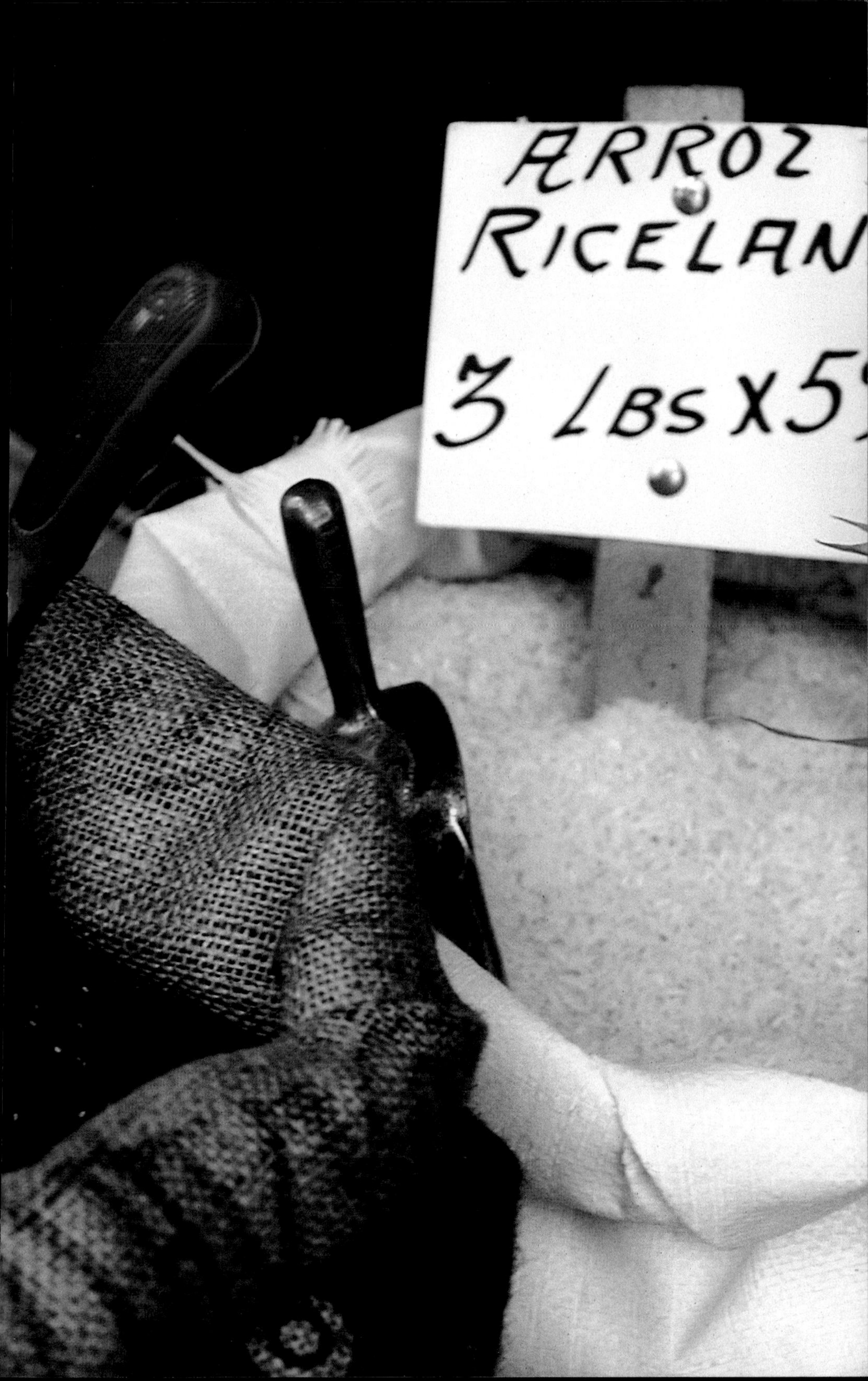
ARROZ
RICELAN
3 LBS X 5

Feeding time in the United States... oh, where the fickle flow. Grazing on sea urchin sushi, warm squab salad with okra, rabbit chili? Steak is for New York strips. Chicken wings belong in the Midwest. Pot-au-feu? Not for many.

Be brave. This is Miami, the simmering stockpot of the tropics. Curry up to goat, a splendid, lean meat found along Mediterranean coastlines but not in Milwaukee. Miami's many Jamaican and Haitian restaurants specialize in goat and kid, most often curried or stewed, slow cooking being the manner preferred. Also look for such dishes as oxtail, jerked pork and chicken, even cow's foot.

Too native? Consider the Queen of the bays: conch. Conch meat must be tenderized, usually with a severe beating, and is often further broken down by a soak in lime juice. But the result is delicious, slightly chewy but with a flavor unlike any other seafood. Cracked conch, a sort of conch cutlet, is breaded and then quickly fried, served sizzling hot with a wedge of lime, superior to veal. Conch also makes a superlative fish chowder.

For the fainter of heart, work up to conch in fritter form. If done right, not puck-like from the National Hockey League recipe book, conch fritters are light, airy, crisp on the outside, moist, steaming hot inside, flavored with bits of ground conch, sweet red pepper and onion.

Even a cliché like Key lime pie, an overexposed dessert served everywhere in Florida, has a distinctive side. Originally made without refrigeration, consisting of little more than the juice of tiny, yellowish Key limes, eggs and sweetened, condensed milk, the pie must be yellow, not green. It should also make the lips pucker.

**Simmering seafood:** Remember that nothing goes into this city's big pot without first

**Preceding pages**: rice and beans, a Miami staple. **Left**, *paella* for a multitude. **Right**, a Sunday brunch.

being brought from some place else and the sea is the factor that binds it all together. The provender making the leap from the Atlantic and the Gulf of Mexico to Miami's kitchen is impressive. Look for fresh yellowtail, a smallish snapper with moist, elegant meat that doesn't have an abundance of bones. A ceviche, which is raw fish marinated in freshly squeezed lime juice and flavored with hot peppers, onions and cilantro, is wonderful if it is made with local yellowtail.

Dolphin, listed on many menus, is a lean, blunt-headed fish and no relative of the famous mammal. Lobster in Florida is really a clawless crawfish, a seasonal food that may be legally caught from August through March. It is completely unlike Maine lobster, not as rich, tougher. Pompano is a dark-meated, more flavorful fish.

But all this is mere warm-up food to the main course. Stand outside Miami's most famous restaurant, Joe's Stone Crab on Miami Beach, within a block of the ocean and several hours' wait for a table.

People lust for stone crabs, most often

served chilled. The fat claws are plump with firm, pure white meat, like well-fed baby's arms. And if the meat has little flavor and most of the taste comes from the mustard sauce or the melted butter dip, no one seems to notice. Stone crabs are exotic. Stone crabs are part of Miami.

**Latin spices:** Another Miami flavor is that most humble of foods, the bean. Not just any bean, but the earthy black bean. This bean, full of Spanish heritage, is a basic of culinary Cuba. Poor man's food, beans and rice combine to a nearly perfect protein, the equal of red meat but without the fats. Black beans and rice cooked together is called *moros y*

Many foods identified with a culture often become clichéd and trite, but young Cuban cooks improvise with this staple, along with such things as *yuca*, a starchy root vegetable, and *plantain*, a starchy, hard green banana that is usually fried like a sweet chip.

But Hispanic Miami is more than just Cuban cooking. The city's large Nicaraguan population has spawned numerous restaurants, too. The specialty of the house is steak, grilled and served with a pungent sauce. Several Argentine restaurants also satisfy the beef lover.

Colombian cooking, heavily reliant on seafood from the Pacific's abundant

*cristianos,* after the famous collision of Charles Martel and the Arabs in AD 732.

Black beans have a slightly mealy texture but more taste than those found in Boston. They are used in soup, in stews, served cold in salads, simmered with an onion and a bay leaf to be poured over rice as a side dish. In recent years cooks have drained cooked black beans, mashed them into a paste, flattened it and fried the result into crêpe-like black bean cakes, served with salsa and a dot of sour cream. Black beans are even found in stuffing. *Bolichemechado* is a beef dish, eye of the round, stuffed with rice and beans.

Humboldt Current, is popular. Brazil and Peru are also represented. The Miami telephone directory divides restaurants by ethnic persuasion.

**Southern roots:** If modern Miami dining is an international buffet, old Miami is more connected to Dixie. For real roots, look toward the Everglades. Of the indigenous creatures found in early Miami, the alligator was the only marginally harvestable, edible item on the list. But through the years, millions were killed for their hides. One estimate was

**Above**, outdoor cooking. **Right**, Cuban coffee.

# CAFE CUBANO

**A**t Cafeteria Café Cubano on Miami's Calle Ocho, a dark-eyed waitress slides a thimble-sized paper cup across the clean counter. Sweet and swampy, the liquid idiosyncrasy is raised to the lips and a local ritual begins. Soon, the caffeine and sugar infusion that is café Cubano will sharpen the mind and loosen the tongue. The steamy antithesis to a soothing shot of bourbon, Miami's favorite drink transforms a 10-second sip into a cerebral celebration that winds you up instead of down.

From the chrome-and-glass skyscrapers of downtown Miami to the ham-and-cheese lunch counters of Little Havana, the potent aroma of Cuban coffee percolates throughout the city. While across the country many Americans have become caffeine conscious and sugar phobic, Miamians have cross-culturally adopted this coffee beverage, rendering it as much a local staple as sweet Florida sunshine and salty sea air.

Imported from Latin America, the beans used in Cuban coffee are roasted at a slightly higher temperature and for a longer time than beans used in American coffee. But both the temperature and roasting time are less than those used for roasting Italian espresso coffee beans.

Brewed in traditional, red-and-white espresso machines, each cup is individually prepared with extreme care and precision. Three scoops of freshly ground coffee are dropped into the filter. In about 10 seconds, an ounce of scalding water pushes through the tightly packed coffee and a foamy, molasses-thick nectar drops into a tiny metal pitcher below. Two teaspoons of sugar are stirred in and the liquid is poured into a tiny paper, plastic, or china *demi-tasse* cup.

At home, many of Miami's older Cubans still brew the coffee the old-fashioned way – in a cheesecloth funnel, or sometimes an old sock, filled with coffee and boiling water. To create the foam, a drop of coffee is added to two spoonfuls of sugar and mashed into a paste. The grounds are then saved for the flower garden.

Coffee and sugar, the ingredients of café Cubano, have been two of the main ingredients of the Cuban economy for the past 200 years. The coffee bean, which grew wild, was first cultivated by European settlers as early as the 1500s. By the 1800s, *cafetals* – coffee plantations – flourished throughout the island's fertile, mountain land. Concurrently, sugar plantations prospered.

During the early 1900s, cafés along the elegant boulevards of old Havana sold the local drink from enormous machines that clamored and chimed with each freshly brewed batch. Later, cafés improvised their own Pavlovian call by ringing a bell on the streets to entice people in.

The popularity of café Cubano took hold in Miami in the 1960s, when the first wave of Cuban immigrants peppered the streets with hand-painted signs advertising the potent brew.

Café Pilon, one of the major coffee suppliers in Miami, services over 800 restaurants in the area, along with supplying beans, grinders and machines to almost 5,000 Miami businesses. Many bankers, doctors, lawyers and business people offer complimentary cups to their clients. Unlike the cold-weather tradition of lingering over a large, steaming mug of coffee, drinking the tiny, concentrated "shots" is a sensible way to take coffee in a semi-tropical setting.

Café Cubano is served ubiquitously, from the lace-table-cloth restaurants to the beauty parlors, dress shops, Art Deco hotels, hospitals and funeral homes. Take-out windows sell it in large plastic containers with a supply of tiny paper cups. Even the McDonald's restaurant in Little Havana offers café Cubano to go with the Huevo McMuffins. While the decors vary, the coffee is a constant.

Taken alone as a pick-me-up, or with a guava-filled Cuban pastry, café Cubano is sipped throughout the city from morning till night. Sometimes, bite-size pieces of bread dipped in sugar are dunked in the coffee. After meals, it is served in the company of a hand-rolled cigar. While *café con leche* – Cuban coffee with warm milk in a regular-size cup – is often served and frequently given to children, in true café Cubano, cream is a sacrilege, a social taboo. ∎

that 3½ million alligators were slaughtered during one 50-year span.

By the 1960s the alligator's survival was threatened and hunting was prohibited. Quickly, the alligator came back. By 1988, it was again legal to hunt alligator and people were beginning to experiment, to actually bite back. Alligator, specifically alligator tail, became a menu item.

The tail is all lean, white meat and people will say to try it because it tastes like chicken. That is what they say about anything that slithers, crawls, hops, hisses, croaks and lives in the swamp.

In fact, alligator tastes the way it is cooked.

Most often it is breaded and fried, served as an appetizer with a red tomato sauce like fried clam strips. It is stewed like conch and turtle or made into sausage.

Venture into the swamp and one finds the cook fires of Miami's native Americans, the Miccosukee Indians. Many of the Miccosukee ceremonies are kept a secret but their cooking is an open book. Two items, if you can find them, are worth the trek. Everglades frogs' legs consist of delicate, alabaster meat that gently pulls away from the tiny bones. Local frogs' legs are a dying tradition because no one wants to hunt them, not even the

Indians. The Indians' own fry bread – dough dropped in hot oil and fried to a golden puff – is another seldom-sampled taste of Miami.

**Garden of Eden:** If Miami is sea and swamp, it is also like a green garden. Certain exotic fruits, all brought from elsewhere, grow on the southern tip of Florida and in no other region of the US. While the rest of the country is cold and gray in winter, Miami is growing strawberries, tomatoes, beans and squash. Once citrus was the coveted crop, the rest of the world breathlessly in awe of oranges, tangerines and grapefruit in January. But most of the early citrus is gone, limited now to backyard growers.

What still flourishes in Miami is virtually the total US crop of Persian limes, that plump little twist of green which is dropped into a gin and tonic. The sour orange is another tiny little fruit, but it plays a catalytic role in producing one of Miami's most flamboyant dishes, whole roast pig. People spend hours squeezing these baby oranges to make a marinade for the pig, called *lechon*. The roasting, at Christmas or for major celebrations, takes a day and is often done in a backyard pit. The juicy, slow-cooked meat comes off in great chunks from the crackling skin that protects it from the heat.

Because of its geography, Miami's future belongs to exotic fruits that command a good market price. Consider the atemoya, a green, rough-skinned fruit with a white, custard-like interior that tastes like piña colada. Atemoya looks like a cross between a hand grenade and a mutant artichoke.

But the biggest exotic cash crop in Miami is the sacred fruit of India, the mango. Called the apple of the tropics, mangoes come in colors: red, orange, yellow and purple, the sweet flesh is yellow to golden orange. Mango, first an import, is now a thriving export to other US markets.

It has been adopted and made part of the flavor of Miami. Mango trees, 40-ft tall at maturity, line streets and pop up in side yards, their heavy fruit hanging down in clusters. In India, they sing songs of love to the mango. In Miami it is part of the movable feast, part of the exotic landscape.

Left, sweet treats. Right, ripe mangoes.

# PLACES

At dawn, a red-headed rooster crows his morning call through the inner-city neighborhood of Little Haiti. Across town, an elegant old peacock fans his iridescent tail and struts past the palatial homes of Coconut Grove. Miami's cityscape is a picture of incongruity – part American dream, part Third World struggle.

The Places section that follows is designed to evoke that often-elusive "sense of place." It is a portrait of Miami's neighborhoods and nearby cities and the quality of life within them – from the high-power offices of downtown Miami to the low, lush strawberry fields south of the city. But more than casual descriptions of Miami's neighborhoods, the Places chapters are keen assessments of the settings that cradle the mingled destinies of its people.

Although not every inch of the city is detailed, what is included is an eclectic array of sights and sounds that will put you in touch with where you find yourself and set your feet and mind in motion. Whether actually visiting, or just armchair traveling from home, the upcoming pages will make it clear that Miami is much more than just a beach.

This is followed by a series of daytrips from the city that will guide you through the South Florida environs, from the underwater spectacles of the Upper Keys and the womb-like wonders of the Florida Everglades, to the beer-guzzling bars of the Fort Lauderdale strip and the old-money mansions of extravagant Palm Beach.

While, for most, travel will never mean the rugged contours of continents or the sensuous smells of spices that Ulysses found on his journeys, there is still time to uncover corners of Miami that are very different from your own home town, and to bask in its simple secrets of where to find the best fried bananas or the most enticing *salsa*-filled nightclub. In essence, the things that make a place a place.

**Preceding pages: windsurfers set sail; Deco delights in South Beach; fishing for an urban catch; pulsating to the rhythms. Left, aerial view by NASA of the Miami coast.**

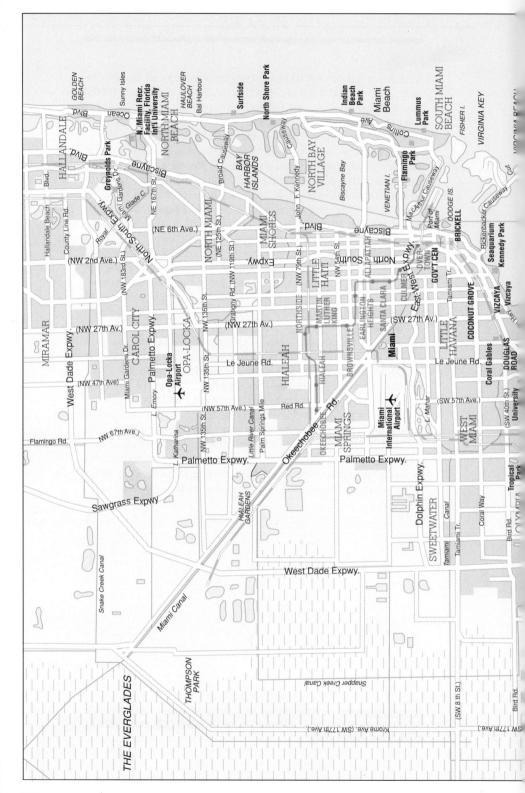

THE EVERGLADES

GOLDEN BEACH
Sunny Isles
Ocean Blvd.
HALLANDALE
Blvd.
Hallandale Beach
County Line Rd.
Royal
Miami Glade C.
Miami Gardens Dr.
N. Miami Recr. Facility, Florida Int'l University
HAULOVER BEACH
Bal Harbour
Surfside
North Shore Park
Indian Beach Park
Miami Beach
SOUTH MIAMI BEACH
VIRGINIA KEY
Greynolds Park
Biscayne Blvd.
North-South Expwy
NORTH MIAMI BEACH
BAY HARBOR ISLANDS
Broad Causeway
NORTH BAY VILLAGE
Biscayne Bay
VENETIAN I.
Lummus Park
Collins Ave.
FISHER I.
MIRAMAR
(NW 2nd Ave.)
NE 167th St.
(NE 6th Ave.)
NE 125th St.
NORTH MIAMI
(NE 119th St.)
MIAMI SHORES
Expwy.
John F. Kennedy Causeway
Flamingo Park
MacArthur Causeway
Port of Miami
DODGE IS.
Rickenbacker Causeway
(NW 183rd St.)
Trailnigy Rd. (NW 119th St.)
(NW 79th St.)
LITTLE HAITI
NW 54th St.
North South Expwy.
East-West Expwy.
OVER TOWN
GOVT CEN
BRICKELL
Seaquarium
Kennedy Park
CAROL CITY
Palmetto Expwy.
OPA-LOCKA
135th St.
(NW 27th Av.)
NORTHSIDE
MARTIN LUTHER KING
EARLINGTON HEIGHTS
SANTA CLARA
CULMER Expwy.
Tamiami Tr.
VIZCAYA
Vizcaya
DOUGLAS ROAD
(NW 27th Ave.)
(NW 47th Ave)
Opa-Locka Airport
Le Jeune Rd.
HIALEAH
BROWNSVILLE
Miami
(SW 27th Av.)
Le Jeune Rd.
LITTLE HAVANA
COCONUT GROVE
Coral Gables
Emory
L. Katharina
NW 135th St.
Palm Springs Mile
Red Rd.
HIALEAH
L. Mahar
University
(SW 40th St.)
(SW 57th Ave.)
Flamingo Rd.
NW 67th Ave.)
Little River Canal
Miami International Airport
WEST MIAMI
West Dade Expwy.
Palmetto Expwy.
Okeechobee Rd.
OKEECHOBEE Rd.
MIAMI SPRINGS
Palmetto Expwy.
Dolphin Expwy.
SWEETWATER
Bird Rd.
Tropical Park
HIALEAH GARDENS
Sawgrass Expwy
Tamiami Canal
Tamiami Tr.
Coral Way
Snake Creek Canal
Miami Canal
West Dade Expwy.
THOMPSON PARK
Snapper Creek Canal
Bird Rd.
(SW 8th St.)
Krome Ave. (SW 177th Ave.)
SW 177th Ave.)

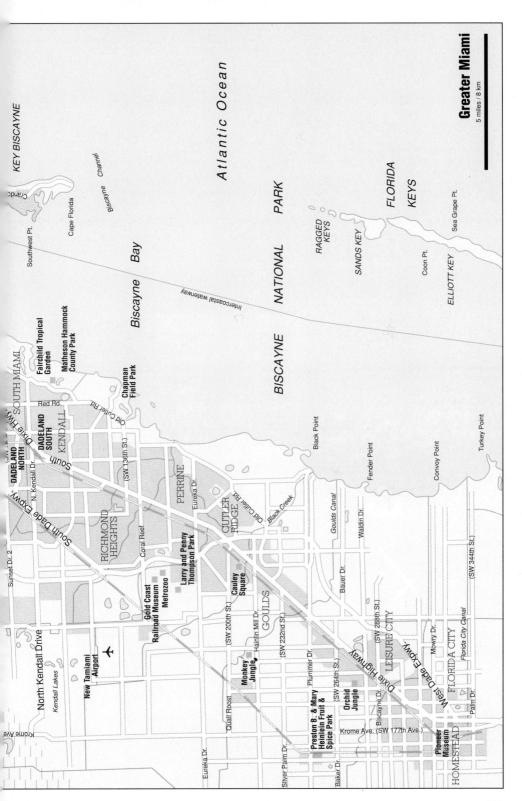

**Greater Miami**

5 miles / 8 km

KEY BISCAYNE

Grande

Southwest Pt.

Cape Florida

Biscayne Channel

*Atlantic Ocean*

Biscayne Bay

Intracoastal waterway

BISCAYNE NATIONAL PARK

RAGGED KEYS

SANDS KEY

FLORIDA KEYS

Coon Pt.

ELLIOTT KEY

Sea Grape Pt.

Black Point

Fender Point

Convoy Point

Turkey Point

Fairchild Tropical Garden

Matheson Hammock County Park

Chapman Field Park

SOUTH MIAMI

Dixie Hwy.

DADELAND NORTH

DADELAND SOUTH

Red Rd.

KENDALL

South Kendall Dr.

N. Kendall Dr.

Old Cutler Rd.

(SW 136th St.)

PERRINE

Eureka Dr.

CUTLER RIDGE

Old Cutler Rd.

Black Creek

Goulds Canal

Waldin Dr.

Sunset Dr. 2

South Dade Expwy.

RICHMOND HEIGHTS

Coral Reef

Larry and Penny Thompson Park

Gold Coast Railroad Museum

Metrozoo

Cauley Square

(SW 200th St.)

Hainlin Mill Dr.

GOULDS

(SW 232nd St.)

Bauer Dr.

(SW 288th St.)

LEISURE CITY

Mowry Dr.

Dixie Highway

West Dade Expwy.

Florida City Canal

(SW 344th St.)

FLORIDA CITY

North Kendall Drive

Kendall Lakes

Krome Ave

New Tamiami Airport

Quail Roost

Monkey Jungle

Plummer Dr.

(SW 264th St.)

Orchid Jungle

Preston B. & Mary Heinlein Fruit & Spice Park

Biscayne Dr.

Krome Ave. (SW 177th Ave.)

Silver Palm Dr.

Baker Dr.

Eureka Dr.

Palm Dr.

HOMESTEAD

Pioneer Museum

# DOWNTOWN MIAMI

It is a toddler in the family of America's big cities. Some of downtown Miami's older buildings are younger than many of the folks who have come here to retire. But since April 15, 1896, when Henry Flagler brought his Florida East Coast Railway into Miami, literally putting the town on the map for subsequent waves of settlers, the little devil has turned into a spunky, scrappy city. With its notable, excitable Latin edge, downtown feels more like the northern tip of the southern hemisphere than the other way around.

From a distance, especially at night, downtown Miami looks like a throbbing megalopolis, its bank of skyscrapers floodlit and twinkling in colored neon, creating a magic-show skyline quite unlike any other in the United States. Yet, for visitors walking its streets, from the **Morningside** neighborhood, south along **Biscayne Boulevard**, through the central grid of one-way streets, across the **Miami River** and into the gleaming **Brickell Avenue** quarter, Miami runs very much on a human scale.

There are cops walking beats along wide sidewalks; hawkers selling fruits and juices and cakes from corner pushcarts; cabbies dozing in taxis queued up along **Flagler Street** like bright yellow bonbons; hot-dog vendors and shoeshine men on the steps of the **Dade County Courthouse**. The city seems more like a street fair than the cultural, political and administrative nerve center of a sprawling metropolis.

**A walker's delight:** Start a downtown tour at the intersection of Flagler Street and **Miami Avenue**. It's here that the rest of Miami gets its bearings: the two streets divide Dade County into four quadrants of the compass. Flagler runs east–west; Miami north–south. This is the eye of Miami's urban storm. Walk east on Flagler and it's quickly appar-

ent: the street, with the scent of freshly squeezed oranges, the palette of subtropical clothes, and the sound of businessmen haggling in Spanish, Creole, Hebrew and English, is a real-life cartoon strip, an eight-block-long signature of the urban subtropics, Miami in shorthand.

At the intersection of **N.E. Second Avenue** sits a collection of the wonders of Miami's brief past. **Walgreens**, on the southeast corner, is a Streamline Moderne architectural gem, opened in 1936 as one of the drugstore chain's most attractive shops. Next door is the classy **Ingraham Building**, a Florentine Renaissance beauty that opened in 1926. Its lobby is crowned by an ornate ceiling, with original light fixtures, mailbox and office directory. Scenes of South Florida wildlife play out on the gold of the elevator.

West on Flagler is the **Olympia Building**, its Spanish-eclectic style boasting the glorious **Gusman Cultural Center**. Built for Paramount Pictures in the mid-

1920s, the theater is a romantic re-creation of what might be an Andalusian courtyard at night, replete with billowing clouds painted overhead and stars a-twinkling. The tall, smooth organ pipes tower in the cool cavern near the left of the stage.

Over on East Flagler Street the severe lines of the **Alfred I duPont Building** define Miami's ode to Rockefeller Center. An Art Deco jewel built between 1937 and 1939, the duPont served as the southeastern seat of the Florida National Bank and Trust system. It was regional headquarters for the US Navy during World War II. Its appearance has remained relatively unchanged. Inside the lobby, the Deco-styled café and directory seem like remnants of a Miami that flared, then faded, half a century ago. At the foot of the escalator, near the front door, the view up is toward beautiful murals inspired by Florida history and its natural landscape.

Next, it's back on the street to the buzzing of contemporary Miami. Electronic hardware outlets are everywhere; they are what many Miamians first think of at the mention of "downtown." The shops, lined door-to-door throughout downtown, are magnets to shoppers from around the Caribbean. They cart off stereos, TV sets and video recorders by the bagful. Some even come with empty suitcases in order to carry the goods on the next plane out.

A few doors down, in the **Capital Mall** on Flagler, is **Floridita**, a restaurant famous in Cuba before its owners migrated north. Walk through the mall and on to **N.E. First Street**. This corridor might be downtown's best-kept secret, with its cluster of architectural delights dating back to the 1920s. First, there is the **Dade Commonwealth Building** with its majestic eagles resting atop neo-classical columns. Born of the boom era, the Commonwealth is really a truncated version of its former self; the killer hurricane of 1926 obliterated the top 10 stories.

West, on the south side of First Street,

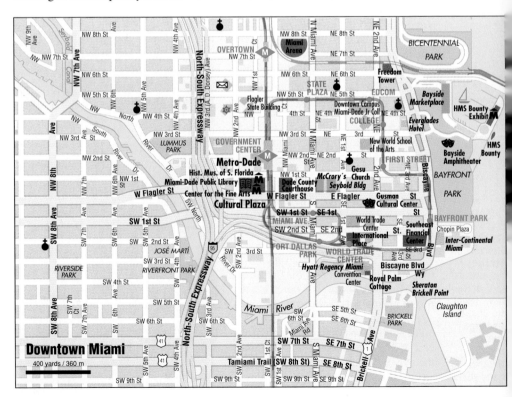

sits the **Shoreland Arcade**. The arcade once housed the Shoreland Company, a huge boom-era developer. The structure dates to the mid-1920s. The highly ornate, classical design remains intact, its huge arched entranceways boasting elaborate friezes. The original chandeliers, decorative terrazzo floors and mailbox remain as well.

West of the Shoreland is the old **Dade Federal Bank Building** with its trademark Art Deco highlights near the roof. Across the avenue stands the **Ralston Building**, built in 1917 as one of the city's earliest skyscrapers.

Carefully cross First Avenue – Miami drivers are notoriously reckless – then turn toward the northeast. The French-inspired mansard roof, rare for Miami, tops off the slim, imposing **Capitol Bank Building**. Next-door is the **Gesu Catholic Church**, the oldest Catholic parish in Miami. This is a beautiful, Mediterranean-Revival structure constructed in the mid-1920s. Covering the ceiling is a mural, restored in its

entirety by a lone Nicaraguan refugee in the late 1980s.

Farther west along First Street, pass by the rear of the old Jackson Byron's Pharmacy. A couple of doors past that is the 10-story **Seybold Building**. Built in the 1920s, it's the heart of downtown's booming jewelry business, one of the busiest in the country.

Next door stands **McCrory's**, housed in one of the oldest buildings in downtown – parts of it date back to 1906. The American civil rights movement made history in 1960 when blacks staged a daring lunch-counter sit-in at the cafeteria. The store is a real nugget of Miami history, reminiscent of a time when Five & Dime stores flourished across America.

One block south along Miami Avenue is **Burdines**, flagship department store of downtown. Burdines began near this spot back in the late 1800s and today the chain is the largest in Florida. Note the foot-bridge that ties the old Burdines to its newer counterpart on the

Gold sold by the inch.

west side of the street, crossing Miami Avenue, oldest thoroughfare in town.

**Heart of the county:** West on Flagler is the **Dade County Courthouse**, the unofficial hub of downtown. It was built between 1925 and 1928 and at the time of its opening prided itself on being the tallest building south of Baltimore, Maryland. Its style is neo-classical. The building once housed both the city and county jails, which were stacked safely on the top 10 floors. Earlier, along the building's north side, gallows used to be erected from time to time for executions. Each fall, turkey buzzards that have migrated from Ohio take over the courthouse's ziggurat-stepped roof as their winter home.

The courthouse area is the center of downtown's civic and cultural life. It sits beside the heart of Dade's rapid-transit system as well. The two sets of overhead tracks constitute the county's fledgling transit network. The first carries **Metromover**, a driverless rubber-wheeled train that runs along a 1.9-mile loop through downtown, stopping at 10 spots. It's a convenient and quick way to hop from one place to another.

The higher set of tracks carry **Metrorail**, mother ship of the system. Metrorail is a high-speed rail that pierces the county out of downtown along a 20-mile arc. It carries passengers northwest to Overtown, the civic center and on to Hialeah, and south to Coconut Grove and Kendall. Metrorail is a great way to see Miami and its environs. The trains soar high above the streets, tree canopies and tile roofs that make this such a lush, lovely city to ponder from the air.

Get off back at the **Metro-Dade Government Center**, home office to the massive county government. Wander the lobby shops and cafés, then hop an elevator to the higher floors for sweeping views of turquoise Biscayne Bay, its islands and port, downtown streets and curling Miami River.

Across First Street is the **Metro-Dade Cultural Plaza**, designed by renowned architect Philip Johnson. The Center is

Metro-Dade Cultural Plaza.

home to the **Miami-Dade Public Library**, the **Historical Museum of Southern Florida** and the **Center for the Fine Arts**. Costs are minimal and the library, of course, is free. The plaza connecting the Center's components is an architectural delight. A grand stairway skirting a seven-stepped granite fountain leads to the plaza, a quiet world unto itself, reminiscent of the *piazzas* of Italian hill towns. This is an urban oasis, a great place to buy a sandwich and relax in the sun.

**Table with a view:** Leaving the center, walk or drive west on Flagler to **East Coast Fisheries**, a Miami institution since 1926, and a fine place for lunch on the river. Grab a table upstairs, order from the large menu, then sit back and absorb the animation.

Several blocks north is **Joe's Seafood Restaurant**. Tables offer close-up views of the river and the people who work on it. A few blocks southeast is **Lummus Park**, with two of Miami's most historic structures: the **William English Slave Plantation House**, commonly known as **Fort Dallas**, a limestone fortress built in the 1840s and moved to this site in 1925 from just down the river, and the **William Wagner House**, crafted from Dade County pine by a 19th-century homesteader.

Another interesting area on the periphery of downtown is the **Overtown-Park West** development around N.W. Sixth Street and Second Avenue, the first major redevelopment of a central city neighborhood in South Florida. Backers are betting this project, which began in 1988, will bring suburbanites back downtown to live, lured by new apartments and the **Miami Arena**, home of the Miami Heat, a member of the National Basketball Association.

Just north is **Overtown**, one of the city's oldest black communities. Today, it's a shell of its former self, ripped apart by a freeway system and hobbled by poverty and crime. It's not an area to wander into alone, by day or by night. It was once a much prouder place, home to

Published in two languages.

a largely self-sufficient black community and famous for its lively jazz clubs and theaters.

**On "The Boulevard":** Leading out of downtown along the bay is Biscayne Boulevard, a palm-lined passageway that passes through several small cities north of Miami. The **Sears Building** at 13th Street, built in 1929, is the oldest Art Deco structure in Miami. At 14th Street are the **Boulevard Shops**, another fine Art Deco specimen. Behind it on the bay is the *Miami Herald* **building**. Just north on Biscayne, the **Omni International Mall**, hotel and movie complex towers above the boulevard.

To the west a few blocks on N.E. Second Avenue, the **S&S Restaurant** serves up home-cooked fare at Depression-era prices, a real Miami institution. Run across the street to the **Miami City Cemetery**, the city's oldest burial spot and home to many of its original settlers. The cemetery is known for its late-Victorian architecture and a wide variety of subtropical trees and plants.

Back on Biscayne, the next several miles are a bit worn at the edges; prostitutes and drug dealers lend a tattered air to an otherwise gorgeous thoroughfare. One break in this dreary picture is the historic district of **Morningside**, just east of the boulevard and north of 55th Street. Here, one finds a fantastic collection of Mediterranean-Revival and Art Deco homes, facing wide tree-lined avenues leading down to the bay. Even Pope John Paul II saw fit to spend the night at a home in this district during his visit to Miami in 1987.

**Bankers' row:** Back on the other side of downtown, Brickell Avenue serves as the southern counterpart to Biscayne Boulevard. Cross the bridge on to "bankers' row." Many of these are international banks that symbolize Miami's strong connections to South American and Caribbean economies. Tall green-glass buildings now dominate what was once the corridor for Miami's most stunningly beautiful mansions, a veritable millionaires' row. Rounding the turn at

**The Jamaica National Dance Company performs downtown.**

**15th Road** and Brickell Avenue, the banks give way to Miami's most famous high-rise residential real estate. Arquitectonica, a daring and avant-garde architectural firm, made its mark here. The firm's most famous works include the **Palace Condominium** and the **Atlantis** on Brickell Avenue. There is also the **Villa Regina**, a rainbow-colored condominium that's impossible to miss.

One of the most interesting spots in the downtown area is **Tobacco Road**, a bar/restaurant on South Miami Avenue that claims the city's oldest liquor licence (1912). Dark and smoky with walls covered with old newspaper clippings about the club, the Road cranks out live blues and jazz most nights, as well as occasionally hosting open-mike poetry readings.

**A working man's river:** Coursing through downtown is the last sloping bend of the Miami River just before it spills into Biscayne Bay at **Brickell Point**. The river, a working waterway full of foreign freighters, gives definition to the downtown and adds a certain mystique to an already mystique-filled town. Start at the strip of land at the foot of the steps behind the **Hyatt Regency Miami Hotel**. One of Miami's earlier and premier housing subdivisions occupied this site. The river was originally just 5 miles in length and served as a highway for the early pioneers, its banks holding the first residents.

A few hundred feet west is the **Royal Palm Cottage**, a yellow-framed house built in 1897. Today it's a waterfront restaurant. Take the **Riverwalk** northeast, following the contours of the bay. Towering above the thicket of skyscrapers is the 47-story **International Place**, opened in the late 1980s and designed by the internationally renowned architect I.M. Pei. At night, the tower is floodlit in different colors – red, white and blue on the Fourth of July, emerald green on St Patrick's Day.

Closer to the bay is Miami's tallest tower, the **Southeast Financial Center**, another product of the early 1980s

*International Place changes color on command.*

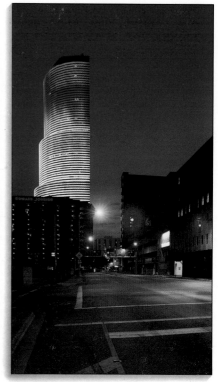

building boom downtown. Part of the complex rests on the site of an ancient Indian burial mound. Its 55 stories also make it the tallest skyscraper in Florida. At the edge of the bay the Riverwalk passes the **Hotel Inter-Continental Miami**, one of the city's finest.

**Downtown playgrounds:** Next comes **Bayfront Park**, a large greenery built in the early 1920s from bay bottom. At the southern end stands a memorial built by the late Japanese sculptor Isamu Noguchi and dedicated to the crew of the ill-fated *Challenger* space shuttle. This is the spot where, in 1933, an assassin attempted to kill President-elect Franklin D. Roosevelt. He missed Roosevelt, but mortally wounded Chicago's mayor, Anton Cermak.

The park has recently undergone a $30-million facelift. Evenings, horse-drawn buggies carry sightseers from nearby Bayside Marketplace to the **Claude and Mildred Pepper Fountain**, named after the late congressman and his wife. The park also features a

sprawling amphitheater, host to concerts and festivals, and nightly a laser show, throwing beams of colored light into the night above Miami. At the eastern edge stands a celebrated statue of Christopher Columbus, presented to the city by the people of Italy on Columbus Day in 1953.

To the north of the park is **Bayside Marketplace**, a 16-acre extravaganza of over 140 shops, restaurants and attractions. Along the water's edge, private boats dock for lunch and dinner as mimes, jugglers and bands entertain the crowds. The 65-foot-long neon guitar in the background marks the entrance to the **Hard Rock Cafe Miami**, one of the many rock memorabilia clubs around the world. With an emphasis on the city's Latin personality, this Hard Rock Cafe includes memorabilia from local superstars Gloria Estefan and John Secada. North of Bayside, **Bicentennial Park** often comes alive with outdoor concerts and festivals.

A few blocks north, the restored **Freedom Tower** rises on the west side of Biscayne. Built in 1925 as home to the now defunct *Miami News*, the tower served in the 1960s as a processing center for Cuban immigrants, hence its name. It was abandoned for years, until Saudi Arabian investors in the late 1980s sunk money back into the 17-story gem, once called "Miami's Statue of Liberty," and restored it to its former grandeur. It's now an office building.

Due west two blocks is **Miami-Dade Community College's Wolfson Campus**, the largest community college in the United States. Wolfson has given downtown Miami another boost of energy; the campus has hosted huge paella cook-off parties and, each November, the Miami International Book Fair. Directly west of the campus is the **United States Post Office and Federal Courthouse**, the latter housing the small jail cell that in 1990 was the unluxurious home-away-from-home for Panamanian dictator Manuel Noriega, while he awaited trial on drug charges.

**Left, downtown at night. Right, Bayfront Park afternoon fun.**

130

# MIAMI BEACH AND SOUTH BEACH

The Bulgarian artist who calls himself Christo was prophetic when it came to Miami Beach. After more than a year of battling environmentalists, politicians and tourism honchos, Christo convinced the doubting dozens to allow him to use gleaming Biscayne Bay as the backdrop for his art. On May 7, 1983, when Miami Beach was for the most part a has-been Riviera of the South, Christo and a band of loyal subjects finished wrapping 11 islands in Biscayne Bay in 6½ million sq. ft of flamingo pink plastic.

For two weeks, the islands floated among the shiny pink fabric for all to see. The grim opposition had given way to gasps of delight and civic pride. After decades of being ignored, Miami Beach was once again in the pink.

Soon after, *Miami Vice* arrived and Miami Beach, particularly **South Beach**, with its white sand beaches and cotton candy-color hotels with whimsical Art Deco designs, never looked better. Miami Beach has always been more vice than nice, making it a frustrating place to live, but an astoundingly beautiful spot to visit. And if it looks as if the "grass is greener" in Miami Beach than in other parts of the city, it is. Occasionally, officials have been known to hook up high-pressure hoses and literally spray paint the sun-burned grass with 50-gallon vats of non-toxic dye.

**Another comeback:** "Miami Beach," as one observer put it, "has had more comebacks than Peggy Lee." In the early 1980s, residents knew and tourists were warned not even to drive through blighted and deserted South Beach at night. Now, tourists not only drive through; they stop, stroll, eat, drink, dance, and sleep in renovated and historic South Beach hotels. South Beach is no longer the place to avoid. It's the place to be – and be seen. Nowhere more than on South Beach are the boundaries between trendy and tacky so well fused. Tacky is trendy in South Beach. Kitsch is cool. And the beach beckons all year-round.

**SoBe:** Developers have spent hundreds of millions of dollars transforming run-down and forgotten hotels and apartment buildings, inhabited for decades by retired Jews from cold northeastern cities, into chic buildings where artists create, yuppies entertain, and tourists vacation. Though still shaky, like the shifting sand banks it sits on, South Beach has made another comeback; this time as a trendy urban neighborhood of Art Deco apartments, nightclubs, restaurants, oceanfront cafés, second-hand furniture and clothing stores, art galleries and theaters. South Beach even has a spiffy nickname: SoBe – inspired by Manhattan's SoHo.

Although there are several bridges linking Miami to Miami Beach, the **MacArthur Causeway**, which joins South Beach with downtown Miami, offers the most stunning view of the islands. Formerly a drawbridge that was

lifted often for passing boat traffic, the causeway was rebuilt in the mid-1990s and is now a massive expanse of concrete above Biscayne Bay.

Driving over it, tourists and even some locals stare transfixed at the yachts, sailboats and condominium-size luxury cruise ships, or gaze back at the panorama of Miami's downtown skyline. Many open their car windows to catch that first tantalizing whiff of Miami Beach's salty sea air.

On both sides of the MacArthur Causeway is **Watson Island**, a park named for three-time mayor James Watson, who came to Miami during its infancy in 1898. On the north side of the MacArthur is a tiny jewel called the **Japanese Garden**, a one-acre respite from the boat, air and automobile traffic that surrounds it. As an expression of his friendship, Japanese industrialist Kiyoshi Ichimura gave the garden to the City of Miami in 1961. Ichimura would have been dismayed at what became of his gift. The city ignored the Japanese

Garden for years, until it was nothing but an eyesore. Finally, in 1988, the garden was restored, and once again visitors could walk along the rock garden and the little foot-bridges of the tranquil park under the watchful eyes of the 8-ton, 8-ft tall statue of Hotei, the Japanese god of prosperity.

Watson Island, more than anything, looks like a Madison Avenue-inspired advertising campaign for the wonders of modern transportation. The sounds are diverse: the drone of jets flying overhead to or from Miami International Airport, the whoosh of propellers from helicopters that lift tourists above and around Miami Beach, the bellow of horns announcing cruise ships and yachts crossing, the slap of tug boats dragging tankers and cargo ships across the choppy cut, and, on the causeway, the ever-present sound of automobiles. It's a symphony of engines.

The most startling sight – and sound – for tourists not familiar with amphibious machines, are the bulbous airplanes **A homeless man with all that he owns.**

that circle the Miami skyline and splash into Biscayne Bay, only to crawl up to Watson Island. These seaplanes make up **Chalks International Airlines**, the world's oldest airline, headquartered on Watson Island. In the 1930s, Ernest Hemingway flew frequently on Chalks.

**The Port of Miami:** The grand old airline, founded in 1919, had some rough times recently. The huge leisure conglomerate, Resorts International, threatened to shut down Chalks because it was losing money, and the City of Miami was insisting that the company pay a hefty rent for the land it leases on Watson Island.

The very idea that the chubby planes would fly no more so upset Miamians that many of them wrote angry letters to the editor of the *Miami Herald*. One *Herald* columnist began an unofficial campaign to keep the airline on Watson Island. The public outcry worked. In early 1996, Chalks merged with Pan Am, a recent company that bought the rights to the defunct airline's name, and

it is now officially called the **Pan Am Air Bridge**. Chalks, however, has a loyal fan club and most customers and Miami locals insist on calling it by its original name.

Beyond the flurry of activity on Watson Island are **Dodge** and **Lummus Islands**, home to the largest cruise port in the world, the Port of Miami. The old port facilities stretched from the Freedom Tower to the *Miami Herald* building in downtown Miami. They were replaced in 1964 by the complex on Dodge and Lummus Islands and have since captured the majority of the cruise ship market. Well over 3 million passengers pass through the port each year. There are 12 passenger terminals that serve as home base to 10 cruise lines. The Port of Miami also handles close to 50 cargo lines.

There is no better spot than Watson Island from which to watch the huge cruise ships slowly making their way out to sea. At night the view is even more spectacular, when the lights on the

The *Fantasy* leaves the largest cruise port in the world.

inside and outside of the row of luxury liners are turned on.

On the northside of the MacArthur Causeway are three bridges leading to **Palm**, **Hibiscus** and **Star Islands**. These posh islands, dotted with mansions with yachts moored in their backyards, have had their share of famous and infamous residents. Al Capone, the American gangster whose gambling and prostitution syndicate terrorized Chicago in the 1920s, lived at 93 Palm Island. Fiction writer and journalist Damon Runyon, best known for his humorous stories written in the slang of New York City's underworld characters, lived at 271 Hibiscus Island.

As does Don Johnson, the actor who made unconstructed clothing in pastel hues and unshaven stubble on the chin and cheeks the "Miami look" during the days of *Miami Vice*.

Once past the islands, the teasing is over: the real Miami Beach has been reached. The 400-slip **Miami Beach Marina**, from where dive boats depart for artificial reefs offshore and charter fishing boats, filled with knowing captains and eager anglers, head out to catch The Big One, is to the south – along the end of South Beach.

Following the tip round to Biscayne Street is **Joe's Stone Crab** restaurant, a South Beach institution since 1913. Only at Joe's is pride given over to pleasure. Only at Joe's do Miami's politicos and movers-and-shakers wait with the common folk – sometimes for as long as four hours – for a table. Joe's takes no reservations, although a little cash placed in the palm of the *maître d*'s hand has been known to hurry things along a bit.

And only at Joe's do otherwise reserved adults allow themselves to have huge paper bibs tied around their necks and tucked over their clothing by waiters in tuxedos. To what end? After they've dipped the first succulent claw into butter or mustard sauce, customers understand that there are no better stone crabs' claws to be had than at Joe's. And they are grateful for those claws, despite

**Beyond the boatyard, one of the posh islands west of Miami Beach.**

the fact that they've waited for hours, donned bibs, and depleted their wallets.

Across from Joe's is the entrance to **South Pointe Park**, a 17-acre slice of meandering sidewalks, grassy walkways, a beach (although the beach is not the park's strong suit) and a fitness course. The 50-yard **Sunshine Pier**, which joins the mile-long jetty at the mouth of **Government Cut**, is another prime spot for fishing and watching the cruise ships head out to deep water.

South Pointe Park also has benches along the water, an observation tower, charcoal grills, picnic pavilions, and a playground for children. On Friday nights, South Pointe Park comes alive with free concerts and a craft market. Mimes and magicians compete with basket-weavers and jewelry makers for attention – and sales.

On the beach at lively **First Street** is **Penrod's**, a big, rollicking sports bar, complete with 12 televisions, a jacuzzi, a pool, and volleyball nets on the beach. Loud is the key word here. Long before the sports bar crowd is awake, the action is at a tiny park between Second and Third Streets, where a group of elderly women exercise every morning at 8am. Under the palms, they stretch, kick and gossip away their aches and pains. In the afternoons, retired men and women play cards. On some days a woman practices on her mandolin.

The area south of Sixth Street to the southern tip of the island is technically part of South Beach but it hasn't shared in the renaissance of the Art Deco District. In the southern portion of the island live some of the oldest and poorest people in the country. In the early 1970s the City of Miami Beach had this portion of the island designated a redevelopment area – bureaucratic parlance for urban renewal. The city put a moratorium on building improvements and came up with a plan to hire a master developer to create a Venice-like community in the 255-acre area, complete with canals and gondolas. That idea, not surprisingly, fell apart.

The southern tip of South Miami Beach lacks the luster of the Deco District.

The city still wants to transform the land into an upscale yuppie urban neighborhood with townhouses, shopping and, of course, a mammoth resort hotel. But at the moment, many of the buildings are dilapidated or deserted. At night the streets become mean with drug dealers and criminals preying on the poor and homeless.

Still, this area should not be ignored (if only for a trek through South Pointe Park and lunch or dinner at Joe's Stone Crab). It is ethnically, racially and culturally diverse. Artists, yuppies, wannabes and hippies live among the elderly Jewish retirees, many of whom fled Eastern Europe during the 1930s and 1940s. They visited South Beach during the winters and settled here when they retired. The most recent immigrants are Cubans.

**Fifth Street**, the main road that leads from the MacArthur Causeway to the actual beach, has seen a great deal of improvement in recent years. Health food stores and restaurants are popping up, and the entire street is slowly, but surely, coming to life.

Between Jefferson and Meridian on Fifth is **Tap Tap**, a combination Haitian restaurant, art gallery, and popular gathering spot for artists, journalists and film-makers. Amid floor-to-ceiling murals of bold, primitive art, Tap Tap is the only authentic Haitian restaurant outside of Little Haiti. Along with poetry readings and lectures, it hosts some of the best live Haitian music this side of Port-au-Prince. At the corner of Fifth and Washington is **The China Grill**, a New York transplant famous for its Asian/New World cuisine.

**Deco delights:** From Sixth to 23rd Streets the look of the beach drastically changes. In the 1960s and 1970s, this area fell out of vogue and became a crime-ridden, seedy retirement ghetto. With so many ailing elderly people, it was often referred to as God's Waiting Room. But thanks to diehard Deco lovers who petitioned and lobbied and fought with politicians and state and

**Tap Tap restaurant.**

federal agencies, in 1979 this portion of Miami Beach, with more than 500 playful, rounded buildings built in the 1930s, became the youngest historic district in the nation. Its official status and name is the Miami Beach **Art Deco National Historic District**.

Soon after, developers, salivating over the potential of owning a piece of what was now being heralded as "The American Riviera," sunk millions into renovations. Since the late 1980s, fast-talking speculators have treated the Deco District like a Monopoly board game, gobbling up properties as quickly as they can. Without the capital to live through the off-season, many have found themselves entangled in financial fiascoes, and end up filing for bankruptcy.

A fickle business, nightclubs and restaurants in this part of South Beach, referred to as **SoBe**, have high mortality rates, and the in-spot of today may likely be gone tomorrow. Even the international celebrities have gotten caught up in the high-stakes action. Among them:

Mickey Rourke, Spike Lee, Oprah Winfrey, Michael Caine, Madonna, and the artist formerly known as Prince. Some have had better luck than others.

As SoBe grew to become an international playground of the rich and beautiful, area rents and taxes skyrocketed. Many locals, who for years lived in low-rent heaven, were forced to move elsewhere. New Yorkers, accustomed to high-rent highrises, bought relatively inexpensive condos for use as weekend retreats, and made dirt-cheap apartments a thing of the past. Although Dade County is indeed happy with SoBe's transformation, there is a certain amount of local resentment toward the new SoBe phenomenon.

**A Gay Renaissance:** Along with the arrival of developers, Miami Beach in the past decade has experienced substantial growth in its gay population. The *Miami Herald* recently reported that gay tenants occupy one-third of the Art Deco District apartments.

In addition to finding South Beach an

SoBe's café society.

ideal gay vacation destination where same-sex couples can check into gay hotels, dine in gay restaurants, and kiss in public without scornful looks, hundreds of gays and lesbians have invested in the area, opening book stores, cafes and boutiques. They have also played a major role in the urban gentrification of the area.

Businesses owned by gays, or by those who are supportive of the gay movement, place a pink dot in their storefront windows as a symbol of welcome. There's even a well-established gay chamber of commerce and several support groups to help newcomers.

So important is the gay population to the city, that some Miami Beach commissioners take their campaigns into gay bars as a way of garnering votes, and the Miami Beach Police Department now requires its officers to attend gay sensitivity training programs.

Several South Beach nightclubs offer weekly "drag-dining" nights when male diners are encouraged to dress up in sequined gowns, feather boas, and very high-heels. And it is not uncommon to see outrageously dressed drag queens – such as local celebrity Kitty Meow – vamping on public streets.

**A street with a view:** For the most historic, modern and dramatic architectural view of the SoBe Art Deco revival, head up **Ocean Drive**. To the east is **Lummus Park**, eight blocks of glorious beach with white sand that stretches 300 feet to the Atlantic Ocean. Little old ladies in sensible shoes and umbrellas, surfers in slick gear and teenage sun worshippers in tiny bathing suits, sprawl on towels or sit in lawn chairs.

Beach-goers listen to suitcase-size radios, fly kites, play paddle ball or go roller skating on the busy sidewalk. Refreshment vendors hawk snow cones and sodas. To the west are restored hotels and apartment houses, as well as chic little European-style outdoor cafes, restaurants and stores. The sidewalks have been enlarged and painted. The color: pink, of course.

**Ocean Drive.**

As a popular cruising street, the traffic on Ocean Drive is horrendous. The parking situation is even worse, with overly zealous meter maids constantly prowling for tardy parkers. Adding to the congestion – and to the view – is the ubiquitous row of jeeps, BMWs, convertibles, Harley Davidsons and other fashionable vehicles that trawl along Ocean Drive. Drivers peer into restaurants and onto porches, and people in the restaurants and porches stare back; dates have been known to be secured this way.

SoBe is also a place where people walk, a rarity in car-addicted South Florida. The colorful locals – the eccentric gentleman who wears his 6-ft boa constrictor around his neck; the born-again Christian who straps a 5-ft long cross on his back; and Haydee and Sahara Scull, two buxom Cuban twins who are as well known for their campy Carmen Miranda-style outfits as for their brightly colored street scene collages – blend easily with the growing number of sophisticated European tourists who converge on the beach.

**Model society:** Several modeling agencies and professional film processing shops have moved in along Ocean Drive, creating a constant beautiful-people alert. A few trendy cafes appear to employ only models. Each waiter and waitress is more stunning than the one who came before. Problem is, they spend a lot of time flaunting their looks, forgetting about the customers completely.

By 7am, there's a photographer on almost every Ocean Drive corner, taking advantage of the bright morning light. Reflectors in hand, they shout instructions in German, French, Italian and English, as the models toss their hair in the air. Huge, air-conditioned motor homes line the streets, and serve as changing rooms and resting spots for the women. The modeling business has in fact become a multi-million dollar industry for Miami Beach, with magazines like *Vogue* and *Paris Match* vying for the best locations.

The pink and green cafe at Ocean Drive and Seventh Street is the **Booking Table**, an eatery that attracts models, model wannabes, and photographers. A block away is the **News Cafe**, one of Ocean Drive's big winners in the restaurant business. Since it opened in 1988, the **News** has been jam-packed day and night. With jazz playing in the background, and an assortment of foreign magazines and newspapers, it has a faithful European and local clientele. At Eighth Street and Ocean is **Larios on the Beach**, a Cuban restaurant owned by Miami singer Gloria Estefan.

Just north on Ocean Drive is the **Carlyle**, the first Art Deco hotel and restaurant to be refurbished. It, like many of the other small hotels on Ocean Drive, has been used as a backdrop for movies, movie videos and modeling sessions. Along with the Carlyle, the **Leslie** and the **Cardozo** were also restored early. The **Cavalier**, with its soaring glass windows and small Art Deco lobby, is rented regularly by photography crews

rtists
aydee and
ahara Scull.

from other cities. The Cavalier, Leslie, and the **Casa Grande**, also on Ocean Drive, are owned by Jamaican-born Island Records founder Chris Blackwell. A shrewd entrepreneur, Blackwell has also brought his **Island Trading Company**, an art and clothing boutique with a Caribbean flair, to Ocean Drive where it is housed in the ground floor of the **Netherland Hotel**.

Directly on the beach at 10th Street is the **Miami Beach Ocean Front Auditorium**. Here, beach residents both young and old gather for music, lectures and lunches. About one block away on Ocean Drive is **Casa Casuarina**, a magnificent Mediterranean-style mansion hidden behind towering pine trees. Formerly a run-down apartment building , this structure was designed to resemble Christopher Columbus' home in the Dominican Republic, complete with 15-ft high antique wooden doors. It is now the private home of Italian designer Gianni Versace, who bought it in 1992 for $2.9 million. A year later, he

bought its neighbor, the Revere Hotel, for $3.7 million, then tore it down to put in a private courtyard and pool.

At 12th Street and Ocean is the **Art Deco Welcome Center**, operated by the Miami Design Preservation League, the non-profit preservation group responsible for the movement to preserve the Art Deco properties and listing them on the National Register of Historic Places. The Welcome Center offers a wealth of Art Deco information. It also sells maps, books, postcards, souvenirs, and Art Deco antiques and jewelry. This is the place to buy presents, because a portion of the asking price goes back into preserving the district. The center also sponsors informative and entertaining walking tours of the district.

**A walking avenue:** There is more to SoBe than Ocean Drive. Two blocks west is **Washington Avenue**, a frenetic, clamoring kind of thoroughfare that feels and sounds more New York City than Miami Beach. A walking avenue, Washington is a dichotomy of **Business and the beach.**

new and old. Fruit markets, second-hand stores, Kosher markets, and just plain junk stores share the street with restaurants serving the trendiest of meals – from sushi to Thai cuisine, over-priced antique and Art Deco shops, and tattoo and body piercing parlors.

But it's the people who bring vibrancy to Washington Avenue. Cuban men who stand at outdoor cafes sipping cafe Cubano, Hasidic Jewish men with flowing beards, babushka-clad East European women, businessmen, bag ladies, New Wave punks, Hip-Hop kids – they're all on Washington Avenue.

Also on Washington is the gaudy **Clay Hotel and International Youth Hostel**, with flamingo pink facade and wrought-iron balconies. A clean, cheap and interesting budget hotel, the hostel is filled with people from other countries. Hand-written notices on lobby bulletin boards are clearly penned by people who speak English as a second language. The European-style hostel is only two blocks from the Atlantic Ocean.

The entrance to the hostel is on **Espanola Way**, a narrow street of Mediterranean-Revival buildings, with white buttresses and gas lamps, which was constructed in 1925. A charming little street that was often used as a set for *Miami Vice*, Espanola has the distinction that Desi Arnaz, the Cuban bandleader and TV star Lucille Ball's husband, played in the Village Tavern (now the youth hostel) in the 1930s. In recent years it has attracted starving artists who rent tiny studios on the second and third floors.

At street level are several expensive but interesting Deco-era clothing and furniture stores, coffee houses, and restaurants. And, **Ba-Balu**, a boutique that pays tribute to Cuban culture. With the decor of an old Cuban country house, Ba-Balu sells antique Cuban post cards, Cuban cookbooks, cigars, coffee, and ever-so-popular Cuba Libre! T-shirts. Ba-Balu, by the way, is the song that made Desi Arnaz famous.

Back out on Washington Avenue is

the **Cameo Theater**, the premier hall for international films when it opened in 1938. After years of refurbishing, the 980-seat theater now draws the younger set to concerts given by punk and New Wave bands. A few blocks to the south is the Miami Beach Main **Post Office**. Built in 1937, this building is crowned by a marble and stained glass lantern. Inside, murals and bronze grillwork decorate a vast rotunda. Nearby is the Miami Beach **Police Station**, an aqua and white streamline structure with a glass brick front.

At 10th Street and Washington, housed in the pretty, renovated Washington Storage Company building, is **The Wolfsonian**. Opened in 1995, the Wolfsonian is the pride and joy of Mitchell Wolfson, Jr, heir to the Wometco movie theater fortune. For three decades, Wolfson has traveled the world collecting propaganda artworks of the 19th and early 20th centuries.

Now, his eccentric collection is on display, including such oddities as Hitler propaganda posters, bronze busts of Mussolini, furniture designed by architect Frank Lloyd Wright, and metalworks, industrial products, trains, appliances, comic books, ceramics and paintings that have had an impact on modern design techniques throughout the world.

**Added culture:** Known in its heyday in the 1950s as the Fifth Avenue of the South, the **Lincoln Road Mall** has recently awakened from a long, sad slumber. Designed by Morris Lapidus, Miami Beach's flamboyant "architect of joy," **Lincoln Road** is a pedestrian-only thoroughfare that was neglected for years. Some cheap luggage and trinket stores remain, but the Road, as it is called by locals, is coming into its own with a younger, arty and more cultured crowd. There's even an Art Deco Burger King here, painted flamingo pink and aqua blue, with big, rounded windows.

Three blocks of storefronts, known as the **South Florida Art Center**, have been transformed into galleries, bou-

There are over 500 Art Deco buildings in SoBe...

tiques, cafes, and studios where more than 100 artists work and display their art. The main office is at 924 Lincoln Road, but there are several galleries that belong to the center.

The **Colony Theater**, a former movie house, now a city-owned performing arts center, is located on the Road. As is the **Lincoln Theater**, home to the New World Symphony, America's only national training orchestra for musicians from ages 21 to 30. These 90 young musicians have played to wide acclaim in Paris and at New York City's Carnegie Hall. No longer is that tired, old joke true: "What's the difference between Miami and yogurt? The answer: yogurt has culture."

In 1993, **MTV Latino**, the Spanish language version of the popular music video TV station, moved in to Lincoln Road and established a state-of-the-art studio in a remodeled Deco building. Soon after, Sony's Latin Music Division did the same. Together, the two have triggered a boom in the production of Spanish-language music videos in the SoBe area.

**Books & Books**, a sister of the Books & Books store in Coral Gables, is on Lincoln Road, and in just a few short years has become South Beach's favorite literary hang-out, with book signings and lectures by prominent authors almost every night of the week.

Several one-of-a-kind restaurants on the Road make dining here a treat, and a stroll around will produce intriguing results. But the best thing about Lincoln Road is free: ballet watching. Old ladies in polyester pedal-pushers, and wide-eyed children gather in front of a storefront window – formerly the Bonwit Teller department store – to gaze at the **Miami City Ballet** at work. Noseprints on the floor-to-ceiling windows suggest that something good is going on inside. The taut, young dancers, dressed in tights and warm-ups, leap and stretch their way to perfect dance movements. Other dance troupes located on Lincoln Road are **Ballet Flamenco la Rosa**, and the

.the ▪ungest ▪storic ▪strict in ▪e country.

**Middle Eastern Dance Exchange**, which offers African, Caribbean, and belly-dancing classes to the public.

A few blocks away from the Road is **Hank Meyer Boulevard**. In Miami Beach, streets are not named for presidents or war heroes, but for entertainers and publicists. Formerly known as **17th Street**, Hank Meyer Boulevard was named for a publicist who encouraged comedian Jackie Gleason to broadcast his television program from Miami. Gleason did so – for 22 years.

A 3,023-seat performing arts center is named for the popular entertainer who immortalized Miami Beach as the "sun and fun capital of the world" on his weekly show. Broadway shows and major ballet and symphony productions are held in the **Jackie Gleason Theater of the Performing Arts** (more commonly known as **TOPA**), another Art Deco building where the national show originated. In front of the theater is *The Mermaid*, a sculpture by Roy Lichtenstein. There is even a street named for Arthur Godfrey, who also broadcast from Miami Beach.

On **Meridian Avenue** is the **Holocaust Memorial**, a somber testament to the tragedies of World War II. Situated near the **Miami Beach Garden Center and Conservatory**, the memorial, designed by Kenneth Treister, is a 42-foot bronze sculpture of a hand reaching towards the heavens. Set against a backdrop of photographs of Nazi death camps and the names of those who died, the sculpture has life-size renditions of terrified victims struggling to the top.

There is one art museum on Miami Beach. Just one. Small though it is, the **Bass Museum of Art** on Collins Avenue is a good museum with a diverse collection of European art, including *The Holy Family*, a painting by Peter Paul Rubens, and a 16th-century Flemish tapestry called *The Tournament*.

Two bars that couldn't be more different or more South Beach are the **Irish House Pub** and **Club Deuce**. The Irish House, on Alton Road, is a real neighbor-

**The area used to belong to the elderly; dog-day afternoon.**

150

hood bar with a great jukebox, greasy food and locals – from sailors based in the area to reporters. Deuce, at 14th Street in the heart of South Beach, is a tougher and funkier nightspot whose clientele ranges from aging transvestites to fresh-faced kids on spring break from college. A pool game at Deuce is not to be undertaken lightly.

**The Main Drag:** One of the most scenic and strangest thoroughfares on the beach is **Collins Avenue**, which takes visitors northward and out of the SoBe area. At 16th Street and Collins is one of the most interesting new/old hotels on the beach, **The Delano**. Built in 1945 and topped off with a modernistic finned tower, the Delano was remodeled in 1995 by French designer Philippe Starck and his partner Ian Schrager, the *haute* hotelier who founded New York City's famed nightclub Studio 54. Austere but elegant, the Delano has white walls, white floors, white beds, white chairs, and even white TV sets; a darling of the rich-and-famous set. In its lobby is the

**Blue Door**, a restaurant and bar owned by Madonna.

At 21st Street and Collins Avenue sits a Miami Beach eating (not dining) institution: **Wolfie's**. The menus here are as large as tabloid newspapers, the waitresses wear name tags and eavesdrop on conversations, offering unsolicited advice along with a basket of free rolls and pastries. Wolfie's is an old-fashioned delicatessen where you can still find a steaming bowl of matzoh ball soup and pastrami sandwiches that are almost four inches thick.

Across Collins Avenue is something that has endeared Miami Beach politicians to the people – a public boardwalk, stretching 1.8 miles from 21st to 46th Streets along the ocean. The action that takes place on the boardwalk is a study of the people of Miami Beach. Hasidic Jewish families stroll around, couples jog, teenagers hold hands and gaze at the water and each other. After dark, portions of the boardwalk, though well-lighted, become dangerous with crack

*he Delano otel was emodeled y Philippe tarck.*

dealers and other shady characters, so watch out. But the boardwalk view can't be beat. With the ocean on one side and fancy high-rise hotels and apartment buildings on the other, it's both a tropical paradise and a voyeur's dream.

The most celebrated hotel in Miami Beach has always been the **Fontaine-bleau Hilton Resort and Spa**. Built in 1954, it reeks of post-war confidence, a time when large families drove to Florida in big gas-guzzling cars for a winter retreat of sun and fun, away from the frozen, gray north. Everyone who was anyone in those days, including Frank Sinatra and Bob Hope, either performed or stayed at the Fontainebleau.

Excess personified, the hotel consists of two curving 14-story buildings that face the Atlantic, along with marble staircases, crystal chandeliers, 1,206 rooms, two pools (one a two-story lagoon with a floating bar) and an entire indoor shopping center. Because of its size and amenities, the Fontainebleau also does a brisk convention business.

If the hotel itself is too much to bear, try a mirror image of it painted on one of its walls at 42nd Street and Collins Avenue. Covering 10 stories is a mural of – that's right – the Fontainebleau Hilton. The hotel is expensive, but a peek at the **Fontainebleau mural** is free.

The Fontainebleau is the grandest of the dinosaur hotels of the era, but it is by no means the only one. From about 42nd Street and Collins Avenue to the north are wall-to-wall hotels and high-rise condominiums, a testament to post-World War II America's "bigger is better" philosophy. Running along Collins Avenue on the west side is **Indian Creek**, a body of water behind which lie stately mansions with kidney-shaped pools and boats moored on private docks.

At 71st Street near Collins is the **MoJazz Cafe**, a hopping jazz joint that features live music six night a week. From 79th to 87th Streets on the ocean is the **North Shore State Recreation Area**. You don't have to be a diehard swimmer or sunbather to enjoy this se-

**Mural of the Fontainebleau**

152

rene beach. A fitness trail winds its way through groves of trees, and there's a series of boardwalks that meanders into natural surroundings. There are also sheltered areas with picnic tables and bicycle rental shops.

**The other Miami Beach:** The towns and villages in the north portion of Miami Beach are vastly different in scope and style. **Surfside** was a 1930s settling ground and winter destination resort for French Canadians. Every spring for the past 35 years, Surfside has thrown a week-long bash, Canada Week, to honor its Canadian population.

Today, Surfside is a comfortable, low-key neighborhood where young and old, established and still-striving, mingle. The **Surfside Community Center** on Collins bustles with locals and tourists playing canasta and gossiping. Along **Harding Avenue**, the main commercial street, mothers stroll with baby carriages and retirees gather for coffee.

A flashback to small-town America, the street still has a beauty parlor where a shampoo and set cost less than you imagine. At the corner of Harding and 95th Street is **Sheldon's Drugstore**, an old-fashioned lunch counter that sells ice-cream sodas. It was after eating bagels and eggs at Sheldon's that the late Isaac Bashevis Singer learned he had won the Nobel Prize for Literature. Singer lived for about 20 years in Surfside, and 95th Street is now known as **Isaac B. Singer Boulevard**.

The international crooner and most tanned man alive, Julio Iglesias, lives nearby in **Indian Creek Village**. Just west of Surfside, Indian Creek has a lush – and private – golf course and over 30 lavish mansions. For art galleries in the area, try **Bay Harbor Islands**, a tiny town full of narrow canals and small-scale apartment buildings. The most unusual collection here is at **Kenneth R. Laurence Galleries**. Mr Laurence, a retired builder with a penchant for what he calls "esthetic collecting of historic documents," has on display framed documents, diaries and letters signed by

Napolean, Gandhi, Churchill, Kennedy, Pasteur and Chopin. Also in Bay Harbor is the **Palm** restaurant, under the same ownership as its namesake in New York.

To the northeast of Bay Harbor is **Bal Harbour**, a 250-acre enclave of concrete condos and minutely landscaped medians. A flashy and ultra up-scale town, Bal Harbour is home to the **Bal Harbour Shops**. This exclusive mall is one square mile of elegance and opulence. Elegant outdoor eateries in the mall offer designer foods to go along with the designer fashions.

**Haulover Park**, north of Bal Harbour and south of Sunny Isles, is a mile-long beach uninterrupted by high-rises – a rarity in South Florida. Fishermen spend days and nights casting their lines from a 1,100-ft pier at Haulover, where snapper and yellowtail are plentiful.

In recent years, the northern part of Haulover Park has become a mecca for nude sunbathers. Although park officials are uncomfortable about the bounty of exposed body parts, they have allowed it to continue because, they say, at least it is contained. Shielded from the highway by sea-grape trees, the nudists are not narcissistic, just happy to enjoy the beach *au naturel*.

**Sunny Isles Beach**, about 2 miles long behind condominiums, is covered in rocky sand. The winds and rough surf here lure surfers and sailors. The **Newport Beach Pier**, built in 1936 and thrice destroyed by hurricanes, is another great fishing hole.

Capping Dade County's northernmost beaches is **Golden Beach**. Like its name, the coastal community here is wealthy and the beach is private. Residents live in palatial, Venetian-style homes along two miles of Atlantic shoreline. There are about 300 homes in Golden Beach, the most famous being **461 Ocean Boulevard**, which rock star Eric Clapton immortalized by naming his album after the house in which he was staying.

**Right**, the family that styles together smiles together.

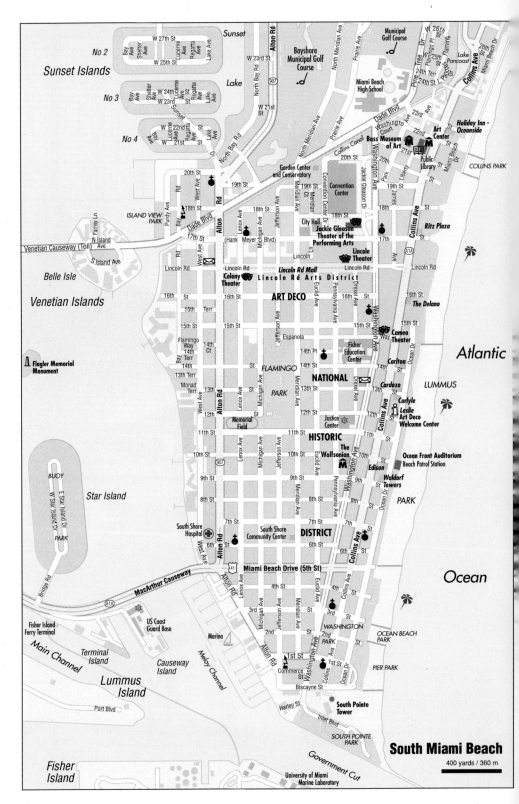

South Miami Beach

# ART DECO

**S**liding across the rainbow from erotic pink to lizard green, the Art Deco structures on Miami Beach were built to uplift the spirits of America and to offer a distraction from the Great Depression. Over 60 years later, they still create that exuberant confetti-like feeling. Critics have called the head-turning, eye-candy buildings tacky, faddish and full of show-girl simplicity, but preservationists say they are some of the most architecturally significant structures in America. For Miami's tourism industry, they represent the ultimate pink flamingo.

The roots of Art Deco go back to 1901 when the Société des Artistes Decorateurs was formed in Paris with the goal of merging the mass production of industrial technology with the decorative arts. It borrowed styles from Bauhaus, Cubism and Constructivism and eventually came to represent an avant-garde attitude that spread its aesthetics from architecture and furniture to ceramics and jewelry.

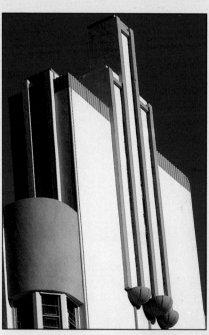

It was proudly introduced to the world in 1925 at the Paris Exposition Internationale des Arts Decoratifs et Industriels Modernes. The nickname Art Deco actually came about in 1966 at a retrospective of the 1925 Paris show.

Typical characteristics of Art Deco architecture and the Art Moderne which followed it are streamline designs using rounded corners, geometric forms, flat roofs, racing stripes and porthole windows. The structures copied the aerodynamic designs of the sleek ocean liners and cars of the period. Strong vertical lines, thick glass blocks and, for the first time, neon lights were used. In celebration of the discovery of King Tut's tomb in the 1920s, occasional Egyptian details were thrown in for effect.

Between the two world wars, over 500 Art Deco structures were built in the southern part of Miami Beach. They were designed, as in other parts of the country, to move the mood of America away from the prevailing gloom by creating an attitude of hope and happiness about the future. Tourists flocked to Miami Beach's Art Deco hotels to indulge their fantasies and to bask in the big band sounds under the moon over Miami.

Miami Beach's Art Deco buildings developed a unique personality and became known as Tropical Deco, with their very own pastel concoctions of semi-tropical Florida style. The stark, white stucco exteriors lent themselves well to the outrageous tropical colors used to decorate the exteriors, as did the bright sunny skies and brisk ocean breezes that cooled the popular verandas.

The etched-glass panels common in Art Deco structures used mermaids, sea horses and waves to evoke the nautical Miami Beach flair. Flamingos, egrets, pelicans and palm trees became common. Eyebrows – overhanging canopies above porthole windows – were introduced to create shade from the South Florida sun.

For the next few decades the Art Deco hotels continued to enjoy prosperity and served as a welcome refuge for Americans escaping the brutal cold of northern winters. But by the 1960s they had begun to decay and in the 1970s Miami Beach's Art Deco structures slipped rapidly into rampant decline. The many layers of paint cracked and peeled and several of the once-glamorous hotels became low-rent housing for the elderly, nervously awaiting the savage swing of the wrecking ball.

In 1976, the Miami Design Preservation League was formed to stop the demolition of the Art Deco buildings and to encourage the restoration of the structures without disrupting the elderly community they housed. In 1979, what is now called the Art Deco District – the approximately 125 blocks that run from 6th to 23rd Streets along the Atlantic Ocean and west to Alton Road – was placed on the National Register of Historic Places, the only 20th-century structures ever granted such a distinction.

Many South Beach Art Deco hotels have been restored to their original condition. A few have been treated to some extra helpings of cartoon colors and now scream of ripe peach, lively lavender and Indian turquoise. Miami Beach's buildings represent the largest concentration of Art Deco architecture in the world. ■

# MY LOVE AFFAIR WITH MIAMI BEACH

*Before he died, Isaac Bashevis Singer, winner of the Nobel Prize for Literature, recalled his early days.*

In 1948 when my wife, Alma, and I visited Florida for the first time, the face of Miami Beach resembled a small Israel. From the cafeterias to the streets, Yiddish resounded around us in accents as thick as those you would hear in Tel Aviv. It was remarkable: Jewishness had survived every atrocity of Hitler and the Nazis. Here, the sound of the Old World was as alive as ever.

Alma and I had not had a vacation since 1940, when we were married. (I was lucky to have a wife who did not resent being married to a poor writer.) But it was a particularly cold winter in New York in 1948, so we decided to buy two train tickets to Miami.

All night we traveled, sitting up in our

seats, until the early morning, when the conductor told us to step out of the train at Deerfield Beach for a glass of fresh orange juice. That first sip was nothing less than ambrosia. In my native Poland, orange juice was considered a most healthful drink. Even today, Alma carries home oranges from the grocery and squeezes fresh juice for breakfast.

When we arrived at the train station in Miami, a taxi took us to Miami Beach. As we rode over the causeway, I could hardly believe my eyes. To me, being at a summer place in winter was a great event. It was almost unimaginable that in Miami it was 80°F while in New York it was 20. Everything – the buildings, water – had an indescribable glow and brightness to it. The palm trees especially made a great impression on me. The driver let us off at the Pierre Motel. Owned by the brothers Gottlieb, it was a modern place but still had its own charm and good clientele. We were given a nice room with a balcony, where I worked every day. It was in those years that I wrote chapters of the *The Family Moskat*, my first big novel, which ran as a serial in the *Jewish Daily Forward*.

In the 1940s and 1950s, Miami Beach was in its so-called heyday. During the day, planes with long streamers flew over the beach advertising dinners with seven courses for $1.50. Rather than eat in the hotel, we often had dinner with acquaintances and old friends at one of the many cafeterias. We ate heartily: borscht, sweet-and-sour cabbage, salad, bread, coffee and dessert.

The cafeterias were nostalgic places for me, and I loved going to them. They reminded me of the Yiddish Writers Club of Warsaw, where I had rubbed elbows with not only some of the greatest Yiddish writers and poets but English and German writers as well. The same food was served and the same conversations took place. I noticed that often people met here again accidentally after a long separation during the Hitler era and a lot of tears were shed.

For some reason we stopped coming

The late Nobel Laurate Isaac Bashevis Singer.

to Miami Beach in the 1960s. Then, in 1973, I was invited to give a lecture in downtown Miami. A former neighbor of Alma's in Munich happened to come to my lecture. Afterward, she invited us to her apartment on Collins Avenue.

By then, we had fallen in love with Miami Beach all over again, and we considered buying an apartment. For five days, we struggled with the decision: Should we, could we, afford to buy an apartment? In the end, we bought one with a splendid view of the ocean where we live all year round today.

One morning in 1978, I went to Sheldon's Drugstore to have eggs and bagels. Earlier, a friend had called to tell me she had heard on *Good Morning America* that I had won the Nobel Prize, but I had dismissed it as just a nomination and not the real thing.

When I returned after breakfast, Alma was calling out to me excitedly. My editor at the *Forward* was on the telephone. He told me that he had heard on the transatlantic wire that I had won the Nobel. My hands grew cold and Alma says I turned as white as a sheet. Two months later, after many hectic shopping trips to buy clothes for the big event, we flew to Stockholm. It was an ecstatic moment for me when the King of Sweden handed me the prize.

But just because someone has won the Nobel Prize does not mean that life changes dramatically. After the ceremonies had ended and the rush of interviews was over, life went on as before. Alma and I returned to our apartment and I continued to write each day.

From this oasis of comfort, I have pondered the many changes that have taken place on Miami Beach since 1948, not all of them for the best.

Nevertheless, for me, Miami Beach is still one of the most beautiful places in the world. Nothing can equal the splendor of nature. Every day, as I sit on the beach looking out at the ocean, each palm tree, each wave, each sea gull is still a revelation to me. After all these years, Miami Beach feels like home.

Historic postcard of Miami Beach.

Lummus Park, a Public Bathing Beach, Miami Beach, Florida

# KEY BISCAYNE

En route to **Key Biscayne**, passing the tollgate and crossing the causeway, you will drive smack into blue sky and bluer water. You might begin to think, much like other Key Biscayners: "I'm home." That peek back at Miami's skyline, so intense in white light, is just enough to confirm: *this* is the perfect distance from bustle, from busy-ness.

"Home" is a 7-mile-long, 2-mile-wide sliver of land off Miami proper, only 15 minutes' driving from downtown Miami and a secret so convenient and comfortable that Key Biscayners, in their laid-back way, will not rush to tell. Despite their "Island Paradise" boast on their welcome, Key Biscayners will insist, out of small-town courtesy, "There's nothing special here."

Part truth, part conspiracy, the secret of Key Biscayne is the mesh of ordinary life and extraordinary setting. Without much ado, Key Biscayne envelops visitors in small surprises, unfolding quietly, even slyly, its history and its heart.

To reach Key Biscayne and its mate, **Virginia Key**, take the **Rickenbacker Causeway** across Biscayne Bay from the mainland at Brickell Avenue and S.W. 26th Road, about 2 miles south of downtown Miami. Originally part of the city proper, residents voted for secession, and in 1991 their island became Dade County's 28th municipality.

Two of hundreds of islands that surround the tip of Florida, Key Biscayne and Virginia Key are sedimentary barrier islands, strung north–south, parallel to the South Florida mainland. They began as sandbars, millions of years ago. As ocean waves and winds piled limestone and quartz on top of hard coral rock, islands emerged, a barrier between the Atlantic Ocean and the mainland for that same water and wind.

Its topographical quirks are hidden. East along the island's sandy northern shore, for example, lies a small reef,

obvious at low tide, barely awash at high. Here Key Biscayne has its own petrified forest – a black **mangrove reef** of fossilized wood and roots, the only such site reported in the world.

Put on your sneakers and hike the waters near **Bear Cut**, the narrow gap which separates the two keys. Small but serious, the unique reef stretches along shore for about 425 yards, jutting seaward 115 yards.

Even with living trees and shrubs, the island was not appealing – a tangle of mangrove swamps, jungle, coral rock and sand dunes infested with snakes, monkeys and mosquitoes. Nevertheless, this place captured attention. English explorer John Cabot spotted the southern tip in 1497, calling it Cape of the End of April. Juan Ponce de Leon claimed it for Spain in 1513.

Its name changed, depending on the mapmaker: Promentorium Floridae, Cape Florida, even Sandwich Gulf. "Biscayne", appearing on Spanish maps as early as 1765, may honor a wealthy

merchant-mariner, the Keeper of Swans at the Spanish Court, or a ship owned by El Biscaino and wrecked in the mid-1500s. Is the confusion artful? Perhaps even the earliest Key Biscayners thought: If they don't know, they won't find us. But surveyors left a marker in 1655. (Look between the 10th and 18th fairways as the pros play at the **Key Biscayne Golf Course**.)

Indeed, the **Cape Florida Lighthouse**, completed in 1825, beckoned travelers. Keeping ships afloat despite storms, uncharted waters, sandbars and submerged reefs, it promised newcomers a smooth landing and easy life. Hardly. In 1836, Seminole Indians attacked the lighthouse. Barely escaping a roasting, the lightkeeper clung to its platform until rescued by a Navy schooner. During the Second Seminole War, US troops arrived, but settlers fled to other keys. Damaged by Confederate sympathizers during the Civil War, the lighthouse lantern was extinguished in 1878. Paradise Lost?

But location, location! Developers arrived in the early 1900s to clear land, dredge shallow Biscayne Bay, fill swamp, and – presto! – create a synthetic island and shore. Under the supervision of Dr William "Commodore" Matheson, Key Biscayne was transformed from a wasteland.

Matheson opened yacht basins, 18 miles of roadway, and then planted, planted, planted: 100,000 Nucifera coconuts, Australian pines, sea grapes, tropical almonds, mangos, bougainvilleas and date palms. From his bayside mansion, he set the early tones of exclusivity.

The modern Key Biscayne community began when the Rickenbacker Causeway opened in 1947, with a daunting 25-cent toll. Named after a World War I flying ace, it loped over Biscayne Bay, a waterway shared with Miami. With the bridge came "mainlanders," out to exploit, according to local Key Biscayners.

Until then, unlike other resorts, Key

**Cape Florida Lighthouse; a bird looks for lunch.**

Biscayne had successfully avoided over-crowding. In the early 1950s, the Mackle Brothers developers built modest track housing in order to lure World War II veterans with GI loans to the desolate island. Working-class neighborhoods emerged.

Then, like other points in Miami, Key Biscayne caught construction fever, and zoning went well awry. Apartments turned into condominiums. Units such as the 27-floor **Casa del Mar**, an anatomical anomaly in an island of low buildings, went up almost overnight in the early 1960s. Irked neighbors, vocal in protest about island aesthetics, still say the Casa del Mar "snuck" past them.

After that, President Richard Nixon brought the winter White House to the island in the 1970s, and homeowners watched as the world discovered Key Biscayne. Amid gentrification, a Mackle home, bought for $15,000 in 1955, sold for $200,000 in 1985. Today, real estate ads fatten *The Islander News*, the island's weekly paper, and many who work on the island cannot afford to live there. Paradise Found?

In the push, developers also claimed famous sites, such as the **Key Biscayne Hotel**, demolished to make way for a massive condominium complex. Amid community protest, financially strapped developers tossed prime acres on to the market. The Key's history remains hidden. Efforts to protect such landmarks have at times been lackadaisical or late. Noting how special status bars some development, one long-time resident cynically observed: "After all, we're capitalists."

But, despite the onslaught, a quiet tempo, an isolation, still clings. Life in "the village" makes this clear. There are few traffic lights and few traffic jams. Tourist season often means only a few seconds' wait before a left turn, a few minutes' longer search for parking near the grocery. Visitors get the same treatment as locals, with no routes designated scenic, no tourist foldouts, no crucial road signs.

**Bill Baggs Cape Florida State Recreation Area.**

Shops are more retro than trendy, delivering the basics with an old-fashioned service. "Doing the mall" means circulating among four, all but one clustered along **Crandon Boulevard**, the 2-mile stretch that bisects the island north to south.

Consider the oldest, the **Key Biscayne Shopping Center**, established in 1950. Or **Key Hardware**, where you can still buy one nail or screw.

Many eateries are just as *local*. The **Donut Gallery Restaurant** in **Harbor Drive Shopping Center** caters to "the most loyal locals." With its 14 swivel stools at a jam-packed counter, it offers hearty egg combos from 5.30am to 1.30pm. Its speedy service pleases waves of regulars.

But because a slow pace is also acceptable, entrepreneurial shopping replaces few fast-food services. Stop by the **Crandon Park Marina** at day's end, as charter boat owners clean and sell a catch. Anchor at **Sundays on the Bay** for a spot of brunch or night-time

reggae. Watch the sunset hues tinge Miami's skyline from **The Rusty Pelican**'s prime vantage. Dip your feet in the surf as you eat at the **Sandbar**. Fax a gourmet order to **Stefano's**, or close the bar in person at 5am.

Even festivals are blissfully local – such as a 100th birthday party in 1990 for writer Marjory Stoneman Douglas. The Key Biscayne Chamber of Commerce sponsors the **Fourth of July Independence Day Parade**, one of the oldest in Dade County. A fly-over from nearby Homestead Air Force base salutes floats and bands. More than 250 artists – shapers of stone, wood and ceramics – offer wares at a juried festival near the Cape Florida entrance in January. Listen for the Key Biscayne Marching and Chowder Chompers Parade Band.

A dense canopy of Australian pine and sea-grape trees was once the main attraction at **Bill Baggs Cape Florida State Recreation Area**, but Hurricane Andrew changed all that. Situated at the southern tip of Key Biscayne, with nothing nearby to break the winds, **Cape Florida** suffered a major hit in the 1992 storm and was one of the most devastated areas in Miami proper. Although it will take decades for the park to regain its original look, rangers began an industrious re-greening effort in the mid-1990s, planting millions of tiny seedlings. Even without trees, however, Cape Florida attracts nature and sun worshippers in both the winter and summer months, for it is now the state's third busiest park, attendance edging near to a million people annually.

The litany of outdoor fun is well-known to all the hedonists: you can swim, sunbathe, picnic, fish, cycle, jog, hike or, in the words of Baggs himself, the *Miami News* editor whose crusade preserved the park, "listen to the drawl of the sea."

White sand, albeit dingy, and often studded with seaweed and stinging man-o'-wars, reaches along the oceanfront. On-the-spot treats include tropical fruit

**Restaurant on the Key at sunset.**

drinks and Key lime pie at the island's most eclectic concession.

A bayside seawall hosts fishers in search of bonefish, grouper, jack, snapper and snook. Fishing here is just as scenic as from the pier of the old Rickenbacker Causeway bridge, where you can toss a line into the gap where the drawspan was removed over the **Intracoastal Waterway**.

Historical buffs can visit the 95-ft red-brick lighthouse, perched in a sand dune. Years ago, 122 steps led to the top of the oldest structure in Dade County. Now, crumbling bricks keep it closed, while funds for repair are sought. The nearby surf is classic. It was here that John Wayne waded, 1940s Hollywood-style, escaping from a smoking PT boat in *They Were Expendable*.

Toward the northern end of Key Biscayne is **Crandon Park**. Donated by the Matheson family, its 1,400 acres carry a few reminders – royal palms, mangroves – of its heyday as a coconut plantation. Slogs through the seagrass

and coastal hammocks in the northeast wildness take visitors back even earlier.

The 3-mile wide swatch of ocean beachfront, with broad concrete walkways, turns into pandemonium when fun-seeking visitors fill four parking lots in mid-summer. Its 493 acres of land include several soccer and softball fields, an 18-hole public golf course, 75 barbecue grills, and is considered by many to be the very best "party beach" in Miami.

Captains of charter boats – Hatteras, Bertram or Monterrey – dock at the park's marina, near slips for more than 200 boats. Half-day and full-day excursions can search for sailfish and dolphin year-round.

**Virginia Key** offers one of the most pristine beaches on the relatively untouched keys, though developers and preservationists are still facing off. Most of the action is on the eastern tip at the 647-acre **City of Miami Park**, with its 2-mile stretch of beach and water deep enough to truly indulge swimmers.

**Birds gather for a communal squawk.**

Families, hammocks swaying, move in for the day.

As a break from the sun, follow dirt roads to the magnificent skyline views from the northern tip to the moviemakers' village set and to the fish smokehouse, guarded by old-timers chewing tobacco on the verandah.

The southern tip houses a mecca for marine scientists. Environmental research, especially about ocean and atmosphere, is under way in federal and academic laboratories, on land and sea – the **National Oceanographic and Atmospheric Administration**, the University of Miami's **Rosenstiel School of Marine and Atmospheric Science**, and the **Maritime Science and Technology Academy**.

Across the causeway, about 200 ft east of the tollgate, discover **Hobie Island,** with one of the most popular stretches of beach, nationwide, for owners or renters of twin-hulled catamarans. Ribbons of cement, pebbles and sand edge the bay, with parking and picnicking sites tucked under a canopy of Australian pines.

Adjacent **Windsurfer Beach** (first past the tollbooth) captivates windsurfing *aficionados*. Averaging 18 knots in March through April, winds from the east and southeast move sailboards along at an easy pace. Flat, shallow, waveless water makes surfing idyllic for beginners. Late summer hurricane winds thrill daredevil pros. Equipment rentals and lessons are negotiable on the spot. Stretching parallel, north of the causeway, is **Jet Ski Beach**, where motorized skiers roar free, banned by law as a safety hazard from other territories.

Just as Key Biscayners long for *their* park (these others are playgrounds for mainlanders), they also stick to *their* beaches – with a claim to beachfront a right for most property owners. Decades ago, when the town centered on the beach, members of the **Key Biscayne Beach Club** gathered weekends on the ocean strip near the prominent hotel. Now, 850 families who currently own

original Mackle property belong to the club free, a legacy of developers who years ago guaranteed a spot on the beach to lure reluctant buyers. Catering to those who wanted to be set apart, the **Key Biscayne Yacht Club** gained prestige and privacy. The beach club stayed grassroots, democratic. With the Atlantic as a backdrop, two hotels and a motel – **Sonesta Beach**, **Grand Bay** and **Silver Sands** – also provide beachfronts.

Accommodation ranges from efficiency to villa with heated swimming pool. What's an ordinary little space elsewhere becomes a romantic hideaway on Key Biscayne, taking on new significance (and higher prices) with sand and sea.

Each offers the requisite view and Ocean Drive address. At the many pools, bars, lounges and restaurants, you can dive into decadence. With massages and salt-glo loofahs for anxieties, plus a place to stash kids from 10am to 10pm, Sonesta is a popular family spot.

For other hidden oddities, head just

**Hiding from the sun.**

offshore. Near the Key's southern tip, where the Atlantic Ocean meets Biscayne Bay at Cape Florida, float into **Stiltsville**. Built as weekend getaways, only a few of these 14 structures remain, planted in the water like concrete-and-wood flamingos.

The bungalows, constructed decades ago by Miami sportsmen, are now off-limits even to their owners. Tossed around by ordinary wind, then sideswiped by Hurricane Andrew, they are mere remnants of their old selves and collectively look like an eery ghost town. Unwilling to tear them down, local officials are waiting for Stiltsville to die a natural death.

Day charters pass fast, en route to deep-sea fishing in the Gulf Stream. Most move far from the sandbar, a center lane where high tides push water to 2 ft. Their wakes rock bonefishers, upright on flat-bottomed boats. Then, it's placid, restful even, with outside intruders rare; usually it's only the cormorants that are curious. Key Biscayne's oceanside waters also nurture artificial reefs, new habitats for fish and other marine life. In the early 1980s, government and private interests heard the clamor of fishers and divers for sites.

How to *build* a reef? To start, look for water at least 65 ft deep, with a barren sandy bottom, a few miles offshore. For a large habitat, dynamite a barge or a ship – a "clean" one, free of pollutants and debris, of course. For a small reef, sink construction rubble, a culvert pipe and plastic tossaways.

Within a half-year, colonies of algae, soft and hard corals, sponges, sea anemones and marine worms call this home. Such bait, the food chain under way, attracts crabs, lobsters, shrimp and brittle stars. In time, with no differences between natural and artificial reefs, larger fish – of interest to fishers and divers – come to foray and southeast Florida gets top-ranking for clear-water wreck diving. Then, battle to limit fish traps, spearguns, or long-lining that drastically cut fish numbers.

Stiltsville, dying a natural death.

The causeway also holds indoor entertainment. Along it stands the 6,538-seat **Miami Marine Stadium**, where audiences on land or on water can watch hydroplane races, boxing matches, boat shows or concerts such as "Pops by the Bay." Miami skyline and Biscayne Bay vistas distract entertainers, also awash on a floating stage.

Down the causeway at the 35-acre **Miami Seaquarium**, visitors can meet, pet and feed sea lions and dolphins, plus view sharks feeding at exhibition halls. Flipper, the world's most televised dolphin, and Lolita, a 5-ton killer whale, perform daily. Endangered birds and reptiles nest in The Lost Islands, a wildlife sanctuary where official efforts to rescue, rehabilitate and reproduce threatened species have been under way since 1955. But no one – locals or visitors – stays indoors for long. For a clue about island style and pace, look to outdoor sports. Key Biscayne tantalizes spectators and participants.

Nearly 300 top-ranked tennis players compete in the **Lipton International Players Championship** for two weeks in March at the **International Tennis Center** located in Crandon Park. As many as 200,000 visitors have watched top players like Chris Evert, Jimmy Connors, Ivan Lendl and Steffi Graf compete for a $2 million purse.

"In training" year-round, residents bike, walk or jog along the beach, causeway or park tracks. Join the locals for a bike's-eye view of the island, with no-sweat cycling on terrain that rises to 16 inches, maybe. Enquire for rentals at the **Mangrove Bicycle Shop** in the Square Shopping Center. Or join the more than 1,000 runners who tackle the 10K **Lighthouse Run** each November.

For the real Key Biscayne experience, join beachcombers for a walk to the lighthouse, arguing all the way about how far it is. Walk into the state park along the beach adjacent to the neighboring condominium, and for heaven's sake, don't pay at the entrance. Only *tourists* do that.

**Miami Seaquarium.**

# HURRICANE ANDREW

I t was South Florida's worst nightmare. Just before dawn on August 24, 1992, a storm packing 160-mph winds and a 12-foot tidal wave slammed into the southern tier of the state, leaving in its wake a surreal scene of devastation.

Hurricane Andrew, the worst natural disaster ever to hit the United States, destroyed over 60,000 homes and left 150,000 people – 10 percent of Dade County – homeless. The category five hurricane, so rare that only one or two occur every century, left a 20 to 35-mile wide swath of damage estimated at around $20 billion. Over 35 people died in storm-related deaths.

Hardest hit were the rural and suburban areas about 20 miles south of downtown Miami – Homestead, Florida City, Kendall – most of which were totally destroyed. South Miami and parts of Coconut Grove and Coral Gables were also badly damaged. Cape Florida, at the tip of Key Biscayne, suffered a direct hit, and it is only through the intense replanting efforts of park rangers that the Bill Baggs Recreation Area will reclaim its former glory.

Along with piles of debris around the city, Andrew left a battlefield of wounds: houses, high schools, gas stations, shopping centers and churches were demolished; cars smashed and overturned; boats damaged and blown ashore; airplanes crumpled, all leaving a severely scarred landscape of uprooted trees.

In the days and weeks that followed, thousands of civilian volunteers from around the country, along with the American Red Cross, poured in to help. The president deployed over 20,000 US troops to the area to help deter looting, clean up the debris, and build temporary tent cities. The soldiers, many of whom had served in the war-torn areas of Lebanon and Kuwait, said that they had never seen such massive destruction. But locals complained that state and national officials, caught in a bureaucratic confusion with no one in charge, took too long before mobilizing government assistance –

tens of thousands of people went for days without food, water, medical care or shelter in the 95° heat before help arrived. So desperate was the situation, that Florida City police officials hijacked a water truck that was headed for nearby Homestead.

Along with the human suffering, animals also fell victim to the storm. Thousands of dogs and cats, not allowed into the pre- or post-storm shelters, were left on the streets to fend for themselves. One Coconut Grove homeowner woke up to find a shark, washed over in the storm, floating in his swimming pool; others found fish in their television sets.

Over 2,000 monkeys and baboons, used by the University of Miami and a private scientific foundation for medical research, escaped when their cages were destroyed. A nasty rumor – that the animals carried the AIDS virus and should be shot on sight – quickly spread throughout the county. Hundreds of the animals were gunned down by police and frightened residents who armed themselves when they heard the news.

When the images of the hurricane hit the news media, foreign aid flowed in from around the world as if Dade County – one of the most cosmopolitan counties in the US – were suddenly a Third World country. Canada, Japan and Taiwan all sent relief. Even President Boris Yeltsin offered to send Russian workers and machinery to help with the clean-up. Despite these offers of help and masive rebuilding projects, it will take years for the area to recover.

Hurricane Andrew, however, did leave Dade County, an area often beleaguered by ethnic and racial conflicts, a more cohesive community. Residents, whether white, black, Cuban, Haitian, Guatemalan or all-American, worked together. "As one we will rebuild" was the spirit.

And, fortunately for the county's vital tourism industry, the damage wrought by Andrew to most busy tourist areas was minimal. Miami Beach suffered only broken windows and fallen trees; downtown Miami the same. Had the hurricane's eye hit just a few miles to the north, the city would likely have been wiped out. Hurricane Andrew, the awesome force of nature, could have been much worse. ■

# COCONUT GROVE

It has been likened to New York's Greenwich Village and London's Chelsea, and it does have some of the abandoned, freewheeling, Bohemian lifestyle of both, as well as the reputation of attracting writers and artists. These people have invariably been off-the-wall types, from the huge, leonine Eugene Massin, an award-winning sculptor/painter with a booming laugh that could shatter glass, to the nomadic Bill Hutton, New York advertising man-turned-painter, who would record his scenes of Grove life on pieces of wood and hawk them on the street to buy food and wine.

The annual three-day Coconut Grove Arts Festival in February attracts at least 300 just as varied artists from around the country who display and sell their works in watercolors, oils, graphics, ceramics, photography and sculpture to more than a million visiting spectators.

Coconut Grove has managed to survive beautifully, a blending of the long-established and the ever-changing, the constant and the capricious. The well-heeled who have just parked their Porsches and Jaguars on their way to dine on **Commodore Plaza** rub shoulders with the tattered jeans set whose hairdos stick up sharply like stalagmites. The fads come and go. For a time, teenagers wearing tight shorts and halters will weave in between the cars on **Main Highway** on roller skates; then, that thrill gone, they switch to skateboards and bicycles.

Strollers will stop and sit down to a spinach salad at the always-busy **Green Street Cafe** across the street from **The Barnacle**, a pioneer home that has sat stolidly overlooking Biscayne Bay for over 100 years. What was once Bert's, the chi-chi, carpeted grocery store that stocked the most exotic comestibles, is now a popular people-watching outdoor café that serves sandwiches and beer. And new Mediterranean-style townhouses have gone up close to turn-of-the-century, bougainvillea-draped homes, built by pioneers.

In the Grove, the old do not frown on the new; they have learned to drift with the winds of change, even when those winds introduced the miasma of marijuana in the late 1960s and the village was suddenly invaded by runaway long-haired "hippies" protesting the Vietnam War. Long-term residents' only lingering regret about the Grove is that the community lost its independent status as the area's original settlement when it was annexed (surreptitiously, they will tell you) by the City of Miami in 1925. Many of them still staunchly have their mail addressed to Coconut Grove, zip code 33133.

Nowhere else in crime-conscious South Florida are streets still so alive at midnight, with diners lingering over coffee at one of the village's many outside cafés after an evening at the theater and couples strolling the red-bricked sidewalks lined with trees and street-

lamps. This is where they come to dream, to plan, on one another's shoulders. If, in other, darker parts of the Grove, nefarious deeds are being committed, here in the village at least the mood is carefree, almost Disneyesque.

Because it is part of Miami, Coconut Grove's boundaries are vaguely defined, though the village itself really starts at **Peacock Park**, at the end of **South Bayshore Drive**, about 6 miles south of downtown Miami. It was here that the first hotel was built in 1882 by Charles Peacock; at that time, it was the only hotel in the 230-mile stretch between Lake Worth and Key West. The park is taken up now mostly by a baseball mound and the woodsy **Chamber of Commerce** building.

But let's backtrack a little, for there's much to explore before getting to Peacock Park. On the way to the Grove, a minute's drive after turning off the US 1 highway on to South Miami Avenue, stop and visit two of the area's most intriguing attractions.

**Vizcaya** is an Italian Renaissance-style 70-room mansion surrounded by manicured gardens and nature trails with a superb collection of 15th through 19th-century art and European furniture. The 10-acre bayfront estate was completed in 1916 as a winter retreat by James Deering, the International Harvester tycoon. There are daily guided tours. Across the avenue is the **Miami Museum of Science and Transit Planetarium**. The museum explores the mysteries of space with more than 150 exhibits, live demonstrations of scientific phenomena and unusual natural history specimens. The Planetarium has astronomy and laser shows.

South Miami Avenue becomes **South Bayshore Drive**, and the ambiance of the Grove can be felt shortly thereafter at **Kennedy Park**, where Groveites jog in the early morning or exercise on the vita course, pausing only to watch the sun come up from behind Key Biscayne on the boardwalk over an inlet that separates the park's two sections. Between

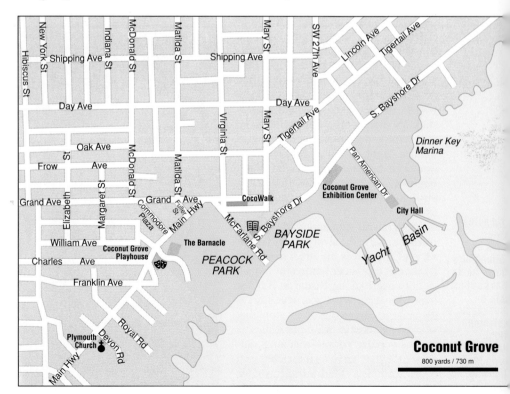

**Coconut Grove**

800 yards / 730 m

there and Peacock Park lie no fewer than three sailing clubs: **Coral Reef Yacht Club** (established in 1955), the **Coconut Grove Sailing Club** (1946) and, between them, the grand-daddy of them all, the **Biscayne Bay Yacht Club**, founded in 1887 by pioneer Commodore Ralph Munroe, but occupying its present site since 1932. If one wishes to join the prestigious Biscayne Bay Yacht Club, one must be recommended by three of its 250 members, then, once accepted, sit back and wait for one of them to die.

On the way along South Bayshore Drive is one of Florida's classiest hostelries, the 13-story, 181-room **Grand Bay Hotel**, which even ascribes to itself in the telephone directory the accolade of the Mobil 5 Star Rating for Excellence. Shaped like a Mayan temple, its entrance is dominated by a bright red steel funnel-shaped sculpture tied with what looks like a convoluted bow, an untitled work by Alexander Liberman. The hotel's top floor is occupied by **The**

**Penthouse Club**, which is open to both private members and guests of the hotel.

On the east side of South Bayshore is a colorful restaurant named **Monty's Bayshore**, which can serve its special fish and seafood dishes to up to 700 people at a time. There is no Monty now connected with the restaurant, though Monty Trainer was one of Miami's best-known personalities and the previous establishment on the same site carried his name. Trainer's flamboyant career took a sudden dip in 1989 when he was charged with tax evasion; however, such was his charisma that a host of local politicians and businessmen threw a lavish farewell party for him on the eve of his going off to spend some time in a federal prison.

On the bay, just before Peacock Park and the Sailing Club's yacht-filled lagoon, is the **Dinner Key Marina**, the city's largest, with 575 moorings; the boats, their myriad masts almost blotting the landscape, are home to many of the owners. Here, too, at the end of **Pan**

e gardens
Vizcaya.

**American Drive**, is **Miami City Hall**, where the local commission has its weekly meetings, and nearby the renovated **Coconut Grove Exhibition Center**. The road was named for the airline that built the structure originally as a terminus for its seaplanes making flights to Latin America in the 1930s.

Where South Bayshore Drive ends, **McFarlane Road** takes over as the highway into the Grove village. Situated at the bottom is the **Public Library**, a coral rock building with a sloping tiled roof and verandah that would not look out of place as a luxury jungle safari lodge. The land was donated by Commodore Munroe – his first wife is buried in the grounds – and the library was started in 1895 by writer Kirk Munroe (no kin) and his wife as a reading group called the Pine Needles Club. After the original building opened in 1901, the group used to send books by boat to the new Miami settlement that was growing just up the coast. The present building opened in 1963.

At the top of McFarlane, a sheer left (southerly) turn takes one on to Main Highway, the Grove's main drag, where the cafés, shops and boutiques are painted in bright colors and reflect an eclectic, sometimes tacky, architecture of bold sweeping curves, a sort of updated Art Deco. Nowhere is this more evident than in the orange-hued **Coconut Grove Realty building** on Commodore Plaza, its design all circles and swirls. A sanctuary in all of this flamboyance is **The Barnacle**, shielded from bustling Main Highway by a forest of trees. This is the home Commodore Munroe constructed in 1891 on a coral ridge overlooking Biscayne Bay. He was a builder of sailboats, and one of them, the ketch *Micco*, is on display at the house, which retains many of the original furnishings and is open to the public for tours.

The **Taurus Steak House** really marks the south end of the village. A one-story cypress restaurant built in 1922, with oak beams and tables fash-

**A minute massage on Main Highway.**

ioned from ships' doors, it is a popular stopping-off place for commuters heading towards South Dade. But one must go a few hundred yards farther along Main Highway under a canopy of long-rooted trees for a peek at one of Florida's most beautiful churches.

Although it looks like a Spanish monastery with its bell towers and niche containing a small sculpture of a saint carved out of the coral – and, in fact, its iron-framed black wooden door came from a 17th-century monastery in the Pyrenees – this is actually **Plymouth Congregational Church** on Devon Road, which goes back only to 1916. Its facade makes an imposing backdrop for wedding photographs.

The **Memorial Gardens** behind the church, with borders of impatiens flowers, a huge poinciana tree and varied palms, is an oasis of peace. On the practical side, the church's **This 'n That thrift store** sells various items of clothing, books and kitchenware. Now and again, the church and its environs re-ceive some unusually exotic and colorful visitors: South American macaws and cockatoos that are residents of the **Parrot Jungle** tourist attraction, but who like to spread their wings and visit the neighborhood.

Returning to Main Highway, one finds the **Coconut Grove Playhouse**, another aspect of the village's culture. The building, with its red Mediterranean-styled roof and white curlicued pillars, was the brainchild of industrialist George Engle, who opened it as a cinema in 1926. It became a legitimate theater in 1965, attracting stage luminaries like the maverick Tallulah Bankhead, who once conducted a press interview while seated on a toilet. It was a gesture that left Groveites, long since inured to such drollery, unfazed. The 1,100-seat theater was taken over by the state of Florida and now stages mostly Broadway-bound musicals and bedroom farces imported from London.

Two short streets of shops – Commodore Plaza and **Fuller Street** – separate

ymouth ngregational urch; enaissance ess-up for n.

Main Highway and **Grand Avenue**, which runs into the Grove's original black settlement, immigrant "conchs" from the Bahamas and Key West. (Grand Avenue comes into its own during the first weekend in June with the Goombay Festival, when residents celebrate their Bahamian roots with music, dancing, and an ethnic food splurge along the length of the avenue.)

On Commodore Plaza, look for the **Carlos Art Gallery**, which sells the latest in Haitian primitive art, with works by Andres Saul, Brasil and Armand, and the fine antique furniture at the **Ted Stahl Interior Design Shop**, which has bas-relief sculptures of weird, bearded warlock-like types over the window.

The Plaza also contains two of the Grove's best-known restaurants. At the second-story **Kaleidoscope**, diners order French cuisine under whirring fans and sit surrounded by tropical plants. **Café Europa**, with its floor of Italian marble tiles, serves French and Italian food in an intimate atmosphere of sub-dued lighting with both indoor and outdoor seating.

Outdoor tables in the Grove, incidentally, are not used exclusively for eating. Here, one takes in the passing show or finds oneself sitting next to an artist putting the finishing touches to a wooden sculpture. Fuller Street, the other side street, starts at the **Old Bank Building**. Here, the local bank did business until 1960 when it moved into a spanking new building on South Bayshore Drive. Here, too, are the **Florentino Shops**, 22 of them, the majority being boutiques and sportswear outlets. Upstairs is **Fuddrucker's**, a self-service restaurant, whose balcony chairs overlook Main Highway.

Not far away is **Joffrey's Coffee Company**, one of those oh-so-trendy coffee houses that seem to be popping up on every street corner in America. Although the service can be poor – customers must collect their coffee from the counter themselves – Joffrey's has a loyal clientele who sit at the outdoor

The Bahamian neighborhood of Coconut Grove.

tables for ages, sipping their exotic coffee concoctions.

At the bottom of Fuller Street and over to the west on Grand Avenue stands what is perhaps the Grove's most anachronistic store: the **Krest Five & Dime**, which continues to stock the little necessities of life. Also on Grand Avenue are **Mandarin Garden**, an excellent Chinese restaurant that does a thriving business with take-away types as well as sit-down diners, and the **Hungry Sailor**, a small English-style pub in a mall that is decorated with nautical charts and marine flags, and serves English fare like shepherd's pie and half a dozen brands of English beer.

If one is in the Grove on a Saturday morning, a visit to the **Farmers' Market** on Grand Avenue between McDonald and Margaret Streets is in order. The first stalls are set up around 8am, and until they pack up and leave at 3pm, vendors offer vegetables and fruit fresh from the South Dade fields (there's a particularly wide variety at the bustling

oconut rove armers' Market.

Juanita's stall), honey, fish and seafood, plus handcrafts, jewelry and clothing. John Balz, a tall ascetic, gives what he calls mini-massages while lecturing customers on the valuable properties of garlic. It's a regular weekly meeting place with the local laid-back types, who tend to indulge in a lot of kissing and hugging with old friends.

Across from the market is **Dade Cycle**. One of the friendliest bicycle shops in the city, Dade offers a huge selection of rental bikes ideal for a cruise through the Grove.

Just north of the intersection of McFarlane, Main, and Grand, is the **Oak Feed Store**, where the health-conscious seek out nutritional candies, drinks, vegetables, bread and vitamins; its presence is registered by a huge carrot sign on the front. And, farther along, between here and Mary Street, are the Grove's two most ornate expressions of the sumptuous life: Mayfair House and **Mayfair in the Grove**.

**Mayfair House** is a grand, 180-room

hotel with Japanese tubs in its suites. Its semi-circular entrance contains a mosaic pool and fountains with statues of anhinga birds standing on one leg. The front door, guarded by a liveried doorman, is of carved mahogany, as are the walls in the small marbled reception area inside. Its rooms, with balconies spilling over with ferns, take up the top three floors of the five-story mall that is Mayfair in the Grove.

The mall contains more than 30 shops with names like Charles Jourdan, Polo/Ralph Lauren, Yves Saint Laurent, and Benetton, doing business in a flamboyant atmosphere of mosaic tiled floors and stairways, copper sculptures, noisy fountains and a profusion of greenery. It is the work of Miami architect Kenneth Treister, who was once a student of Frank Lloyd Wright.

Mayfair is also the home of the world-famous **Planet Hollywood**, a 425-seat restaurant and member of the chain of eateries owned by movie stars Sylvester Stallone, Bruce Willis, Demi Moore,

and Arnold Schwarzenegger. Fun, flashy and flamboyant, this particular restaurant has *Star Trek* masks and boxing outfits as worn by Stallone in the film *Rocky* on display. Next door to Planet Hollywood is, appropriately, Mayfair 10 Cinemas, a 10-screen movie house.

Across the street from Mayfair is **CocoWalk**, a big, pink, Mediterranean-style open-air mall with towering palms and three levels of terraces and balconies. Ultramodern and in some ways a bit too commercial-looking for this old Miami neighborhood, CocoWalk has nevertheless brought new life to the Grove in recent years. It houses several restaurants, dozens of boutiques, and its own 16-screen movie theater.

It also features free, live concerts on weekends and, some weeknights, artists who sketch caricature portraits or sensual flamenco dancers who really work up a sweat.

To sample one of the most glaring contrasts from the glitz and glamour of CocoWalk and Mayfair, one must drive up Mary Street for five blocks to Bird Avenue and turn right to where the road connects with S.W. 27th Avenue. At the corner is what looks like something out of a dilapidated Western ghost town, but the **E–Z Kwik Kuntry Store** is, in fact, one of the area's liveliest spots, both day and night. It could almost be said that it never closes, for its hours are 6am to 2am, seven days a week. The myriad bottle caps stuck into the parking lot surface attest to its reputation as a popular hangout.

But the Kuntry Store's faded wooden front belies the quality of the gourmet goodies inside. Its deli has a wide variety of imported cheeses, fresh fish and seafood. A sign urges: "Boat people identify yourself so we can pack your sandwiches properly." There are a dozen long shelves of domestic and foreign wines, and beers from New Zealand, Australia, Canada and Europe.

In Coconut Grove, there really is just about everything one could need to gratify the five senses.

**Left**, flamingo mailbox. **Right**, Grove boutique.

# CORAL GABLES

Entrepreneur/developer George Merrick called it the City Beautiful, and Coral Gables is certainly that. Its most notable features include towering Mediterranean and colonial-style houses with manicured lawns and carefully tended shrubbery, and quiet, tree-lined streets, monumental gateways, pergolas of flowing vines and ornate fountains that look as if they have been transplanted from a square in Seville.

It is also the City Prosperous. Its 45,000 residents – 63 percent of them non-Latin whites – earn nearly twice as much as their neighbors throughout Dade County, and their homes are worth an average of over $107,000; its healthy economic atmosphere attracts prestigious firms such as IBM Corp., Seagram's Overseas, Texaco, and the Latin American division of American Express to set up headquarters here.

**Easy recycling:** It is without doubt the City Confusing. Its streets, with small, white, sometimes illegible identifying markers, have mainly Spanish names in no alphabetical or rational order, so that visitors have to contend with a hodgepodge system where avenues like Caligula, Savona, Gerona and Luenga run randomly one after the other off LeJeune Road. Street numbers are nonexistent.

It is the City Fussy. Its strict zoning laws forbid the parking of boats or trucks in house driveways (they must be kept out of sight in garages or behind homes), the removal of a tree without city permission, and the keeping of more than four cats or dogs per household. Residents putting out their trash for the weekly pick-up must separate items like milk cartons, newspapers, soft drinks cans and plastic bottles to ensure easy recycling.

It can also be the City Infuriating to absent-minded drivers who park their cars in Coral Gables' streets and forget to check the meters. The city employs an unusually aggressive army of sharp-eyed meter maids, known uncharitably as the Witches on Wheels, who tool around in three-wheeled vehicles and can effortlessly spot a red "Expired" sign at a hundred yards.

But Coral Gables is an immaculate and fascinating city of restaurants whose architecture is as inviting as the fare, of bright shops with red-tiled roofs and arched windows, of winding waterways where sleek yachts are moored at the foot of sloping gardens. It's a city that, in the words of Ellen Uguccioni, its historic preservation administrator, "tries to maintain the quality of life."

That quality was born in the early 1920s in the mind of George Merrick, son of a Congregational minister who had settled in the area from Massachusetts and developed citrus and avocado groves. George, in turn, slowly turned the plantation into a residential community, assembling a team of architects and landscape artists to create a South

**Preceding pages: Coral Gables and its fancy cars; a scene to savor. Left, classic coral rock planter. Right, home on historic Coral Way.**

Florida city with a Mediterranean theme; the homes and buildings would reflect the best of Spanish and Italian design. He named it Coral Gables after his childhood home.

The flamboyance of the period is no better exemplified than in the huge **Venetian Pool** on DeSoto Boulevard; once a rock pit, it featured lush landscaping, coral rock caves, diving platforms and waterfalls amid Venetian-inspired architecture. Beauty pageants were held there in its early years. Open to the public, the pool recently underwent a $2.3 million renovation.

A graceful, towered building with a 40-foot arch was built in 1924 as an entrance to the city from Douglas Road. By the mid-1920s, Merrick's showplace hotel resort, the Biltmore, had opened, some 600 homes had been built, roadways constructed, and thousands of trees, shrubs and flowers planted. It was boom time.

But it was a brief era of prosperity. Land values dropped because of artifi-cial inflation and over-speculation; the disastrous 1926 hurricane put a halt to further building; the depression of 1929 ended the frolicking Jazz Age; and the city declined into bankruptcy.

The city, however, rose from the ashes. The **University of Miami** boasts one of the best football teams in the US. It has long discarded its derisive image as Suntan-U, whose students were purportedly more interested in frolicking in the sun than learning, and has an enrollment of close to 14,000 and a full-time faculty of 1,500 on its 260-acre campus northwest of **Ponce de Leon Boulevard**, off highway US 1. It opened its **School of Medicine** in 1952, and the **Rosenstiel School of Marine and Atmospheric Science** in 1969. Its **Lowe Art Museum** has a permanent collection of 8,000 works, including Renaissance and baroque art.

Coral Gables is really cut into two parts. It starts just north of the **Tamiami Trail** in the north, and encompasses the next 5 miles or so south, through the

Spanish-style Coral Gables home.

194

Granada and **Biltmore golf courses** (public), the **Riviera Country Club** (private), and the University of Miami, to **Sunset Road**, where it takes up the area east of **Old Cutler Road** for three miles south to a few blocks past **Fairchild Tropical Garden**.

On the east, the Gables starts at Douglas Road, about 7 miles from downtown Miami, reached by Brickell Avenue to **Coral Way**, which then meanders west and south. Gableites will sniff that the striking **Miracle Center** on Coral Way is a couple of blocks short of actually being in the city, but it is worth a visit, for there is no mall like it in the Gables. Its three floors contain 30 shops, a health spa, four restaurants and a five-theater cinema.

The Gables' main shopping area, **Miracle Mile**, is only four blocks long, between Douglas and Le Jeune Roads. Here are 160 boutiques, shoe stores, bookshops and a Woolworth's which serves a tuna sandwich for less than you thought possible. Near the western end

of the Mile is the **Miracle Theater**, a 600-seat, 1940s Art Deco movie theater that was transformed into a playhouse in 1995 and now has its own resident company that performs year round.

The most dominant structure on the Mile is the **Colonnade Building** at the corner of Ponce de Leon Boulevard. Built in 1925, featuring a huge baroque front door, a rotunda with marble floors and a central fountain, it is the home of the Florida National Bank, but it is also connected to the elegant 13-story **Colonnade Hotel** on Aragon Avenue.

Before leaving this area, incidentally, pop into the neat little **Chamber of Commerce** building (yes, it has a red-tiled roof) at the corner of Aragon and Galiano, and pick up a sheaf of brochures detailing area attractions. Ask for the map of the city, for it details an all-encompassing self-guided tour and a bicycle path.

For further reading on the Gables, and just about any subject under the sun, call in at **Books and Books**, also on Aragon,

Cheerleaders root for the University of Miami's football team.

at the corner of Salzedo. With some 5,000 volumes, this store has reading material to keep the bibliophile entranced for the day. There's not only an old and rare book section, but owner Mitchell Kaplan helps customers track down out-of-print books. Kaplan, co-founder of the Miami International Book Fair, sponsors lectures and authors' parties at the shop.

At the foot of Miracle, on the other side of Le Jeune Road at Biltmore Way, stands **Coral Gables City Hall**. It, too, rose in the late 1920s, a semi-circular building with a facade of 12 columns and a Spanish Renaissance-type clock tower. A few blocks west on Coral Way is the **Merrick House**, where George Merrick grew up. It was constructed in 1899 of oolitic limestone, with a multi-gabled roof of coral-colored tiles. The house is operated by the city as a museum, and is open to the public for a minimal charge.

The 18-story **Biltmore Hotel** on Anastasia Avenue, fashioned after the Giralda Tower in Seville, has gone through several phases since its spectacular opening in 1926. Merrick's brainchild attracted movie stars and industrial barons, and Rolls-Royces were parked in the driveway. But after the hurricane of that year, and the real estate failure, the hotel stayed almost fallow until 1943, when it was turned into a World War II army hospital. It was not until 1987 that guests were admitted again to the luxuriously refurbished 286-room hotel.

In 1994, the Biltmore hosted the Summit of the Americas, when heads of state from North and South America gathered to discuss the future of the hemisphere. It has also become the favored hideaway of Miami-visiting movie stars and royalty, and one of the most sought-after fashion photography locations in the city.

Taking a leaf from Merrick's baroque book, Gables architect John Nichols designed the **Hyatt Regency Hotel**, which opened in 1987 at the corner of

**Even the security force is beautiful in the Gables.**

Douglas Road and Alhambra. The location is appropriate, since the 242-room hotel's Moorish architecture is patterned after the ornate Alhambra in Granada, Spain. The U-shaped complex is composed of archways and columns, courtyards and fountains, topped by a red-barrel tile roof. Inside are stone balustrades, huge, elegant mirrors, silk-draped ceiling-to-floor windows, tapestries and landscaped terraces. The Court of the Lions, the hotel's outdoor patio area, is patterned after the Alhambra courtyard.

And so the influence of Merrick never dies; indeed, it is forever being revived. **Venetian Villas** on Toledo Street, with its Moorish arches, Spanish tile fountains and wrought-iron balconies, opened in 1926 as a winter retreat for wealthy northerners. It was later converted to a 22-apartment building, then it fell into disrepair. But the Edelman Restoration Co., which has gained a reputation for restoring old buildings, gave the villas a $2½ million facelift in 1989, and converted the property into six luxury con-

dominiums valued at more than $500,000 each.

Other influences did manage to creep into the Gables, though, over the years, and the eclecticism of its architecture was reflected in a happy mélange of small, historic communities like the **Chinese Village** (on Riviera Drive at Menendez Avenue) with its sloping tiled roofs; the **Dutch South African Village** (LeJeune Road at Maya Street), patterned on the farmhouses of 17th-century Dutch colonialists; the **French City Village** (Hardee Road at Cellini Street); the **French Country Village** (Hardee at Maggiore Street); the **French Normandy Village** (LeJeune at Viscaya Avenue); the **Italian Village** (Altara Avenue at Monserrate Street), and the **Colonial Village** (Santa Maria Street), which was designed to evoke the image of New England homes.

The Gables is blessed with fine restaurants, most of them on, or just off, Ponce de Leon Boulevard. **Place St Michel** is a favorite place with Gable-

**Courtyard and pool of the Biltmore Hotel.**

ites for continental dining and leisurely Sunday brunches. The restaurant is contained in the exquisite little (28 rooms) **Hotel Place St Miche**l, also built during the Merrick era, with high ceilings and individually furnished rooms of antiques.

**La Palma**, on Alhambra Circle, is a gem tucked inside the **Hotel La Palma** (*circa* 1925), awarded accolades by notable food critics for its continental cuisine. Also recommended are **Charade** and **Christy's**, within walking distance of each other on Ponce de Leon.

Ponce is also one of the starting off points of Gables Gallery Night, a regularly scheduled first-Friday of each month tour that takes art-lovers and lookers to 18 Coral Gables galleries. Free, open-air trolley cars move from gallery to gallery and allow visitors to come and go as they please, to peruse the art, fine photography and antiques, and to sample a little complementary wine and cheese along the way.

To see the other half of the Gables,

turn left (south) at the bottom of Miracle Mile and drive for 4 miles or so, through US 1, and over a waterway to **Cartagena Plaza**, where LeJeune, Sunset, Cocoplum and Old Cutler Roads converge. If the neat homes on the west side of Old Cutler fit quite well into the Gables' average $107,000 value, the Cocoplum mansions lining the waterways leading out to Biscayne Bay are in a world by themselves.

Local authorities insist that these $500,000-plus digs on roads with names like Mira Flores must conform to strict zoning laws in their color and roof styles. New homes have to fit into the same pattern as those already here.

There are two other luxury home divisions, on Casuarina Concourse and Arvida Parkway, before one comes to the 100-acre **Matheson Hammock Park**, which was developed in the 1930s on land donated by pioneer Commodore J. W. Matheson. The park, a popular weekend spot for residents, has a marina and a small beach; a man-made tidal pool is separated from the bay by a walkway. There are picnic facilities and sailboat rentals.

Next door to the park, and the end of the Coral Gables experience, sits the 83-acre **Fairchild Tropical Garden**, the largest tropical garden in the continental United States. The garden, which has been open to the public since 1938, is supported by membership fees, grants, donations, admissions and a small endowment. It was named in honor of the distinguished plant explorer, Dr David Fairchild.

Here, along winding paths and overlooking lakes, is an outstanding collection of tropical flowering trees, and some 5,000 ferns, plants and orchids, with exotic names like the fire tree from Australia, the talipot palm from Sri Lanka and the ponytail tree from Mexico. Tram tours of the garden leave every hour, but walking tour guides give visitors a closer look at the labeled flora. The City Beautiful is that indeed, right to the end.

**Left**, jogging through Matheson Hammock Park. **Right**, shopping on Miracle Mile.

# LITTLE HAVANA

Picture a neighborhood where a flame leaps day and night for veterans of the Bay of Pigs invasion. Imagine a parade where schoolchildren march proudly for a homeland they never once knew. Picture a fast-food restaurant that features hamburgers, French fries and café Cubano, to go.

At the core of **Little Havana** beats an exile's heart, scarred with sadness for a lost homeland, swelled with pride in its past. From pharmacies to restaurants to car washes to grocery stores, the names here speak of far away and long ago: Farmacia Camaguey, Fruteria Los Pinareños, Managua Medical Center, Nicaragua Restaurant.

Havana, Cuba, never looked like this hodge-podge of car dealerships and strip shopping centers, furniture stores and flower shops, run-down 1950s motels and well-kept Mediterranean Revival-style houses. This is Havana, Miami, an immigrants' launching pad, a constantly changing monument to new beginnings and hope.

Today, one can find *guayaberas* in Hialeah, dance *salsa* in Key Biscayne, sip *ajiaco* in Kendall. The neighborhood's Cuban flavor has become diluted in recent years as Central American refugees have taken over entire blocks. Still, Little Havana remains the symbolic center of South Florida's thriving Cuban community, a place to savor a good meal or a good memory.

Very roughly, Little Havana is bounded by the **Miami River** on the east, **37th Avenue** on the west, **State Road 836** on the north and **Coral Way** on the south. It sprawls over a collection of old Miami neighborhoods settled after the turn of the century and first known by the names Shenandoah and Riverside.

Cuban exiles first began settling here *en masse* after their country's 1959 revolution, re-opening boarded-up stores and filling vacant apartment buildings in the deteriorating neighborhood. As the first Cuban settlers moved up economically, they moved out to more affluent areas, leaving room for new waves of fellow Cubans disenchanted with communism.

**Recent headaches:** The 1980 Mariel boat lift, when 125,000 Cubans boarded boats for South Florida, marked a turning point for Little Havana. More than 12,000 of the new arrivals flooded the neighborhood's eastern end, and officials housed many in tents by the Miami River beneath a highway overpass.

The tents came down, but crime rose as derelicts and the homeless flooded the area. In the violence-ridden years that followed, **East Little Havana** became known as Little Vietnam.

Though police say that crime has fallen since the late 1980s, the neighborhood has not recovered, especially east of 12th Avenue in the **Flagler Street** area. Storefronts are boarded up, and derelicts walk the streets. Those unfamiliar with this neighborhood are advised

against wandering here alone, particularly at night.

Since the late 1970s, local merchants and city officials have dreamed of developing the area west of 12th Avenue into a tourist attraction similar to San Francisco's Chinatown or New Orleans' French Quarter. The 60-block area would have hotels and specialty shops and apartments built above businesses to lend the neighborhood an urban, ethnic ambiance. More than a decade later, the Latin Quarter had met with modest success; brick sidewalks lined with black olive trees and scattered shops with white stucco walls and red-tiled roofs were the prime evidence of its existence.

Unprodded by urban planners, change has proceeded at a more rapid pace east of 12th Avenue. During the 1980s, struggling Central American immigrants – the majority of them Nicaraguans – crowded bungalows and patronized the corner *bodegas*.

Little Havana's best-known street is **S.W. Eighth Street** (or **Calle Ocho**), the eastern end of Florida's Tamiami Trail that links Tampa with Miami. In early January, it hosts the Three Kings Day Parade. Later in the month, there is a schoolchildren's march in honor of José Marti, the Cuban writer, philosopher and leader of Cuba's independence struggle against Spain. The major annual event is the Calle Ocho festival in March, a mammoth street party that features Latin food and entertainment.

Another important thoroughfare is **Flagler Street**, a wide, busy street that parallels Calle Ocho to the south, linking downtown Miami with the county's western end.

A good launching point for any Little Havana tour is the corner of Calle Ocho and 13th Avenue, also known as **Cuban Memorial Boulevard**. On the south end of the street is the **Bay of Pigs Monument**, which consists of a flame surrounded by a half-dozen unloaded missiles pointing upwards. On plaques are the names of the 94 members of the invasion team who were killed.

**A heated game of dominoes.**

The monument pays tribute to the April 17, 1961, invasion of Cuba by a team of exile volunteers trained and sponsored by the US Central Intelligence Agency. The invasion, intended to spark a mass uprising against Fidel Castro, did not succeed. After three days of fighting, almost 1,000 men were taken prisoner, and the remainder were forced to retreat to Miami.

A few blocks away, on S.W. Ninth Street, is another Bay of Pigs landmark: the **Juan J. Peruyero Museum** and the **Manuel F. Artime Library**, both named after invasion leaders who are now dead. This is a fascinating place, well worth a visit. It is filled with maps, photographs and old newspaper clippings dating back to the early 1960s. On one wall are black-and-white pictures of veterans who have died during and since the invasion. Also on display are old camouflage uniforms worn during the operation and pilots' maps.

**Local color:** Clustered within walking distance of the Bay of Pigs Monument are a number of Little Havana commercial institutions. **Casino Records** offers a wide range of Latin music on tapes, records and compact discs. There's everything from turn-of-the-century Cuban *danzons* to mambos and *cha-chachas* by the late Cuban bandleader Damaso Perez-Prado to spirited *salsa* by Cuban exile Celia Cruz. The variety here includes Dominican *merengues*, Colombian *cumbias*, Brazilian sambas and Argentinian tangos.

Nearby is **Botanica La Abuela**, a long narrow store filled with herbs, candles, dolls and small images of saints. *Botanicas* are the pharmacies of santeria and voodoo, stores that carry the ingredients and tools for their rites. If you stand long enough inside La Abuela, you are likely to hear customers discussing which herb to use for a particular problem, or which prayer to recite for a loved one.

*Botanicas*, scattered throughout Little Havana and other Miami neighborhoods, were not designed for tourists.

**eft, the ay of Pigs onument on uban emorial lvd. Right, a ffee shop.**

Outsiders are politely tolerated, but not particularly welcome. Practitioners are sensitive about being sensationalized and misinterpreted, and tact and discretion are advised.

Next door to La Abuela is **El Credito**, the largest handmade cigar factory in Miami. Step inside and see two dozen men and women nimbly cutting the leaves, rolling them into cigars and squeezing them into wooden presses. Many of these craftsmen learned their trade in Cuba, where, before the revolution, owner Ernesto Perez Carillo's father and grandfather ran a business.

Another Cuban institution transplanted from Havana to Little Havana after the revolution is the **Casa de Los Trucos**. Also located on Eighth Street, this House of Tricks carries strange hats, uzi machine guns that spit water, maracas, magic tricks and a wide variety of masks, including Fidel Castro.

Close by is **Pinareños Market**, a fruit stand, half indoors, half outdoors, whose displays include a variety of tropical fruits. Depending on the season, one might find papaya, *platanos manzanos* (apple bananas), *boniato* (the Cuban sweet potato) and *malanga*, a white-flesh root that is usually boiled or used in soups.

Down the street stands a **McDonald's Restaurant** that carries Cuban coffee along with its regular fast-food fare. The real reason to stop here is not the food, but the opportunity to see two pieces of original art by Haydee and Sahara Scull, Cuban-born identical twins who conjure happy images of 1950s Havana through their murals that combine painting and sculpture. Hanging here is a charming, bustling scene of the action outside Havana's cathedral: a caped man with a flower; a woman in a tight yellow dress and, in the lower-left hand corner, a pair of brown-tressed women in identical red dresses, the ubiquitous Scull sisters.

The rattle of dominoes and the smell of cigars pervade what must be Miami's most densely populated park. Located

**Nicaraguan child waits for her mother.**

at the corner of Calle Ocho and 15th Avenue, **Maximo Gomez Park** (better known as **Domino Park**) is a collection of game tables topped by red-tiled roofs. Concerned about crime, Miami city officials have limited access to the park to those over the age of 55 and require an identification card to get in. Exceptions are made for tourists.

A few blocks to the west is **La Casa de las Piñatas**, a shop filled with colorful *piñatas* and other accessories for children's parties. Even farther west, near 27th Avenue, is **Almacenes Gonzalez,** a religious artifacts store which is as much a museum as a business. The store features Spanish-made wood-paste statues of Catholic saints popular with Cubans: St Judas Tadeo, the Virgin of Regla and the Virgin of Charity, Cuba's patron saint. Exiles buy the saints and set them in small shrines, often in their own front yards.

Well worth a visit is **Woodlawn Cemetery**. Anastasio Somoza, the Nicaraguan strongman unseated by his coun-try's 1979 Sandinista revolution, rests here in a mausoleum marked only with his initials. Carlos Prio Socarras, the late Cuban president elected in 1948 and deposed in a 1952 coup by Fulgencio Batista, lies beneath a tombstone that carries the red, white and blue of the Cuban flag. Also buried here is Gerardo Machado y Morales, Cuba's fifth president, a harsh dictator forced to flee Cuba following a 1933 army revolt.

**Spicy fare:** Little Havana is at its most accessible through the palate. The neighborhood abounds with restaurants and coffee shops serving up a wide range of Latin foods.

Cuban cooking is homey; people's fare. Starting from the west on Calle Ocho, you will find **Versailles**, one of the most popular eating establishments in town. The large mirrors and bright lights make this place unself-consciously gaudy, and that is part of its charm. Fast-paced and moderately priced, Versailles attracts a widely varied clientele, from large noisy families to groups of busi-

Credito
gar factory
elcomes
sitors for a
ok.

nessmen to theater-goers dropping in for a late-night snack. The menu is huge. Neophytes to Cuban cooking might try the restaurant's sampler of typical Cuban foods: roast pork, sweet plantains, ham croquettes and tamales. Also popular, and with a similar menu, is **La Carreta**, located across the street and one of the only places around that is open 24 hours.

Down the street is **Casablanca Restaurant**, a venerable Little Havana eating institution. Opened in 1962, it is slower-paced than the latter two. Try the guava-and-cheese pastries.

Former President Reagan, wildly popular among many Cuban exiles for his hardline anti-communist stance, made Little Havana history on May 20, 1983, when he stopped for lunch at **La Esquina de Tejas** on S.W. 12th Avenue, also known as Ronald Reagan Avenue. The restaurant, which serves standard Cuban fare (try the Cuban sandwiches), has not forgotten this visit. Reagan's autograph is reproduced on the menus, and the restaurant still serves "The President's Special."

**Islas Canarias** on 27th Avenue is another extremely popular spot, offering fast service and some of the best Cuban cooking around. **Latin American Cafeteria** on Coral Way specializes in Cuban sandwiches. **El Pulpito** Restaurant on Calle Ocho also offers Cuban dishes and sits in the heart of the planned Latin Quarter.

For a quick and very inexpensive snack, drop into **El Rey de las Fritas** on Calle Ocho or the **Morro Castle** on N.W. Seventh Avenue. A Cuban version of the hamburger, the *frita* consists of a beef patty and *julienne* potatoes doused with spicy sauce inside a roll. For dessert, pay a visit to the **Perezsosa Bakery**, which is situated next to Domino Park. Try the *pan de Karaka*, corn bread that, before the revolution, made the bakery famous in the central Cuban city of Camaguey.

For more sophisticated and more expensive cuisine, head for the Spanish

**A father gets a haircut as his son watches.**

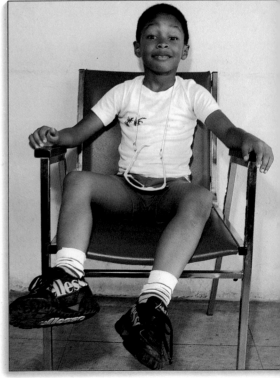

restaurants. On Calle Ocho, there's **Casa Juancho**, bustling with young upwardly mobile Cuban-Americans. Across the street is **El Bodegon-Castilla**, a quieter restaurant and favorite gathering place of many of the older Cuban exile organizations. Nearby and also very popular is **Centro Vasco**. On the eastern end of Calle Ocho is **Malaga Restaurant**, where fast-paced conversations spill out of the restaurant's many rooms; the snapper is delicious.

For good Colombian food, there's **Restaurante Monserrate** on 12th Avenue. Small Nicaraguan restaurants have abounded in the neighborhood since the late 1980s, such as **Guayacan**, where homesick Nicaraguans go for homemade soups and delectable beef-tongue simmered in tomato sauce.

For Little Havana entertainment, try Centro Vasco and Malaga, both of which have popular flamenco shows. If your Spanish is good enough, venture to a Little Havana theater. Depending on what's playing at **Bellas Artes**, you might stumble onto a Spanish tragedy or a contemporary anti-Castro comedy. For music shows and Cuban exile comedy-in-the-rough, try **Teatro Marti** on Eighth Avenue.

**Little Managua:** Twenty years after Cuba's 1959 revolution, upheaval in Nicaragua began sending a new group of refugees to Miami. The result: **Little Managua** – or New Managua, as some exiles prefer to call it. In Miami, Nicaraguans found much sympathy from Cuban exiles, many of whom embraced the anti-Sandinista cause as their own. Cuban exile doctors healed wounded Contra veterans, while local Cuban radio stations staged fundraisers for rebel boots and uniforms.

By the time the Sandinistas were defeated in Nicaragua's February 25, 1990, elections – and Nicaraguan Opposition Union (UNO) coalition candidate Violeta Chamorro triumphed – Miami's Nicaraguan community had grown to an estimated 150,000 residents: former government ministers, ex-Contra fight-

uban
ooking
go.

ers, entrepreneurs, professionals and workers, all in turn alienated by the Marxist-led Sandinistas.

With the Sandinistas' electoral defeat, the mood on Miami's streets was euphoric as Nicaraguans honked their car horns, waved flags and shrieked with joy; Cubans joined in, hoping Fidel Castro would be next.

Though spread from Hialeah to Key Biscayne, Nicaraguan exiles have made their strongest impact in East Little Havana and West Dade's **Sweetwater** area; the latter neighborhood is what has become known as Little Managua, bounded loosely by 97th and 115th Avenues between State Road 836 and S.W. 40th Street.

The neighborhood's main artery is **Flagler Street**. The surrounding area, which includes the tiny city of Sweetwater and the residential development **Fontainebleau Park**, is home to a well-established working and middle-class Nicaraguan enclave.

Today, Little Managua remains a community in transition, its future to be determined as much by events in Nicaragua as the situation in South Florida. But some landmarks are here to stay.

For instance, there's **Ruben Dario Avenue** (a stretch of 97th Avenue near Flagler Street) and **Ruben Dario Middle School**, named in honor of the beloved Nicaraguan poet. Situated on Flagler Street near 104th Avenue is the **Centro Comercial Managua**, a small shopping center where everything from the jewelry store to the bakery to the pharmacy is Nicaraguan-run.

The most famous Nicaraguan eatery around is **Los Ranchos Restaurant** in Sweetwater, owned and operated by José Somoza, nephew of Anastasio Somoza, the late Nicaraguan dictator. Savor the *churrasco* steak with *chimichurri* sauce, then top it off with *tres leches*, a rich cream-soaked cake that is the house specialty.

There are other excellent restaurants which serve typically Nicaraguan fare: the red beans and rice dish known as

**Freighters loaded down with stolen bicycles on the Miami River.**

*gallo pinto*; the charcoal-broiled beef *carne asada*; fried pork rind or *vigoron*, and the snapper in tomato sauce called *pescado a la Tipitapa*. A few blocks from Flagler Street, off 107th Avenue, is the **Galloping Lobster**. On Flagler Street, there's **La Parrilla**.

For Nicaraguan food in other parts of town, there's **El Novillo** in Hialeah (a newer branch is on Bird Road) and **La Choza** on Key Biscayne. **Los Ranchos** has also opened up in Kendall, Coral Gables, and in downtown Miami at Bayside Marketplace.

**River scenes:** From Sweetwater, drive east on Flagler Street and find the **Miami River**. Once a waterway to the Everglades plied by Tequesta Indians in cypress canoes, today's Miami River is a busy, gritty shipping center. Spilling on to its banks are boatyards, marinas, terminals and fisheries.

Just pick a point somewhere close to the water and observe what floats by: rickety Haitian freighters weighed down with stolen bicycles; mattresses or plastic containers; rusty-hulled foreign ships squeezing through with the help of tugboats; fishermen returning with the day's ocean catch.

Criss-crossed by bridges, the Miami River's navigable stretch starting from its mouth on Biscayne Bay measures only 5.6 miles. The draining of the Everglades during the first two decades of the 20th century radically changed the course of the river west of 24th Avenue. Its original source, in Everglades headwaters near what is now 32nd Avenue, was all but eliminated by the dredging of the Miami Canal linking the river to Lake Okeechobee. One doesn't need a boat to appreciate the river. Try visiting the public parks that line its banks.

One of Miami's best-kept secrets is **Sewell Park**, a quiet, gently sloping and somewhat overgrown plot with tall royal palms perched on the south side of the river near the 17th Avenue bridge. On the north bank and upriver is **Curtis Park**, which has picnic tables on the Miami River and the only public boat launch on the river.

Most outstanding is **José Marti Park** on the eastern edge of Little Havana, a vision of pink-stucco buildings and red-brick walks sprawled along the river's south bank. Built on what was once a Tequesta Indian settlement, the site in 1980 became known as Tent City, a temporary shelter for homeless Mariel refugees. In 1985, it became a park dedicated to Cuban writer José Marti. The park includes a pool, a fountain, a bust of José Marti donated by the Cuban government in 1952 and a statue of the late South Florida Congressman Claude Pepper.

A little to the north of the park, on South River Drive, is the **Miami River Inn**. The structures, built between 1906 and 1914, were restored to their original condition in the late 1980s by local preservationist Sallye Jude. The four wood-frame buildings house 40 antique-decorated guest rooms that offer a cozy slice of Miami history.

he Miami
iver Inn.

# LITTLE HAITI

The storefronts leap out at passers-by. Bright blues, reds, and oranges seem to vibrate to the rousing Haitian music blaring from sidewalk speakers. The multilingual signs advertise peculiarly Haitian products – rapid money transfers to any village in Haiti, the latest *compas* records, custom-tailored "French-Styled" fashions and culinary delights such as *lambi* and *griot*.

Unlike so many neighborhood shopping areas in the age of the automobile and suburbs, Little Haiti's streets are filled with pedestrians. Houses wear coats of pink, blue and yellow, the colors found in the Caribbean countryside and far from the subtle pastels of Miami Beach's Art Deco District. When straw-hatted women in floral cotton dresses walk past, it almost seems as if a Haitian painting has come to life.

In spite of this allure, too few tourists visit Little Haiti, which lies about 3 miles north of downtown Miami and just a few blocks inland from Biscayne Bay. Perhaps they are frightened away because it is adjacent to **Liberty City** and a few miles north of **Overtown**, the sites of four highly publicized riots in the 1980s. Or perhaps many have believed the negative stereotypes of "Haitian boat people."

For whatever reasons, people should not avoid venturing into Little Haiti and those who seek something culturally different should definitely go. Little Haiti is quite unlike Little Havana and the rest of Miami, and it is as safe as any urban neighborhood in Miami.

It has been just over a decade since Miami's Little Haiti began to emerge in an historic neighborhood once known as Lemon City. The area was one of the first settled in Miami. Until the 1960s it was primarily middle-class and white. Located at 79th Street and Biscayne Boulevard was one of Miami's most important shopping centers. In the late 1960s, newly -arrived Cuban refugees settled there and blacks from Liberty City moved slowly east.

During the 1970s the area became predominantly black and during the 1980s those blacks were increasingly Haitian. The neighborhood began to appear neglected. Previously crowded stores were empty and streets littered. Tumbledown houses with absentee owners showed the wear of years without care.

In the last half of the 1980s, change unfolded. In ways that were both dramatic and subtle, Little Haiti began to take shape as an enclave of Caribbean culture. The colors of Little Haiti, the vivid hues of the sunlit tropics, are most evident in the folk-art murals on the storefronts, walls and billboards scattered throughout the community. Many signs are hand-painted, often by local artists, their subjects ranging from storefront names to murals of political demonstrations, floral collages and Haitian people. While widely scattered

throughout the neighborhood, they are especially prevalent along **N.E. Second Avenue** and on **54th Street**.

The Haitian community leaders are both businessmen and political organizers. The businessmen are energetic and optimistic. They envision Little Haiti becoming another Little Havana or San Francisco-style Chinatown. The only Little Haiti in the US, it will be a cultural and tourist attraction based on the Haitians' drive and enthusiasm and their unique cultural attributes – world-renowned painting, wood crafts, music, French-inspired cuisine, architecture and numerous skilled trades.

While Little Haiti is not yet famous, the modest accomplishments of Miami's Haitian entrepreneurs remain a notable development even in an area which is well accustomed to rapid and spectacular growth.

**Haitian refugees:** Most significantly, these achievements have come in spite of profound obstacles. Miami's Haitians are one of the most persecuted and suffering of immigrant groups in the US. While Cubans have always been encouraged to come to Miami and have received substantial government assistance, Haitians have always been rejected. The government has labeled them as economic refugees, in contrast to the Cuban political refugees.

In reality, the conditions and motivations impelling both the Haitian and Cuban flows are similar: underdevelopment, desires to improve oneself and political repression. For reasons of US foreign policy and racism, Haitians have not been welcomed into Miami.

But Haitians have resisted US governmental efforts to send them back to their island, and with the assistance of organizations and lawyers they have achieved partial victories. Few have been deported, and a Haitian community has gradually emerged. For a while they were identified as one of the main sources and carriers of AIDS. Subsequently, research revealed that Haitians were not a primary at-risk group and that AIDS was

**Haitian shop along 59th Street.**

probably first imported to Haiti from the US. Haitian refugees are also commonly perceived as desperately poor, illiterate and unskilled.

The facts are that recent Haitian immigrants to Miami are much like any other immigrant group: better off, more educated and more skilled than their typical countrymen back home. Moreover, there's a significant middle and even upper-class group of Haitians in Miami. Some came directly from Haiti, but most are secondary migrants, coming to Miami after living often 20 years or more in New York, Boston, Montreal or some other northern city. They are usually fluent in English, college educated and the business owners and political leaders of the community.

**Business District:** The commercial center of Little Haiti lies along **N.E. 54th Street** between **Miami Avenue** and **N.E. Second Avenue**. Virtually all the businesses on this single, long block are Haitian and they have all been decorated with Haitian colors and designs.

The block contains a Haitian grocery store, restaurant, record store and even a *botanica* (see panel at end of chapter).

Close to Miami Avenue on 54th Street is the site of the **Haitian Refugee Center** (HRC). HRC has been at the forefront of the Haitian struggle to obtain equal treatment from US immigration authorities. With assistance first from Miami's black American churches and later the National Council of Churches and the Ford Foundation, HRC has provided legal assistance to thousands of Haitians, counseling as many as 150 a day in 1980, the peak year of immigration to Miami. The **Haitian Activities Center**, a few doors down from HRC, frequently has evening lectures and discussions, usually on political topics in Miami or Haiti. Outsiders are welcome and participants usually offer to translate from local Creole into English.

On weekends, the corner at 54th Street and N.E. Second Avenue turns into a miniature Third World market, as vendors set up umbrella-covered stalls filled

ıe Haitian
ıtholic
ınter mural
ıpicts the
ıurney of
aitians to
liami.

with fresh Caribbean fruit and vegetables. If you cannot visit on a weekend, then go into any Haitian grocery store. The biggest ones are situated on N.W. Second Avenue, between **58th** and **59th Streets**, and on the corner of N. Miami Avenue and **62nd Street**. Here, you will find ox tail, goat, conch, dried Haitian mushrooms and many other peculiarly Haitian foods.

Outside the grocery stores, gypsy cabs gather to transport people, usually in groups, from home to stores and from Little Haiti to other Haitian settlements in the Miami area.

**Caribbean style:** Along N.E. Second Avenue, all the way from **45th** to **84th Street**, Haitian stores predominate, but the new focal point is the **Caribbean Marketplace**. The Caribbean Marketplace was conceived in 1984 as a tourist center that would spark Little Haiti's sagging economy. Led by the Haitian Task Force, a non-profit, community development organization, community leaders planned an ornate center based on the old Iron Market in Port-au-Prince, a product of Haiti's most fanciful turn-of-the-century architecture.

Created from an abandoned, dusty furniture store at 60th Street, the new Marketplace's twisting gables and brightly colored aeries won three prestigious architectural awards. It is a wonderful building, festive and energetic. Its walls are painted yellow, orange, green, blue and magenta, an intense color scheme that is carried on inside and out.

Inside, the space is left wide open, the ceilings criss-crossed with trusses. Tenants sell fresh produce, clothes, records and other retail goods. The market was intended to serve the community first, but many of the merchants sell items to appeal to tourists. The market operates six days a week, Tuesday through till Sunday.

A few blocks away, on N.E. 59th Street, is **Toussaint Louverture Elementary School**, Miami's only new elementary school built in an urban

*The architectural award-winning Caribbean Marketplace*

neighborhood in the 1980s. It is also the only Dade County school named after a Haitian hero. Toussaint Louverture was a freed slave who led the uprising against the French in Haiti that produced the first emancipation of slaves and the first modern free black republic.

Toussaint Louverture school contains a statue of the hero, donated by the Miami Haitian community, and its stucco walls reflect Caribbean colors all boldly applied, in broad sweeps.

**Spiritual support:** Back on N.E. Second Avenue, just across the street from the Caribbean Marketplace, is Little Haiti's spiritual center, the **Church of Notre Dame D'Haiti** and the **Pierre Toussaint Haitian Catholic Center** which occupy the buildings and grounds of a former Catholic girls' high school. The chapel, which was once the high school cafeteria, was renovated in 1988–89. In the morning the sun illuminates stained-glass windows that cover the full length of one wall.

The splendid windows depict the fam-

ily of the freed Haitian-born slave Pierre Toussaint, who is currently being considered by the Vatican for sainthood. Pierre Toussaint's descendants now live in Little Haiti and attend this church. Another wall is covered with a mural that depicts the journey of Haitians to South Florida.

Mass is held daily, but every effort should be made to attend a Sunday service, especially the 9am or 5pm ones. Then, the chapel overflows with worshippers, immaculately and elegantly attired. A Haitian band and choir provides music and everyone in the congregation joins in. The songs and music are a blend of French melodies and African rhythms, much more mellow and mellifluous than most Afro-Caribbean music. On a good day the service will go on for nearly two hours, although one hour is the norm. On Easter Sunday and Christmas Day, everything is moved outdoors, under the broad shade trees.

Aside from spiritual help, Notre Dame also provides English classes, child-

woman
ads a
salm book
Creole.

care services and financial assistance. English classes for Haitians, both at Notre Dame and elsewhere, are usually over-enrolled and teachers commonly comment that Haitians are remarkably dedicated students. While the English level of most recent immigrants is low, the rate of enrollment in English classes is much higher among Haitians than other immigrant groups in Miami. Moreover, Haitians frequently learn Spanish on the job, since their co-workers and bosses are commonly native Spanish-speakers. It is not unusual to find quadrilingual Haitians, i.e. those who speak Haitian Creole, French, English and Spanish.

Further up N.E. Second Avenue, nearly at 79th Street, is **Les Cousins' Bookstore**, a cultural center of the community. Viter Juste or his son Henri are usually around in their shop of books, newspapers, records and folk art. Customers can buy pastries at the front counter, flip through Creole newspapers or pick up an exposé of the *Ton-Tons Macoute* or a teach-yourself-English (or Creole) primer.

**Haitian rhythms:** If asked, Viter or Henri will provide a quick audio tour of Haitian music with selections from their extensive stock of records demonstrating all of its assorted roots from Africa, France, other Caribbean nations, and even the US. There are recordings of traditional voodoo drums and chants, folk songs, the country carnival music called *rara* with bamboo flutes and junk-band percussion. There are also older Haitian *merengues*, slower than those of the Dominican Republic and typified by the popular tune "Yellow Bird." Les Cousins' also has examples of groups from the 1930s and '40s, when Latin influences (mostly from Cuba) such as *bolero* and *cha-cha-cha* were the rage, and the '50s big-band dance music of Jazz de Jeune and Nemours Jean-Baptiste.

More recent releases include the *engage* (message or protest) songs of Farah Juste and Kiki Wainwright. And there

**A little music on the streets.**

are rows and rows of modern mini-jazz and *compas* albums – big names from Haiti and New York like Tabou Combo and Coupe Cloue as well as Miami-based groups like Magnum Band, Top Vice, Bossa Combo, Macho Band, Khal-Mah Vibrations and others.

**Night spots:** Little Haiti's nightclubs have become increasingly popular with non-Haitians. Beginning around midnight on Friday and Saturday nights, joyous *compas*, politically charged protest songs and stirring African rhythms set feet in motion at clubs such as **Obsession** and **Spirits**. Another nightclub in the neighborhood is **Churchills**, primarily an Anglo club that hosts Miami's upcoming bands.

If you make it to neither a record store nor the nightclubs, then try to catch a Haitian radio program. There is no solely Haitian station, but a number devote time to Haitian programming, which consists of political discussion, virtually all in Creole, and music. Most of the programs air on the weekends.

**Primitive art:** Haitian painting with its distinctive primitive style and bold colors has had an international following for decades. Surreal themes are common including, for example, Haitian heroes, *vodoun* figures, and contemporary political events. Pastoral scenes may include African elephants and tigers that have never been in Haiti. Increasingly frequent are urban scenes that depict the political turmoil and hopes of the late 1980s in Haiti.

A number of accomplished painters live and work in Miami, but it is difficult to find their work locally. If you express an interest at Les Cousins or one of the other Haitian stores, someone will probably be able to introduce you directly to the artists themselves and take you to their studios.

**Creole cuisine:** Haitian restaurants can be found throughout the neighborhood and provide a pleasant and intriguing cuisine. While no Little Haiti restaurant offers the superb French Creole cuisine that can be found back home, many

eft, utching a lver purse. ight, ollecting ottles and ans for sale.

provide excellent food at a low price, under \$15 for a complete meal. *Lambi*, or conch, is a favorite, served in a light tomato-based sauce with a tinge of spiciness. *Griot* (fried pork) is one of Haiti's national dishes, while fried chicken or fish in a French-style sauce are also standard fare. Insiders know to be sure to ask for *picklee* – pickled cabbage and carrots – that truly add spice to any dish. No meal would be complete without fried plantains, rice and beans.

Visitors might also notice brightly colored houses that have a number of people eating in their backyards. These are informal home restaurants that offer eat-in and take-out meals, primarily for the neighborhood's single men who either, for whatever reasons, do not know how or do not want to cook. They offer the same range of food as the established restaurants, but usually charge a dollar or two less.

The **Design District**, just north of I-195 around 36th Street, forms the southern boundary of Little Haiti. It contains a set of showrooms for upscale home "design". Until recently, the showrooms were open only "to the trade" but now most welcome the public. Immediately adjacent to the Design District is a small, integrated neighborhood, **Buena Vista East**, in between Miami Avenue and N.E. Second Avenue, that has significant "old Miami" architecture. A number of the houses have been either maintained by the original residents or gentrified by black Americans, white Americans or Haitians.

Little Haiti is still plagued by poverty, by unemployment of at least 30 percent and by all those forces that prey on marginal neighborhoods. Roads and sidewalks are in bad condition. Empty lots need to be cleared. Like any older, deteriorating urban neighborhood, it needs better lighting and more frequent garbage pick-up.

But Haitians have enlivened and brightened the neighborhood, creating an ambiance not found anywhere else in Miami – or any other US city.

**Haitian woman takes a break from housework.**

# VOODOO BOUTIQUES

The first thing you notice as you enter the door is the smell – sweet, pungent and slightly intoxicating. Listed in the Miami telephone book under religious goods, *botanicas* (shops that sell magical herbs and religious paraphernalia) are living testimony to the controversial fact that African mysticism is alive and well in modern Miami. Usually tucked away in neighborhood shopping centers, *botanicas* cater to the Miami practitioners of the Caribbean/African religions of *santeria* and voodoo.

Stocked on the shelves is a supernatural potpourri: aromatic roots, tranquility balm, serenity salve, virility pills, black cat repellent, sacks of patchouli, incense, dried alligator flesh, face masks, floor polish to ward off greed, rosary beads, statues of saints, bulls' horns, metal spikes, black candles, bile of bullock, bones arranged as crosses, numerology books, aerosol sprays for prosperity, blood of mice, stuffed monkey heads and rag voodoo dolls equipped with pins.

In some shops, special potions and elixirs are stored in the back for serious maladies. Donation plates are set out for cash offerings to the spirits and large ceramic soup tureens hold foods thought to be desired by the gods.

While *botanicas* are most popular in the neighborhoods of Little Haiti and Little Havana, they are also found throughout the city and all have a combination Jesus Christ, Black Magic, Mickey Mouse persona.

Both voodoo and *santeria* have their roots in the religion of the Yoruba tribes of Western Africa. They were carried to the Caribbean by the hundreds of thousands of African slaves who were brought over to work, and took on a Christian character when the slaves were forced by their masters to adopt Christianity. Followers began to worship their African gods in the form of Catholic saints and celebrate Christmas in a most non-traditional manner. Secrecy over the religions was common because the slaves knew the colonizers feared it might unite them and foment rebellion. In Haiti, the African religion became what is called voodoo. In Cuba and some other areas, it became *santeria*. Both were brought to Miami by the Caribbean immigrants who moved to the city.

While there are differences between the two, both are animistic and pantheistic and have remained relatively clannish religions that utilize drum beating, chanting and the offering of animal sacrifices to influence the gods. Also in both, followers communicate with spirits who are found in nature, occasionally beat themselves with twigs to ward off evil spirits, and cast magic spells to change the course of their future. Local sociologists say that the practice of both religions among some of Miami's Caribbean immigrants is a remedy for the pressures they feel to adapt to a new culture and assimilate to American life.

*Botanicas*, which never existed in the Caribbean where the desired medicinal herbs were commonly sold at marketplaces, are a relatively modern phenomenon of Miami. While the *botanicas* themselves are a peculiar-yet-peaceful addition to Miami, the followers of *santeria* and voodoo have caused controversy with other area residents and share a stain of disdain due to their eccentric ceremonies. In some neighborhoods, locals have complained about the disappearance of pet dogs and cats, and animal rights groups have protested against the killing of chickens and goats in religious sacrifices. Practitioners have also been accused of breaking into coffins in city cemeteries and stealing human remains for ritual use.

In defense, the practitioners have squawked of religious persecution and have publicly marched for their rights, saying their worship activities are no more dramatic than those of charismatic Christians or Kabalistic Jews.

It is difficult to determine exactly how many people take part in the African religions in the Miami area because they are predominantly practiced at home and a veil of secrecy remains around them; few people confess to their practice. But the fact that a large number of *botanicas* prosper leads to the belief that the number of practitioners is in the tens of thousands. ∎

# THREE SISTER CITIES

The cities of Opa-locka, Hialeah and Miami Springs provide a totally different perspective on the Greater Miami area than that of the dynamic metropolis along the downtown waterfront or the affluent residential neighborhoods of Coral Gables and Coconut Grove. These three cities, located in northwest Dade County, offer a clear glimpse into the middle-class suburbs created during the real estate boom of the 1920s that used exotic architectural themes as marketing schemes to attract buyers.

Unfortunately, these grand dreams were short-lived due to the financial disasters of the time, but their legacies have left some interesting monuments that continue to delight and amuse visitors and residents alike.

Glenn Curtiss, one of the most important figures in early aviation history along with Wilbur and Orville Wright, came to Miami in 1916 to start an aviation school. In 1921 Curtiss teamed up with cattle rancher James Bright and began the development of **Hialeah**.

Hialeah soon became an entertainment center with movie studios, dog and horse tracks, a Jai-Alai fronton and an amusement park. The city was planned with a mission-style architectural theme, based on the Spanish churches of the California missions.

In 1924, Country Club Estates, later renamed **Miami Springs**, came to life as an affluent, planned community with wide, tree-lined boulevards and a large golf course. Miami Springs used the Pueblo-Revival architectural style inspired by the Pueblo Indians of Arizona and New Mexico. In 1925, without the partnership of Bright, Curtiss embarked on the city of **Opa-locka**. This time the outrageous Moorish-Revival theme was used, inspired by the *Arabian Nights* stories. Buildings sported horseshoe arches, domes and minarets, while streets were given names like Ali Baba and Sharazad. The community offered a zoo, a pool with aquatic shows and an airport holding aerobatic performances.

After some hard times in the late 1920s, the Opa-locka Airport became a US naval air base. In 1937, Amelia Earhart took off from this airport on the inaugural flight of her ill-fated trip around the world. During World War II, the base was expanded to moor Zeppelins and military planes and, although it is no longer a Navy base, it still operates as a civil aviation facility.

**Opa-locka today:** These days Opa-locka is one of Dade County's most economically depressed areas. Like many inner-city neighborhoods in America, crime and drugs have taken their toll. Present revitalization efforts have resulted in the restoration of some of the city's most significant landmarks, while others languish.

Many of the Moorish-inspired houses remain, although most have undergone drastic alterations. Signs of the Arabian influence – minarets and horseshoe

*Preceding pages: Opa-locka City Hall. Left, City Hall employee poses in archway. Right, Arabian Nights mural.*

arches – are still a striking sight and serve as a symbol of pride for the community, which celebrates an annual Arabian Nights Festival each spring.

The Opa-locka Company Administration Building, currently the **City Hall**, is the city's most impressive building located on Sharazad Boulevard. The building has been fully restored to its former splendor, with embellished domes and crenellated parapets. The main entrance through a horseshoe arch leads to an interior courtyard. The flanking wings contain administrative offices with brass light fixtures and hand-painted ceilings.

Adjacent to the City Hall building is a small one-story structure with an oversized dome that once served as the original Police and Fire Station of the city. One of the most interesting buildings in the city is the old Opa-locka Bank, now used as the **First Baptist Church of Opa-locka** on Caliph Street. Rather than the Moorish style of most other buildings in town, the bank was inspired by an Egyptian *mastaba*, or funeral structure. It is solid and austere, giving the impression of permanence.

The **Hurt Building**, at the intersection of Opa-locka Boulevard and Ali Baba Avenue, has a large central dome flanked by two smaller domes and tall, slender minarets. The structure once housed the Opa-locka Hotel.

The **Opa-locka train station** is probably the finest example of the fantasy Moorish-Revival architecture for which the city is known. Located across from the Hurt Building, the structure was built in 1927 and is most noted for the use of multi-colored, glazed ceramic tiles in a variety of patterns. Twin domes facing the direction of southbound trains herald the arrival of visitors to the Arabian wonderland. But visitors are scarce these days. Trains no longer stop, and the station, like much of Opa-locka, awaits the awakening of a new and brighter day.

**Hialeah:** To the south of Opa-locka is the city of Hialeah – home of Dade

**Opa-locka's station has seen better days.**

County's largest Cuban population, estimated at over 60 percent of the city. Its major attraction has always been the **Hialeah Race Track**, considered one of the most beautiful in the country. It also has the unusual distinction of housing what is said to be America's best library on thoroughbred racing.

The park features a grandstand and clubhouse more reminiscent of an opera house than a race track and manicured gardens with fountains and statues. Hundreds of pink flamingos, originally imported from Cuba, live in the park which has been designated a bird sanctuary by the National Audobon Society. The property is listed on the National Register of Historic Places.

**Miami Springs:** South of Hialeah is Miami Springs. Many of its residents are associated with the airline industry since the city is located just north of the very busy **Miami International Airport**. The main attraction is its Pueblo-Revival architecture – an exotic anachronism in South Florida.

The original adobe construction is interpreted in stucco, and the hand-hewn roof beams are applied as decoration. But the flat roofs and hand-molded walls are faithfully reproduced, providing the necessary ambiance of another place and another time.

The center of town has a circular plaza, from which wide boulevards and Curtiss Parkway radiate. The plaza serves as a small commercial center where **Stadnik's Pharmacy** is located. Pure Pueblo Revival, the building houses a "pharmacy museum" featuring an assortment of old chemicals, drugs and local newspapers and photographs of the town's earlier days. The most prominent building in Miami Springs is the old **Country Club Hotel**, now known as the **Fairhavens Retirement Home** on Curtiss Parkway. Built in 1927, it is the largest Pueblo-Revival structure in the city. Its unusual features include its terracing masses, an eccentric, irregular front staircase and a large thunderbird on the front facade.

Fairhavens Retirement Home in Miami Springs; Opa-locka minaret.

# THE DEEP SOUTH

**South Dade County**, situated around the community of Homestead and a disappearing farm area from the early 1900s known as the **Redland**, is 25 miles from Miami but years away in time. This is what Miami once was: rural, small town, Southern, a place for a barbecue rather than a *boulangerie*.

In 1992, Hurricane Andrew charged right through South Dade County, the hardest hit section of the Miami area. Hundreds of buildings, restaurants and homes were totally destroyed, and many tourist attractions took years to rebuild. Rational-minded scientists and botanists insist that South Dade – specifically the Everglades and the rich farmlands – got a much-needed pruning by Mother Nature, and in fact will be better off in the future because of the storm. The foliage may indeed be growing back thicker than before, but the emotional scars on residents and shopkeepers will take longer to heal.

The hurricane notwithstanding, **Homestead**, 12 sq. miles, and its surrounding area, are still "old Florida." It is a place with a smell of earth, a place of pick-up trucks, turnip greens, two-lane streets lined with tunnels of majestic Royal Palms, a hardware store on the main street. This is a town where the mayor regularly attends the Wednesday Rotary meeting.

Drive through farmland in the Redland in winter and smell lime trees in blossom. There is an annual rodeo, and cowboy boots are worn not as fashion but as everyday dress. But change, like the lime blossoms, is in the air. Once as corny as Kansas, South Dade is suddenly a new frontier of yuppification. Volvos are heading deep south.

Once heartland, the area is changing to become the gateway to the Florida Keys; jumping-off point to Everglades National Park and the water wonderland of Biscayne National Park; and a possible home to a spring-training baseball team. It has a French-owned restaurant, an art gallery and a bed and breakfast inn. Homes from the 1920s are being "saved" by yuppies.

But some things remain even if they are as endangered as the Florida panther. This is the county's produce section, where acres of fruits and vegetables still take root among new subdivisions. This is also the winter tomato-and-snap-bean capital of the nation.

**Blushing berries:** From Christmas to April, the rich acres are covered with strawberry fields. When the rest of America is gray and spring is far away, in South Dade there is a blue Florida sky with fluffy white clouds. Below the skyline are rows of vivid strawberry plants stretching to the horizon.

As with the great wines of Europe, local strawberries do not travel well. They are best eaten warm, right here in the field.

Two of the oldest fields are **Burr's Berries** on S.W. 216th Street and

**Knauss Berry Farm** further south on S.W. 248th Street. Burr's has been in business for 30 years, producing homemade ice cream and a spectacular strawberry milk shake, so thick it is impossible to suck through a straw. Use a spoon. Knauss, run by a religious order from Indiana, features fresh berries, freshpicked produce and shakes, and bakes its own pies and rolls.

For those who prefer to do-it-yourself, several fields offer U-pick berries plus tomatoes, onions, squash and other winter produce. Prices are about half of retail. Drive north or south on **Krome Avenue** and watch for signs. Buy more than you can eat because all the way home your car will smell of strawberries and tomatoes, fresh from the earth.

Finding fresh fruits is more difficult. Late-summer mangoes are sold on the roadsides and on card tables in front yards. So are avocados, fatter and less flavorful than the California variety. Exotic fruits are available here only on a very limited basis.

The county's **Preston B. and Mary Heinlein Fruit and Spice Park** on 187th Avenue and S.W. 248th Street is a 32-acre free park dedicated to tropical fruits and spices selected from around the world. Visitors may stroll the ground sniffing and seeing trees and shrubs in bloom, in flower or in fruit, depending on the season. Sampling the fruit is forbidden but a gourmet store on the ground sells dried exotics, jellies, jams and cookbooks. The pioneer **Bauer-Mitchell House** in the park is the oldest house in the area, an example of tongue-and-groove construction.

Across the street is the **Redland Community United Methodist Church**, which was organized in 1912 and built in 1913. The structure, a true country church, is made from virgin Dade County pine, a wood so hard that termites cannot chew through it. The original pines are all gone. The church is open for guided tours from 9am to 12pm, Tuesday and Thursday.

To see the splendor of the tropics,

The humid hot-house of the Orchid Jungle.

take in a free orchid show. South Dade is full of nurseries, many of which sell only wholesale. But its many orchid growers all have sales areas that are open to the public. One of the largest is **Robert Fuchs Orchids** on S.W. 182nd Avenue where you can buy or just look. The firm ships orchids and on some days gives tours of the growing areas.

**Orchid Jungle** is a full-scale private park lush with blooms. The tropical setting, with cool trees, fountains and flowers, is an oasis. Visitors are admitted to the sales area for free.

**Talk to the animals:** If bored by farm and flora, South Dade is also a place for fauna. **Miami Metrozoo** is one of the best zoos in the country, a cageless sprawl over 290 acres that has wisely specialized rather than be a Noah's Ark of every animal, two by two. Opened in 1981, the zoo is dedicated to tropical life; no polar bears here.

The zoo has more than 100 species living in natural-like island sites surrounded by moats. Animals come from the African and Asian plains and jungles, Asian forests, Eurasian steppes and Australia. An elevated monorail travels through the park, which features a lake and various meadows.

There are four first-rate exhibits: a koala park, Wings of Asia Aviary, a petting zoo that features continuous elephant rides, plus an ecology theater and the white Bengal tigers, two of only 150 left in the world.

The koalas arrived in 1988, the first of their kind to have a permanent exhibit on the East Coast. Koalas, which are marsupials not bears, live exclusively on eucalyptus leaves which thrive in Southern California and South Florida. There is a 5-acre eucalyptus grove that was planted just for the koalas at Metrozoo. The koalas have acclimatized so well that in 1989 they produced an heir, the first koala birth in the country outside California.

The aviary is an enclosed 1½-acre, 65-ft high rain forest, waterfall and tropical hardwood hammock that visitors sit in

urtles at
Metrozoo
easting on
alad.

to be surrounded by identified flying objects such as orange-billed leafbirds, swamp hens, magpies and yellow-breasted fruit doves. Birds are fed at 11am and 3pm. The zoo also has frequent outdoor rock and country music concerts.

Adjacent to Metrozoo on S.W. 152th Street is the **Gold Coast Railroad Museum**, featuring 50 pieces of railroad equipment from different eras. The 1942 *Ferdinand Magellan* is the presidential car of Franklin D. Roosevelt, Harry S. Truman, Dwight D. Eisenhower and Ronald Reagan. Walk through the narrow confines of a working dining car, see steam and diesel engines and peer out of a 1948 stainless-steel, domed passenger car used by the *California Zephyr*. On Sundays the museum fires up a train and chuffs up and down a 1.3-mile track.

Just 1½ miles to the south, on 184th Street, is **Larry and Penny Thompson Park**, a 270-acre pineland preservation area that has a lake and 240 rustic camp-

ing sites. Farther south is **Monkey Jungle**, a roadside attraction that features walking tours of shaded grounds full of monkey business. These passive exhibits may be out of fashion but at Monkey Jungle the residents roam free in the trees while the paying public watches from fenced-in enclosures.

**Cauley Square** is a former railroad town that still faces the old tracks and highway US 1 at 224th Street. It is 10 acres of nostalgia featuring several shops selling crafts and antiques, all of which are linked by paths. There is a quaint tea room for lunch. This is not Disneyland, not a mall but the way things used to be, insists the owner.

The nearby flatland is ideal for bike rides and a 20-mile loop can be wound through the Redland. Or pop the top down for a drive in the convertible, poking around country lanes looking out for homes and farmsteads, many of which are officially designated by the county's historic preservation division. A quarter of the county's historic homes and buildings are found here. Because the area is still zoned for agriculture, most homes sit on a minimum of 5 acres. It is the space, and relatively low prices, that attract potential buyers, particularly to old farmhouses with established tropical vegetation.

A rough-hewn, coral-rock front porch is a sure sign of an early homestead. One buyer got an historic 1920 farmhouse with a 26-foot ceiling and 13-foot coral-rock hearth for $150,000 in the Redland, renovated it and now claims it is worth at least $500,000. His biggest complaint is noise from low-flying crop-dusting planes.

One destination to aim for is the **Redland Grocery** on 187th Avenue. A frame, tin-roof store, built before 1920 and once a dance hall, it serves farm workers hot and cold lunches. Two cooks begin at 5.30am, preparing hundreds of sandwiches, main dishes and desserts. Sit on picnic tables in a mango grove out back. The place still sells kerosene, but now also Perrier.

**Antiquarian book room at Cauley Square.**

A spooky roadside attraction, **Coral Castle**, is a coral-rock mansion built by a Latvian immigrant to his unrequited love. The house has a 9-ton gate that swings open to the lightest touch and a 2½-ton Valentine heart.

**Weeks Air Museum** is a small collection of 35 antique aircraft – featuring an all-plywood DeHavilland – based at a regional airport in the middle of crop country. The entire area is like Orange, California, a 1920s center for orange and lemon groves where one-time farmhouses have been swallowed by Los Angeles' growth. Miami has not yet swallowed Dade's deep south. But hurry while it lasts.

Down the road is **Homestead Properties**, the largest single development in Dade County and going up on the eastern edge of Homestead. Some $500 million is being spent on what will one day be 21,000 units on 5,800 acres. Another $51 million worth of projects have been built in the city in recent years, including the **Metro-Dade/ Homestead Motor Sports Complex**, site of the Miami Grand Prix. Located near Palm Drive, the complex hosts car and truck races and test runs throughout the year.

**Shuffleboard:** For all its lofty plans, parts of Homestead are still in a time warp. There's even a public park dedicated exclusively to a game most people have forgotten: shuffleboard. Shuffleboard is all one can play at **Musselwhite Park** on North Krome Avenue. Adults only, says the sign out front: that means 18 or over.

Built for winter tourists, Musselwhite opened in 1958. Soon there were 16 courts, each one standard: 52-ft long, 6-ft wide, green cement with scoring triangles at each end. Players get a rack of eight waxed wooden disks, a cue, a chalkboard eraser and a sausage-like stick of chalk to keep score. The official season ends on March 31. As with big-league baseball, most of the players head north in April.

Shooters get to sit on a park bench in

country ttage-style op.

the shade, smell the gardenias, hear the palms, feel the warm breeze, talk to their neighbors and play shuffleboard in one of the nicest parks that can be found anywhere.

The park manager is called "host". He makes the coffee. He takes photos of the trophy winners. He lays out the mail sent from players who have gone home. But it is that kind of place – for the timid, not for the frail. Shooters, many of whom bring their own cue, are dead game and deft of touch. Musselwhite shuffleboard has odd house rules: one is taht no overhead fans can be turned on until the temperature reaches 90°F.

**Home cookin':** Homestead has a wide variety of restaurants. **Potlikker's** specializes in down-home Southern cooking, featuring at least 11 of those local vegetables every day. The area also has French, Italian, Asian and Indian, plus true Mexican.

It also has a tortilla factory. Most mornings the owner cranks up his corn grinder with twin volcanic lava rocks,

fires up his huge green conveyor machine that says *Hecho en Mexico* and in 90 minutes produces 300 pounds of fresh, still-warm tortillas. The tortillas roll off an assembly line that serves the family's **El Toro Taco Restaurant**.

It was nearly three decades ago that the Hernandez family, mother Estefana, father Pablo and seven sons and daughters, arrived in Homestead from Texas as migrant workers. They had no money, no car, no jobs and only one change of clothing each.

Today, the family owns a square block of downtown Homestead across the street from the police station, a four-unit apartment building, a two-acre farm, 10 cars and two other homes, and supports seven Hernandezes plus various spouses from a central source of jobs at the restaurant. On weekend nights there are lines waiting to get into the 140-seat restaurant, where prices are very, very reasonable.

South of Homestead is a small town called **Florida City**, last stop before the Keys, crossroads for the Everglades and the sea. Originally named Detroit because so many people from the Motor City came here to retire, Florida City now mostly consists of fast-food restaurants and budget motels. At its southern edge is the **Florida Keys Factory Shops**, one of the many discount malls that have sprung up in the state of Florida. It features over 50 major-name clothing stores that sell often high-quality goods at bargain prices.

**Florida Pioneer Museum** is Florida City's railroad site. This place has a collection of memorabilia from Henry Flagler's Florida East Coast Railroad, and photos from the old days. The museum only has afternoon hours.

Florida City has a number of country-style restaurants and breakfast cafés that ladle up hominy grits and serve fresh biscuits with pork sausages. It also has the **Florida City State Farmers Market**, which sells seasonal fruits and yummy orange-blossom honey at discount prices.

**Left**, a stroll in the shade. **Right**, a Florida scene.

# DAY TRIPS

Everything man-made that can be seen in a day tour north of Miami has been built in the past 100 years. Everything natural has been altered. A century ago the land itself told the story about this subtropical shore of mainland America, risen up out of the Ice Age sea. A century later, spacecraft circle billions of miles away, launched from its beaches. The irony of 100 years is that the beachfront resort strip, with all its tourist come-ons, is where the region's history can be found.

The route of choice from Dade County is Highway Alternate 1 Atlantic, or, as commonly known, A1A. For 70 miles from Miami Beach to Palm Beach, A1A, except for the odd few blocks, is everywhere the beach road. Not that motorists can see the beach. Most places the beach is blocked by hotels and condominiums. Some places mom and pop motels hang on, and garden apartments with names like Betsy-Marv or Blue Sea Kitchenettes sit behind white board fences. Interspersed are strips of fast-food restaurants and tee-shirt shops.

Morning and evening, joggers pack the A1A roadsides. On weekend mornings, skin-suited cyclists whirr colorfully close by the curbs. Docks and marinas shelter boats along baysides. As the road extends north, counties and towns more generously preserve beachfront for parks. Ultimately comes Palm Beach, where Henry Flagler's legacy endures most authentically.

**Broward County:** The transition from Golden Isles in northernmost Dade is from one of the last single-family beachfronts to the abruptly soaring canyon of **Hallandale**. Halland was a Swede from New York enlisted by Flagler in the late 1890s to farm tomatoes west of the railroad. However, times change. By the 1930s Hallandale had become a notorious gambling town controlled by the Lansky brothers. Hallandale today

forms a vast "U" along the beach; at the bottom are the four boulevard lanes of a briefly impressive A1A between parallel high-rise walls of condominiums. The **Diplomat Country Club & Resort** has been the city's landmark leisure facility since 1957.

**Hollywood** echoes merely a whisper of its roar through the 1920s. Joseph W. Young, an Alaskan goldminer and sometime newspaper publisher, for a flashing moment rode the crest of the land boom until he crashed into the triple wall of the 1926 hurricane, the land bust and the Depression. The scale of his style, if not the grace, endures at the **Hollywood Beach Hotel**, altered as a time-share and tarted up by two stories of shops and restaurants called Oceanwalk. Take a look at the display of colored photo blow-ups that recall the heyday of the hotel. The Hollywood Beach Hotel was a Mediterranean classic: solid, grand, dripping in grotto moss. Elaborate colonnades lifted high ceilings heavenward for America's boom-

Preceding pages: sailing off the coast; surfing in Palm Beach. Left, making waves. Right, sun and daughter.

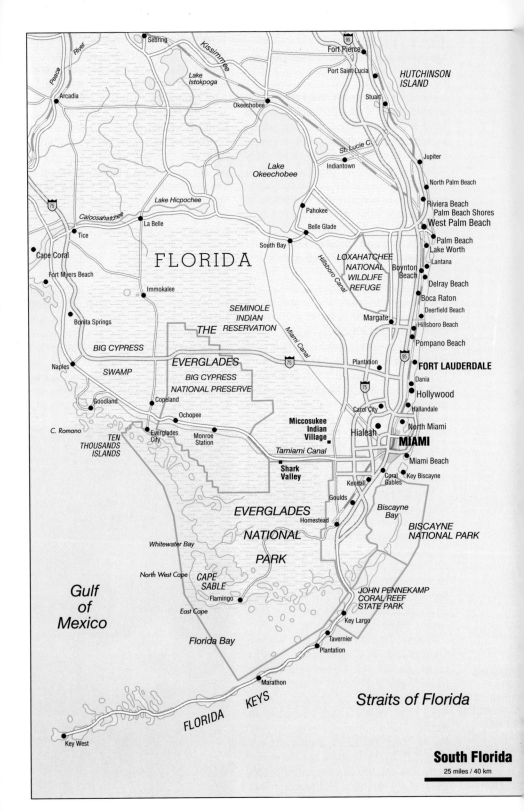

Sebring
Fort Pierce
Kissimmee
Port Saint Lucia
Lake
Istokpoga
Stuart
HUTCHINSON
ISLAND
Arcadia
Peace River
Okeechobee
St. Lucie C.
Jupiter
Indiantown
North Palm Beach
Lake
Okeechobee
Riviera Beach
Palm Beach Shores
West Palm Beach
Lake Hicpochee
Pahokee
Palm Beach
Lake Worth
Caloosahatchee
La Belle
Belle Glade
Lantana
Tice
South Bay
LOXAHATCHEE
NATIONAL
WILDLIFE
REFUGE
Boynton Beach
Cape Coral
FLORIDA
Delray Beach
Fort Myers Beach
Immokalee
Boca Raton
Deerfield Beach
Bonita Springs
SEMINOLE
INDIAN
RESERVATION
Margate
Hillsboro Beach
Pompano Beach
THE
BIG CYPRESS
SWAMP
EVERGLADES
BIG CYPRESS
NATIONAL PRESERVE
Miami Canal
Plantation
FORT LAUDERDALE
Naples
Dania
Hollywood
Goodland
Copeland
Carol City
Hallandale
C. Romano
Ochopee
Miccosukee
Indian
Village
North Miami
TEN
THOUSANDS
ISLANDS
Everglades
City
Monroe
Station
Hialeah
MIAMI
Tamiami Canal
Miami Beach
Shark
Valley
Key Biscayne
Coral
Gables
Kendall
Goulds
Biscayne
Bay
EVERGLADES
Homestead
BISCAYNE
NATIONAL PARK
Whitewater Bay
NATIONAL
North West Cape
CAPE
SABLE
PARK
JOHN PENNEKAMP
CORAL REEF
STATE PARK
Gulf
of
Mexico
Flamingo
East Cape
Key Largo
Florida Bay
Tavernier
Plantation
Marathon
Straits of Florida
FLORIDA
KEYS
Key West

**South Florida**
25 miles / 40 km

time elite. Think of the entire beach as God's golden tunic and the Hollywood Beach Hotel as a button chosen for dress occasions.

These days **Hollywood Boulevard**, dividing around wide circles on its way from town, dumps and collects its traffic along ramps that swerve daredevil-close to the front of the hotel, its elegance forever blighted. Condemning the hotel's remnant to the rear is *hoi polloi* **Broadwalk**, so susceptible to double entendre and misspelling. North beyond the **Dania Beach Boulevard** cut-off, the road extends to **John U. Lloyd State Recreation Area**. Foot-bridges cross a creek into pine forests that border the beach. In winter, old-timers gossip and sun in webbed beach chairs behind their massive campers, living the retirement dream. At the far end of the park road, cruise liners dock across the channel at **Port Everglades**.

Dania Beach Boulevard carries A1A briefly inland to highway US 1 between two sections of **West Lake Park**. Its

1,300 acres makes this the largest urban park in South Florida. Its entrance is south one causeway on Sheridan Street. **Dania**, settled by Danes, is known for its pretty antique shops which line US 1 through town.

**Where the boys are:** The skyscraper landscape of **Fort Lauderdale** pops up like the land of Oz from where US 1 lifts to accommodate the vast spaghetti of the I-595 airport interchange. **State Road 84** bears right into Port Everglades where, 2 miles through industrial cargo operations, **Burt & Jack's** offers romantic waterfront dining in a mission-style setting.

Near Burt & Jack's is a warm-water outfall where tropical fish and pelicans mass for handouts, in winter joined by the endangered manatee, a mammal which resembles the whale.

Other excellent restaurants in Fort Lauderdale include **Casa Vecchia** for northern Italian cuisine; the **Down Under** for seafood and continental fare; and the **Plum Room** for classic French.

pring-break azy.

Fort Lauderdale has come to stand for a seismic shift in young adult behavior, from the teasing 1950s innocence of the movie *Where The Boys Are*, to drug-induced 1980s leaps out of hotel windows into empty swimming pools. Fort Lauderdale better deserves to be known for its one-of-a-kind attractions.

These extend mainly along the north bank of the picturesque **New River**, which filmmaker Rex Beach in the 1920s was known to call "the most beautiful stream in the world."

Downtown to the west are the **Historical Museum** and the **Museum of Discovery and Science**, the largest science museum in South Florida and an ideal attraction for children, featuring hands-on educational exhibits that include video games, a bubble-making machine, an indoor citrus grove, and a 300-seat IMAX theater. A few blocks east is the **Fort Lauderdale Museum of Art**. The museum boasts the country's most extensive collection of CoBrA paintings, sculptures and prints. Pro-duced by artists in Copenhagen, Brussels and Amsterdam between the years 1948 and 1955, CoBrA artworks closely parallel those of the American abstract expressionist movement.

East along the river walk is **Stranahan House**, restored to its 1913 look. Here, 20 years earlier, Frank Stranahan settled the pioneer trading post that was to become Fort Lauderdale. His house is now a museum and gift shop.

Florida's only vehicular tunnel separates Stranahan House from the **Riverside Hotel** and the beginning of **Las Olas Boulevard** shopping. Visitors find quality shops and galleries along a gas-lighted avenue of luxuriant landscaping. The hotel has been a town favorite since 1936, with tropical gardens that extend to the river.

Fort Lauderdale has 500 miles of inland waterways. Its claim to be the "Venice of America" is credible by the striking canalfront subdivisions farther east along Las Olas toward the beach. Water taxis shuttle visitors anywhere along a **Fort Lauderdale's condominium row.**

7-mile inland route. Each December, the city hosts its Winterfest tribute to the good life here with a parade of 100 imaginatively lighted boats.

Perhaps because Flagler never took time with the little settlement, Fort Lauderdale grew only modestly until policy decided that no buildings would go up directly on the ocean between where the **17th Street Causeway** swings alongside the beach to the north end of **Birch Park**. At the south end, the **International Swimming Hall of Fame** is worth a visit.

Just before Birch Park, a curiosity needs explaining that argues a case for visiting here in the summer rather than in the winter.

This is the odd brace of markers in the sand that read "Private Beach Between Signs." The signs bracket the quarter of a mile of the property known as **Bonnet House** that lies behind sea grape trees across the road. Bonnet House was the winter home of artist Evelyn Bartlett, now in the second century of her life.

Mrs Bartlett is the widow of Frederick Bartlett, an esteemed painter, whose father-in-law by an earlier marriage, Hugh Taylor Birch, gave Frederick and his first bride this 35-acre portion of beachfront land. In 1942, at the age of 93, Birch gave the state the 180 acres that now constitute the park in his name just north of Mrs Bartlett's estate.

Bonnet House is a lyrical mansion of art whimsy, with a variety of landscapes from desert to tropical forest. Mrs Bartlett donated the house to the Florida Trust for Historic Preservation, subject to her winter residency. In 1995 she decided to move elsewhere, and the house is now open to the public year-round. The beach which lies between the signs remains the property of the house, but people pay no mind and no one complains.

North from here the **Galt Ocean Mile** is a once chic high-rise district. A public pier extends at **Lauderdale-by-the-Sea**. A mish-mash of condos, apartments and motels follows into **Pompano Beach**. Here, another pier extends from an attractive stone-walled promenade, with dining over the sea at the **Fisherman's Wharf Restaurant**. The light at **Hillsboro Inlet** is on private property, but its site is forever tied to the era of the barefoot mailman.

From 1885 until just before Flagler built the railroad, when there was no land route to the settlements south of Miami, letters were carried by contract mailmen who walked the beaches. They crossed inlets by boats that they tied to trees. When one day his boat was inexplicably on the wrong side of an inlet, carrier Ed Hamilton attempted to swim the channel and was never heard of again. He lost his life to duty at Hillsboro. At least one book, a resort and a lot of yarns have kept the legend of the barefoot mailman alive.

**Hillsboro Beach** is a mere sand spit, though built upon. The road curves between expensive oceanfront estates, buffered by heavy plantings, and the bayside, rimmed by private docks. Un-

and in his hoes.

fortunately, the town's zoning was broken in the 1980s and a large swath of beachside has since submitted to the zealous claws of commercialism.

**Palm Beach County:** But the worst is behind as the road swings across **Boca Raton Inlet** into **Palm Beach County**. To the east hangs the garden facade of the **Boca Beach Club**. To the west rises the pink tower of the **Boca Raton Hotel**. From atop you can see almost to Miami. At ground is the pastiche of the original pink **Cloister Inn** and its arched and barrel-tiled loggia.

Boca Raton was the creation of architect Addison Mizner. Mizner was the darling of Palm Beach society in the 1920s, the aesthetic arbiter after Flagler. His graceful Mediterranean mansions still stand along the ocean road. About the time that George Merrick was creating Coral Gables from tomato fields and Joseph Young was building Hollywood, Mizner dreamed up Boca Raton.

Indulged by the open pocketbooks of his devotees, Mizner formed the substance of a dream resort, "the greatest in the world," he trumpeted. Alas, the boom burst. Boca limped along until after World War II and has since emerged as one of the best-managed communities along the Gold Coast. Its parks and recreational programs are excellent. The town seashore is a varied series of parks and open beachfront.

**Delray**, too, is largely open to the sea. If visiting in winter, drive west a mile along **Atlantic Avenue** and stop at the **Colony Hotel**. Its Moresque stucco facade, its wicker lobby, its small rooms, have barely changed since the 1920s. Guests return year after year as long as they're able. They sit on the porch dressed in their finery daring everything about the moment to deny their permanence. The hotel has hardly run down. True to the old style, the Colony is open only January through March, the season barely extended from Flagler's era.

Three miles farther west along Atlantic Avenue and south on Carter Road is **The Morikami**, a 150-acre park and

La Vieille Maison Restaurant i Boca Raton.

254

museum of Japanese culture that marks the site of a thriving Japanese agricultural community from the early 1900s. Again along the shore in Delray, a marker sites the **Orange Grove House of Refuge**, one of a series of primitive shelters that were spaced along the wilderness beaches between 1876 and 1896 from Cape Canaveral to Cape Florida. The purpose of these shelters was to offer protection to anyone who had the misfortune of being shipwrecked in these remote parts. After the railroad arrived the shelters were abandoned.

**Seaside towns: Gulf Stream** is so private it barely lets on that it's a town. No name appears on the ornate, Mizner-designed **Gulf Stream Club**. The Gulf Stream School is private. The **St Andrews Golf Club** is private. But a beautiful concourse winds under a casuarina canopy that everyone can enjoy.

At **Ocean Ridge** cut east to **Old Ocean Boulevard**. The few blocks pass through an unpretentious little seaside community that, by contrast with its ritzy neighbors, feels slightly downmarket with its stucco cottages and vans parked in driveways. Through **Boynton Beach** bougainvillea and hibiscus spill over masonry walls.

**Ocean Inlet Park** divides Boynton from **Manalapan**. The scene is South Seas languid. Thatch-roofed, open-air chickees line the beach under swaying palms. Rows of drive-out mirrors are placed so that cars emerging from hidden mansions can avoid traffic otherwise obscured by privacy hedges and walls. Coppery sea grape leaves color-coordinate with barrel-tile roofs. No buildings obtrude along the waterway. Look instead for Rolls-Royces and Jaguars, and yachts marked Manalapan on their sterns tied to their home docks. Cyclists pedal by with surfboards under their arms.

High-rises reappear in **Lantana** but are better spaced apart on entering **South Palm Beach**. Across **Lake Worth** is the faintly pink **Gulf Stream Hotel**, a 1920s survivor and now old-fashioned

urty Harry's w bar in eerfield ach.

inn. Up on the paved dune in **Barton Park**, **John G's** is one of the most popular restaurants in the county. Prices are low, the fare is everything Americans most love to eat, the portions are large. John G's is utterly informal. People would think something wrong if they didn't stand in line for a table. The wait is worth it.

**Old-money mansions:** Drive around **Sloan's Curve** and the road fronts beguilingly on the Atlantic. Here at last is the real **Palm Beach**! Even fish swim here in privileged waters, enjoying their own Rolls-Royce, a few years ago added with flourish to the artificial reef. To leeward, mansions. Signs warn that no stopping is allowed. Palm Beach likes to keep people it doesn't know moving, or concentrated in town where shopkeepers and custodians of civic institutions provide extra eyes. Not many years ago blacks were not allowed on the island after dark.

Henry Flagler fell in love with this palm-fringed island in 1892. He bought

out the few landholders who preceded him. The first Breakers Hotel burned down. So did the second. By the time the third Breakers went up in 1926 – no less opulent today than ever – Palm Beach was the winter watering hole for American society. Palm Beach wasn't merely wealthy.

The rich were here at play. They dressed up and partied in the name of charity. Their benefit balls for every worthy cause ennobled their wealth. The Palm Beach way of life became the ultimate sanction for American ambition. For many it still is.

If Flagler gave Palm Beach stature, Mizner gave it grace. His Mediterranean mansions and shops, with their rich ornamentation and colorful shrubbery, were legendary. Mizner's clients adored him because he made them feel divinely gifted.

Mizner's most treasured legacy is **Worth Avenue**, begun in the 1920s and since 1945 one of the world's premier shopping streets. Only three blocks long, the avenue compels because of its human scale. Buildings are mostly two and three stories. Shops are set among villa-like facades, extended by colorful canopies and graced by Palladian windows. Bougainvillea entwines wrought-iron gates that appear on top of ceramic staircases. Little *vias* lead to shops and patios with fountains.

The town epitomizes the *dolce far niente* sensibility. Each beautifully landscaped streets is worth visiting. The best view is by bicycle. These can be rented at the **Palm Beach Bicycle Trail Shop**, close to the 3½-mile lakefront trail untrammeled by automobiles.

Palm Beach's pre-eminent landmark remains **The Breakers**. This Beaux Arts hotel, from its fountains and towers to its frescoed ceilings, dominates the oceanfront like a leviathan at sea, the very articulation of order in a world of chaos, exactly how Flagler esteemed himself in the dog-eat-dog world of 19th-century capitalism.

The Flagler style is personally best

**Mediterranean arches on Worth Avenue.**

expressed at **Whitehall**. Whitehall was the $3 million palace Flagler built in 1901 for his third wife, Mary Lily. Considered the "Taj Mahal of America," the house boasts marble interiors and fabrics of gold, as well as private collections of porcelain, paintings, silver, glass, dolls, lace and costumes. Flagler's private railroad car, *The Rambler*, has been restored alongside. Today, the house serves as the **Flagler Museum**. The house, The Breakers and Worth Avenue are the crown jewels of Palm Beach opulence.

Also worth visiting are the **Society of Four Arts Library and Gardens**, and, in West Palm Beach, the **Norton Gallery** and the **Ann Norton Sculpture Gardens**. West 15 miles from I-95 across **Southern Boulevard** is **Lion Country Safari**, a drive-through commercial zoo where animals roam uncaged. Among outstanding Palm Beach restaurants are **Jo's** and **Chez Moustache** for French cuisine, **Café L'Europe** for continental, **Chuck and**

**Harold's** for informal dining at any hour, and, on the mainland, **La Capanina** for northern Italian fare and **The Explorers** at the **PGA National Resort** for continental.

**A river of grass:** The land to the west of Highway A1A is a non-stop linear city that gives way to faceless suburbs braked only by the near-permanent flood that is the **Everglades**. At first glance the Everglades seems a region of much ado about nothing. Eyes adjusted to the garish beach strip will register a realm without contrast, a philosopher's puzzle, not a sightseer's dream.

Until the latter half of the century, the annual cycle of rainy and dry seasons naturally regulated the flow of water from mid-state marshes into **Lake Okeechobee**. The lake overflowed its banks and flooded the glades south in a permanent shallow river that flowed sluggishly into **Florida Bay**.

Today, water into the lake has been restricted and polluted by dairy herds. The lake has a dyke to keep from flood-

alm Beach's ath and ennis Club.

ing. Locks and dams regulate what actually flows south in a trace of the primeval cycle. Its discharge south has been diverted through canals which drain the land for vast sugar and vegetable plantations that further pollute the lake and its outflow.

Massive tampering of the water supply has stunted animal reproduction throughout the Everglades and is altering the vegetation. Visitors to **Everglades National Park** today see a tenth of the bird life visible when the park was established in 1947. While bureaucrats argue about fault and fate, the park, which has been designated by the United Nations as an International Biosphere Reserve and a World Heritage Site, is steadily dying.

One of the three day-tours south of Miami turns west into Everglades Park. The other trips are east to Biscayne National Park and continuing south to John Pennecamp Coral Reef State Park in the Keys. All link up easily to South Dade tourist attractions.

Everglades is the largest of the parks, with 1.4 million acres. The access road drops 10 miles southwest of Florida City across a large farming district called the **Frog Pond**. Winter fields are busy with broad brim-hatted vegetable and berry pickers. Along the road is **Robert Is Here**, a produce stand since 1960 that sells what's local in season and specialties that include Key lime milk shakes and fruit breads.

A visitor center introduces the park's recreational options with a film, exhibits and publications. There are hiking trails, a half-dozen canoe trails, and multiple overlooks. **Flamingo** is the well-developed outpost 38 miles at the end of the two-lane park road.

Trails and interpretive signs en route to Flamingo establish the complex character of the Everglades. Winter is best for viewing wildlife because during this extended season of low rainfall – indeed drought in recent years – wildlife congregates wherever fresh water can be found. **Anhinga Trail** provides a view

**The Everglades a sunset.**

of **Taylor Slough** which acts as a reservoir for attracting alligators, turtles, marsh rabbits, and many birds. **Gumbo Limbo Trail** is a hardwood hammock whose dense canopy shades a moist forest. Elsewhere alligators scoop holes out of the limestone that collects winter water where animals seek refuge. From May through October rains reflood the glades and wildlife disperses.

Canoes and bikes are available at Flamingo. Tram tours and narrated boat tours are offered. Visitors with more time can camp out or stay overnight in motel-like **Flamingo Lodge**, with its two restaurants, or rent houseboats for up to two weeks at a time.

A Florida Bay cruise is the best way to experience the estuarine ecology. Fresh water flowing into Florida Bay combines with salt water from the Gulf of Mexico. Microscopic marine animals thrive in the brackish mix. These feed on the decaying leaves of mangrove trees that arch stilt-like roots into water. Shrimp devour the micro-organisms,

fish eat the shrimp, big fish eat the little fish. Guides estimate that an acre of mangrove nurtures $4,500 worth of food and gamefish, and here at the edge of the Gulf of Mexico is the largest mangrove forest of North America.

Great flocks of gulls waft in unseen air currents. In winter, white pelicans with 9-ft wingspans migrate here from the west. The bay is full of bird rookeries. Osprey build their nests atop channel markers sturdy enough to withstand hurricane winds. A bald eagle might be seen from one of the 55 active nests in the park. In winter, when the water level is low, egrets and herons stab for their meals in the flats while anhingas dive and spear for theirs.

Odds are good for seeing bottlenose dolphins who like to frolic in the bow wake of fast-moving boats. The dolphins appear as gray projectiles swimming a few feet below the surface, arching their humps into the rushing wake as they clear their blowholes for the next breath before resubmerging.

**pelican**
**oasts along.**

# MARJORY STONEMAN DOUGLAS

For over 65 years, Marjory Stoneman Douglas, the first lady of Florida's environmentalists, has fought her own war against the destruction of the state's most precious natural asset: the Everglades. She has been called opinionated, passionate, poetic, captivating, awe-inspiring, unflappable and frank. Without her, the Everglades, one of the natural wonders of the world, would probably be little more than just a memory.

When the City of Miami threw a party for her 100th birthday in April 1990, Douglas, with her trademark floppy straw hat atop her baby soft curls, typically downplayed the occasion and instead interjected her eloquent assault on the enemies of the Glades. As usual, the crowd hushed to hear her speak.

A former newspaper columnist and short story writer, Douglas moved to Miami from New England in 1915. After a brief marriage with no children, she poured her energies into her work and has lived alone in her one-bedroom Coconut Grove cottage since 1926. She served on the original 1927 committee that pushed to declare the Everglades a national park. Her 1947 book *The Everglades – A River of Grass* first brought to public attention the importance of what many until then considered to be just a big old swamp.

"There are no other Everglades in the world. They are, they always have been, one of the unique regions of the earth, remote, never wholly known. Nothing anywhere else is like them: their vast glittering openness, wider than the enormous visible round of the horizon, the racing saltness and sweetness of their massive winds, under the dazzling blue heights of space. They are unique also in the simplicity, the diversity, the related harmony of the forms of life they enclose." With these opening lines from her book, so began Douglas's life-long crusade.

Years later, she founded the Friends of the Everglades, an organization that closely monitors the Everglades and other connected waters and lands that are in danger. She has been the recipient of more than 50 awards for her work, numerous honorary degrees, and was granted the first "Floridian of the Year" citation in 1983. The building that houses the Department of Natural Resources in the state's capital is named for her. In 1989, *Ms* magazine named her "Woman of the Year" for her continuing battle for a safer, more beautiful environment.

Partially blind and hard of hearing, she still musters the energy to attend book signings for her autobiography *Voice of the River*, and to speak at environmental hearings, all in time to be home at 5pm for her ritual scotch and soda.

A wetland of chaste and subtle charms, Douglas tells her audiences, the Everglades was once a vast ecosystem thick with life that covered 4 million acres of land. But today its problems are many. Encroaching development has depleted much of its water supply. Pesticides have seeped into the water system, killing much of the fish and wildlife. And chemical fertilizers used in agricultural fields have caused rampant growth in some exotic vegetation, choking to death acres of crucial plantlife.

Gone is the natural commotion caused by ospreys, panthers, deer and black bears, for their numbers have dwindled to a few. Ravaged by man for decades, the grassy marshland Everglades are dry and exposed. They occupy a mere 10 percent of their original expanse. Staunch environmentalists argue that the Glades are no longer dying, they are already dead.

Environmental nightmares withstanding, the Everglades are still considered America's richest fresh-water wilderness and are enjoyed by tens of thousands of visitors each year, who come to admire their monotonous sprawl and to feed marshmallows to the alligators.

Through the many battles to save her river of grass, Douglas has never waxed sentimental about her cause. At the close of her autobiography she wrote: "I believe that life should be lived so vividly and so intensely that thoughts of an afterlife, or a longer life, are not necessary."

Even when her tiny and tired body loses its spunk, for many in South Florida the soul of Marjory Stoneman Douglas will live for ever. ∎

**Coral reefs:** A second day-tour south is to **Biscayne National Park**, which lies 85 percent under water 6 to 9 miles east of park headquarters at **Convoy Point**. The park attained its present size of 181,500 acres in 1980 after it was enlarged to keep the islands that now comprise it from development.

Biscayne National Park's appeal (like Pennekamp Park's south along the same reef) is principally in the coral reefs which can be dived and snorkeled. These are the northernmost coral reefs of the Atlantic. Divers and snorkelers view the vivid edge of the sea where the clear shallows in sunlight display nature's brilliance. Coral and fish dazzle – more than 250 varieties. Their spectacle can be viewed from a glass-bottomed boat operated by the park concessioner.

Worth exploring, too, is the string of park islands. Largest is 7-mile **Elliott Key**. A self-guided loop trail introduces visitors to the sharp changes worked in this environment by elevation shifts as subtle as inches. Hardwood hammock gives way to upland forest, in turn succeeded by mangrove swamp as the rocky path turns sandy by the sea.

**Florida Keys:** A third day-trip south of Miami offers a glimpse of the Keys on the way to **Pennekamp Park** and the **Key Largo Coral Reef National Marine Sanctuary**. Reefs here equal those of Biscayne in their natural beauty. Alas, **Key Largo**, nearest of the Keys to the mainland, is over-commercialized.

One worthwhile attraction is the **Key Largo Undersea Park**, which is the commercial arm of the Marine Resources Development Foundation, founded in 1970. The park operates the **Jules Undersea Lodge**, two tiny rooms in a habitat submerged in a 35-ft-deep lagoon kept clear through constant filtration. A cultivated reef is popular with beginner divers and others frustrated by occasional northeasterly winds that in winter can make the offshore reef waters too choppy for good viewing.

Good choices for food include the **Italian Fisherman** at mile marker 104

he world
elow the
urface.

on the Gulf side of the **Overseas Highway,** and **Cracked Conch** at mile marker 105 on the oceanside. Cracked Conch delightfully contrasts the rusticity of unfurnished pine walls, papered with business cards and foreign bank notes, with a sophisticated beer list of no fewer than 75 choices.

Just east of the toll bridge on the back road that returns to the mainland across Card Sound is **Alabama Jack's,** famous for its conch and as a place for watching sunsets. (Key West lies 100 miles in the other direction.)

**Indian territory:** An interesting daytrip can also be made west to **Shark Valley** and to the **Miccosukee Indian Reservation** along the **Tamiami Trail** (US Route 41) on the way to Everglades City at the western entry to Everglades National Park.

Shark Valley lies 35 miles west of Miami at the western edge of the slough that carries the major flow of water through the park. Open-air trams tour a 15-mile loop through an all-encompassing landscape of islands and hammocks that stand above the sawgrass. In winter, visitors at the observation tower can see alligators galore alternately sunning themselves and cooling down in the pond waters.

The Indian reservation features a restaurant, cultural center and scores of artifacts and souvenirs. Colorful patchwork dresses and jackets are the oldest authentic crafts of the region.

Stop for the film showing and interpretive materials at the **Oasis Visitor Center** located in the **Big Cypress Nature Preserve** which abuts the park along Highway 41. **Ochopee**, which is 25 miles farther west, is famous for housing the smallest post office in the United States.

The straight drive across to **Everglades City** takes less than two hours. The road dates from 1928 (when completion linked Tampa and Miami) and veers 3 miles directly south of the **Chamber of Commerce Information Center.** Around the wide circle at the United

**Miccosukee Indian tells visitors the story of his people.**

262

Telephone tower the road leads to the new **Marjory Stoneman Douglas Visitor Center**.

Boat tours carry visitors into the **Ten Thousand Islands** in **Chokoloskee Bay**. Strange sights include raccoons that have adapted to climbing trees during flood tides. Thousand-pound manatee show up in the winter. Floating coconuts turn out to be the heads of mostly submerged turtles. Turkey buzzards soar on the winds.

At land's end in Chokoloskee, **Smallwoods Store** has been restored by the original owner's granddaughter and turned into an area museum. The old cypress and pine structure was the only trading post in the region at the turn of the century.

Next door to the 70-ft **E.J. Hamilton Tower** (too low for impressive views), the **Oyster House** serves gator, turtle, fresh fish, and other seafood. Also in town is the **Rod and Gun Club** built by Barron Collier as a lodge for wealthy friends; in years past, presidents visited

here. Nowadays, the rustic yellow-trimmed, clapboard lodge has a pleasant restaurant-bar and screened porch overlooking the river, with a few ordinary cottages and a swimming pool.

**Heading home:** On the return to Miami consider driving the 23-mile loop road that drops south from **Monroe Station**. Weekdays, maybe only three or four cars pass in either direction. That's because, in sections, the road is so pot-holed that drivers are bewildered as to how they might have taken a wrong turn along this solitary route. In its worst sections, anything over 20 miles an hour comfortably requires a jeep.

The road narrows to one lane, curves and enters a cypress swamp of clear, fresh water, stunningly beautiful. A veritable amphitheater of wildlife hovers. Orchids and exotic red flowers that shoot from cypress-rooted bromeliads fire the imagination. The magic fades as the road improves. The last 8 miles back to the Tamiami Trail are smooth – and only ordinarily beautiful.

Delicate hibiscus.

# INSIGHT GUIDES
# Travel Tips

# FOR THOSE
# WITH MORE THAN
# A PASSING INTEREST
# IN TIME...

Before you put your name down for a Patek Philippe watch *fig. 1*, there are a few basic things you might like to know, without knowing exactly whom to ask. In addressing such issues as accuracy, reliability and value for money, we would like to demonstrate why the watch we will make for you will be quite unlike any other watch currently produced.

### "Punctuality", Louis XVIII was fond of saying, "is the politeness of kings."

We believe that in the matter of punctuality, we can rise to the occasion by making you a mechanical timepiece that will keep its rendezvous with the Gregorian calendar at the end of every century, omitting the leap-years in 2100, 2200 and 2300 and recording them in 2000 and 2400 *fig. 2*. Nevertheless, such a watch does need the occasional adjustment. Every 3333 years and 122 days you should remember to set it forward one day to the true time of the celestial clock. We suspect, however, that you are simply content to observe the politeness of kings. Be assured, therefore, that when you order your watch, we will be exploring for you the physical—if not the metaphysical—limits of precision.

### Does everything have to depend on how much?

Consider, if you will, the motives of collectors who set record prices at auction to acquire a Patek Philippe. They may be paying for rarity, for looks or for micromechanical ingenuity. But we believe that behind each $500,000-plus

bid is the conviction that a Patek Philippe, even if 50 years old or older, can be expected to work perfectly for future generations.

In case your ambitions to own a Patek Philippe are somewhat discouraged by the scale of the sacrifice involved, may we hasten to point out that the watch we will make for you today will certainly be a technical improvement on the Pateks bought at auction? In keeping with our tradition of inventing new mechanical solutions for greater reliability and better time-keeping, we will bring to your watch innovations *fig. 3* inconceivable to our watchmakers who created the supreme wristwatches of 50 years ago *fig. 4*. At the same time, we will of course do our utmost to avoid placing undue strain on your financial resources.

### Can it really be mine?

May we turn your thoughts to the day you take delivery of your watch? Sealed within its case is your watchmaker's tribute to the mysterious process of time. He has decorated each wheel with a chamfer carved into its hub and polished into a shining circle. Delicate ribbing flows over the plates and bridges of gold and rare alloys. Millimetric surfaces are bevelled and burnished to exactitudes measured in microns. Rubies are transformed into jewels that triumph over friction. And after many months—or even years—of work, your watchmaker stamps a small badge into the mainbridge of your watch. The Geneva Seal—the highest possible attestation of fine watchmaking *fig. 5*.

### Looks that speak of inner grace *fig. 6*.

When you order your watch, you will no doubt like its outward appearance to reflect the harmony and elegance of the movement within. You may therefore find it helpful to know that we are uniquely able to cater for any special decorative needs you might like to express. For example, our engravers will delight in conjuring a subtle play of light and shadow on the gold case-back of one of our rare pocket-watches *fig. 7*. If you bring us your favourite picture, our enamellers will reproduce it in a brilliant miniature of hair-breadth detail *fig. 8*. The perfect execution of a double hobnail pattern on the bezel of a wristwatch is the pride of our casemakers and the satisfaction of our designers, while our chainsmiths will weave for you a rich brocade in gold *figs. 9 & 10*. May we also recommend the artistry of our goldsmiths and the experience of our lapidaries in the selection and setting of the finest gemstones? *figs. 11 & 12*.

### How to enjoy your watch before you own it.

As you will appreciate, the very nature of our watches imposes a limit on the number we can make available. (The four Calibre 89 time-pieces we are now making will take up to nine years to complete). We cannot therefore promise instant gratification, but while you look forward to the day on which you take delivery of your Patek Philippe *fig. 13*, you will have the pleasure of reflecting that time is a universal and everlasting commodity, freely available to be enjoyed by all.

*Should you require information on any particular Patek Philippe watch, or even on watchmaking in general, we would be delighted to reply to your letter of enquiry. And if you send*

fig. 1: The classic face of Patek Philippe.

fig. 4: Complicated wristwatches circa 1930 (left) and 1990. The golden age of watchmaking will always be with us.

fig. 6: Your pleasure in owning a Patek Philippe is the purpose of those who made it for you.

fig. 9: Harmony of design is executed in a work of simplicity and perfection in a lady's Calatrava wristwatch.

fig. 10: The chainsmith's hands impart strength and delicacy to a tracery of gold.

fig. 2: One of the 33 complications of the Calibre 89 astronomical clock-watch is a satellite wheel that completes one revolution every 400 years.

fig. 5: The Geneva Seal is awarded only to watches which achieve the standards of horological purity laid down in the laws of Geneva. These rules define the supreme quality of watchmaking.

fig. 7: Arabesques come to life on a gold case-back.

fig. 11: Circles in gold: symbols of perfection in the making.

fig. 3: Recognized as the most advanced mechanical regulating device to date, Patek Philippe's Gyromax balance wheel demonstrates the equivalence of simplicity and precision.

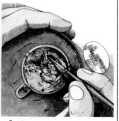

fig. 8: An artist working six hours a day takes about four months to complete a miniature in enamel on the case of a pocket-watch.

fig. 12: The test of a master lapidary is his ability to express the splendour of precious gemstones.

# PATEK PHILIPPE
GENEVE

fig. 13: The discreet sign of those who value their time.

your card marked "book catalogue" we shall post you a catalogue of our publications. Patek Philippe, 41 rue du Rhône, 1204 Geneva, Switzerland, Tel. +41 22/310 03 66.

# INSIGHT GUIDES

## COLORSET NUMBERS

# Getting Acquainted

*Unless otherwise stated, all telephone numbers are preceded by the area code number 305. Toll-free numbers are indicated by the prefix 800.*

## The Place

**Area**: 2,000 sq. miles (5,200 sq. km).
**Population (Greater Miami)**: 2 million.
**Language**: Officially English, although over 50 percent of the local population speak Spanish as a first language.
**Religion**: 65% Christian, 25% Jewish, 10% Muslim, Hindu and Buddhist.
**Time Zone**: Eastern Standard Time (GMT minus five hours).
**Currency**: Dollar.
**Weights and Measures**:
The US uses the Imperial system of weights and measures. Metric is rarely used. Below is a conversion chart.
1 inch = 2.54 centimeters
1 foot = 30.48 centimeters
1 mile = 1.609 kilometers
1 quart = 1.136 liters
1 ounce = 28.4 grams
1 pound = .453 kilograms
1 yard = .9144 meters
**Electricity**: Standard is 110 volts.
**International Dialing Code**: (1).
**Local Dialing Code**: (305).

## The Climate

Although most Northerners cringe at the idea of a Miami summer, daytime temperatures are in fact no hotter than daytime summer temperatures in New York City. The average yearly temperature is 75°F (24°C) with a range from the 60°sF in January to the 90°sF in August 15–35°C).

### MIAMI AVERAGE MONTHLY HIGHS AND LOWS

**January**: High 74°F (23°C), Low 63°F (17°C)
**February**: 76°F (24°C), 63°F (17°C)
**March**: 77°F (25°C), 65°F (18°C)
**April**: 79°F (26°C), 68°F (20°C)
**May**: 83°F (28°C), 72°F (22°C)
**June**: 85°F (29°C), 76°F (24°C)
**July**: 88°F (31°C), 76°F (24°C)
**August**: 88°F (31°C), 76°F (24°C)
**September**: 86°F (30°C), 76°F (24°C)
**October**: 83°F (28°C), 72°F (22°C)
**November**: 79°F (26°C), 67°F (19°C)
**December**: 76°F (24°C), 63°F (17°C)

Definitely part of America's "Sunshine State," Miami sees sun almost 365 days a year. Summer is the rainy season and brief, but intense, afternoon thundershowers can be expected almost daily in July and August. Lightning at this time of year is common.

The hurricane season runs from June to October. Storms that could hit the southeast Florida coast vary annually. While most never make it to Miami, the National Hurricane Center in the city carefully tracks each tropical depression on its path to becoming a hurricane. Warnings are issued if there is even a small hint of a threat.

In previous years, hurricanes were given women's names, but since the 1970s the National Weather Service has given up its chauvinistic ways and hurricanes are now given both male and female names. For news on brewing storms call the National Weather Service in Miami, tel: 229-4522.

## The Economy

Miami is the most urban of cities in Florida and also the largest, even larger than the state capitol of Tallahassee to the north. Tourism has for many decades been a mainstay of the economy, with the city receiving over 8 million visitors annually. Miami also hosts the largest international banking center outside of New York and serves as the headquarters for several national Fortune 500 companies. Major industries in the area include clothing manufacturing, printing and publishing, government, retail, insurance, health services, agriculture and transport.

## The Government

Although Miami often feels more like a South American city than a North American one, it is most definitely a part of the United States and adheres to all US government policies. But since "Greater Miami" is in fact made up of 27 municipalities, local regulations regarding housing, sanitation, recreation and education vary.

## Culture and Customs

Miami's culture, although there is no such thing as one definitive Miami culture, is what many visitors to the city are seeking. It is a hybrid blend of ethnic mixes, with a tendency towards the Latin culture.

## Fascinating Facts

**1)** Fidel Castro, the most hated man in Miami, spent his honeymoon in Miami Beach in 1948.

**2)** Jamaican reggae star Bob Marley spent a great deal of time in Miami, and died in a Miami hospital in 1981. Marley's mother, Cedella Booker, still lives in the Miami home her son bought for her and can often be spotted buying organic vegetables at a health food store in Coconut Grove.

**3)** Many restaurants in Miami offer free champagne or Bloody Marys with their Sunday brunch, but don't think it is out of generosity. Local laws in some areas prohibit the sale of liquor before 1pm on Sunday. These restaurants only give the liquor away because it is illegal for them to sell it.

**4)** Although Miami is not thought of as a music-producing town, in truth it actually is. Criteria Recording Studio in North Miami has been recording well known artists for well over 30 years. Among those who have produced records here are: Abba, The Allman Brothers, Count Basie, Placido Domingo, Aretha Franklin, The Eagles, Little Richard, The Rolling Stones, Tina Turner, James Brown, and Eric Clapton.

**5)** Between 1925 and 1926, the boom years of Miami's early history, the *Miami Herald* ran more pages of advertising copy than any other newspaper in the world.

**6)** The downtown Dade County Criminal Courthouse has a special "Voodoo Squad" group of janitors whose sole job it is to clean up the animal sacrifices and voodoo/*santeria* paraphernalia left behind by defendants who believe their spiritual offerings will alleviate their legal woes.

**7)** The Greater Miami area receives over 8 million tourists a year who create more than $7 billion worth of revenues for the area.

**8)** During the 1980s, a world famous "miracle" tree thrived on SW 4th Street in Little Havana. After a 92-year-old man claimed that the sap from the tree cured his cataracts, hundreds of believers made pilgrimages to the tree with the hopes of curing their own ills. Unfortunately, a swift entrepreneur chopped the tree down and sold the splinters.

**9)** It was in Miami, at the Coconut Grove Exhibition Center, that hard-living rockstar Jim Morrison began his fall from grace. At a 1969 Doors concert, Morrison, after over-indulging on drugs and whisky, exposed himself to the crowd of 10,000. Shortly after, he was arrested for public exposure and convicted on obscenity charges. He died before serving any jail time.

**10)** During his heyday, world boxing champion Muhammad Ali lived in and trained in Miami Beach at the once famous Fifth Street Gym.

# Planning the Trip

## What to Bring

In general, everything you could possibly need can be bought inexpensively in Miami. Some basic suggestions, however, include sun screen lotion, a shade hat, an umbrella, a bathing suit, and any prescription medications.

### Clothing

Casual, cool, lightweight and light colors are the norm. Formal dress is rarely required. For men, a sports coat and open shirt are usually acceptable at finer restaurants with ties being optional. Shorts are acceptable for both men and women even on the streets of downtown Miami. In winter, a sweater or light jacket will usually be enough.

## Entry Regulations

### Visas and Passports

Requirements for both, and vaccination certificates, vary with country of origin. Enquiries should be made to the relevant consulate.

### Animal Quarantine

Birds being brought into the country usually require a minimum of 30 days in quarantine. Small pets like dogs and cats must have a health certificate confirming rabies vaccinations but do not require quarantine.

### Customs

Visitors to the US must declare all items brought into the country to the US customs office at the time of arrival. The duty-free allowance is one quart of liquor (0.946 liters) and one carton of cigarettes. Special forms are required for firearms and certain prescription drugs.

## Health

The US has no socialized medicine so medical care must be paid for by the individual, even in emergency situations. Medical insurance is advisable. However, Miami's medical facilities are considered to be some of the best in the country. In case of any medical emergency, telephone 911 and assistance will be available.

### Sunburn

Severe cases of sunburn are common among visitors and have been known to ruin many a Miami vacation. Use a sunscreen lotion for safety even while bathing or on cloudy days, especially the first few days in town.

### Insects

Mosquitos can be a nuisance during the summer months as well as sandflies – or "no-see-ums" as locals call them – at the beach in the evening. Insect repellent will help protect against both. Also, beware of fire ants – tiny red ants that live in mounds of dirt in grassy areas – which can inflict painful stings that will occasionally cause an allergic reaction.

## Money

Numerous banks and money exchange offices in the area are available to exchange foreign currencies. There are also booths at Miami International Airport (with one operating 24 hours a day). Banks are generally closed on Saturday afternoons and Sundays. The use of US dollar traveler's checks is advised, and a passport or photo identification is usually required. The Florida state sales tax is 6 percent.

## Public Holidays

During some of the holidays listed below, some or all government offices, businesses and banks may be closed. School is also in recess during these times, so area beaches and attractions are usually crowded.

**January 1**: New Year's Day.
**January 15**: Martin Luther King's Birthday.
**February 12**: Abraham Lincoln's Birthday.
**Third Monday in February**: George Washington's Birthday.
**Last Monday in May**: Memorial Day.
**July 4**: Independence Day.
**First Monday in September**: Labor Day.
**Second Monday in October**: Columbus Day.
**November 11**: Veterans Day.
**Fourth Thursday in November**: Thanksgiving.
**December 25**: Christmas Day.

## Getting There

### By Air

Miami International Airport is one of the busiest and best people-watching airports in the US. Over 85 scheduled carriers, both domestic and international, offer more than 800 flights daily. It serves as the main artery to the Caribbean and Latin America and offers numerous flights to New York and the nearby Bahamas throughout the day.

Just 8 miles from downtown, the airport is a city within itself with over 32,000 employees. It offers banks, restaurants, televisions, lockers, a hotel and an airfield sundeck for that last-chance tan. For general information telephone 876-7000.

## Airline Reservations

For information on flights, call the following numbers:

**Air Canada**, tel: (800) 776-3000.
**Air France**, tel: (800) 237-2747.
**American**, tel: (800) 433-7300.
**Bahamas Air**, tel: 305-593-1910.
**British Airways**, tel: (800) 247-9297.
**Carnival**, tel: 305-891-0199.
**Continental**, tel: 305-324-0400.
**Delta**, tel: 305-448-7000.
**Lufthansa**, tel: (800) 645-3880.
**Northwest**, tel: (800) 221-4750.
**Swissair**, tel: (800) 221-4750.
**TWA**, tel: 305-371-7471.
**United**, tel: (800) 377-3461.
**US Air**, tel: (800) 842-5374.

## By Sea

The Port of Miami is the largest cruise port in the world and welcomes well over 2 million passengers each year which represents 75 percent of all cruise passengers worldwide. It is just a five-minute ride from downtown with trolley service available. For general information telephone 371-7678.

### CRUISE LINES

**Carnival Cruise Lines**, 3655 N.W. 87th Ave, Miami, tel: 599-2200.
**Commodore Cruise Lines**, 800 Douglas Rd, Coral Gables, tel: 529-3000.
**Costa Cruises**, 80 S.W. 8th St, Miami, tel: 358-7325.
**Dolphin Cruise Lines**, 1007 N. American Way, Miami, tel: 358-2111.
**Norwegian Cruise Line**, 95 Merrick Way, Coral Gables, tel: 447-9660.
**Royal Caribbean**, 1050 Caribbean Way, Miami, tel: 539-6000.
**Sea Escape**, 1080 Port Blvd, Miami, tel: 379-0000.

### MARINAS

For those who sail into the city on their own, there are over 50 marinas with 350 sq. miles of protected waters that offer dock facilities for almost any size craft:

**Biscayne Bay Marriott Hotel & Marina**, 1633 N. Bayshore Dr., Miami, tel: 374-3900.
**Crandon Park Marina**, 4000 Crandon Park Blvd, Key Biscayne, tel: 361-1281.
**Mathesson Hammock Marina**, 9610 Old Cutler Rd, Coral Gables, tel: 665-5475.

**Haulover Park Marina**, 10500 Collins Ave, Miami Beach, tel: 947-3525.
**Dinner Key Marina**, 3400 Pan American Dr., Coconut Grove, tel: 579-6980.
**Miamarina at Bayside**, 401 Biscayne Blvd, Miami, tel: 579-6955.
**Rickenbacker Marina**, 3301 Rickenbacker Cswy, Key Biscayne, tel: 361-1900.
**Maule Lake Marina**, 17201 Biscayne Blvd, N. Miami Beach, tel: 945-0808.
**Miami Beach Marina**, 300 Alton Rd, Miami Beach, tel: 673-6000.

## By Rail

Amtrak is the passenger line that services Miami from most points across the country. Sleeping berths and restaurant cars are available on most trains. Extended travel passes are available. A trip from New York City takes 26 hours and costs about the same as an airline ticket. For information telephone (800) 872-7245.

Tri-Rail links Dade County with the two northern counties of Broward and Palm Beach, with service available from the Metrorail station at 79th St. Trains operate on a varied schedule. For information telephone (800) 874-7245.

## By Bus

Greyhound and Trailways provide bus service to Miami from across America. For information on both, telephone (800) 231-2222.

## By Car

The major Florida highways leading to Miami are I-95 along the east, I-75 along the west, and the Florida Turnpike which connects the central part of the state to the south. On all of them, the roads are excellent with safe, clean rest stops along the way. Speed limits range from 55 to 65 mph, so watch for changes. Normal city speed limits are usually 30 mph and all are strictly enforced with radar monitors.

## Special Facilities

### Disabled

**Deaf Services Bureau**, tel: 668-4407
**Lighthouse for the Blind**, tel: 856-2288.
**Metro-Dade Office of Handicapped Opportunities**, tel: 375-3566.

## Baby Sitting Services

**International Nanny Services**, tel: 949-0360.

## Gays

**Gay and Lesbian Community Hotline**, tel: 759-3661.

## Marriages

**Marriage License Bureau**, 140 W. Flagler St, tel: 375-3721.

## Alcoholics Anonymous

**AA**, 665 Mokena Dr., Miami Springs, tel: 887-6762.
**Alcohol Helpline**, tel: (800) 252-6465.

## Immigration & Naturalization Offices

**District Headquarters**, 7880 Biscayne Blvd, Miami, tel: 536-5741.

## Useful Addresses

### Tourist Offices

**Greater Miami Convention and Visitors Bureau**, 701 Brickell Ave, tel: 539-3000 or (800) 283-2707.
**Greater Miami Chamber of Commerce**, 1601 Biscayne Blvd, tel: 350-7700.
**Florida Division of Tourism**, Tallahassee, tel: 904-487-1462.

## Embassies and Consulates

**Argentina**: 80 S.W. 8th St, tel: 373-7794.
**Austria**: 1454 N.W. 17th Ave, tel: 325-1561.
**Bahamas**: 25 S.E. 2nd Ave, tel: 373-6295.
**Bolivia**: 25 S.E. 2nd Ave, tel: 358-3450.
**Brazil**: 777 Brickell Ave, tel: 377-1734.
**Chile**: 1110 Brickell Ave, tel: 373-8623.
**Colombia**: 280 Aragon Ave, Coral Gables, tel: 448-5558.
**Costa Rica**: 28 W. Flagler St, tel: 377-4242.
**Denmark**: 2655 LeJeune Rd, Coral Gables, tel: 446-3052.
**Ecuador**: 1101 Brickell Ave, tel: 539-8214.
**El Salvador**: 300 Biscayne Blvd, tel: 371-8850.
**Finland**: PO Box 248216, Coral Gables, tel: 444-7555.
**France**: One Biscayne Blvd, tel: 372-9798.

**Germany**: 100 N. Biscayne Blvd, tel: 358-0290.

**Great Britain**: 1001 S. Bayshore Dr, tel: 374-1522.

**Guatemala**: 300 Sevilla Ave, Coral Gables, tel: 443-4828.

**Haiti**: 259 S.W. 13th St, tel: 859-2003.

**Israel**: 330 Biscayne Blvd, tel: 358-8111.

**Italy**: 1200 Brickell Ave, tel: 374-6322.

**Jamaica**: 25 S.E. 2nd Ave, tel: 374-8431.

**Japan**: 2801 Ponce DeLeon Blvd, Coral Gables, tel: 445-1477.

**Netherlands**: Two S. Biscayne Blvd, tel: 858-7617.

**Norway**: 1001 North America Way, tel: 358-4386.

**Paraguay**: 7205 N.W. 19th St, tel: 477-4002.

**Peru**: 444 Brickell Ave, tel: 374-1305.

**Portugal**: 100 Biscayne Blvd, tel: 444-6311.

**Senegal**: 200 S. Biscayne Blvd, tel: 371-4286.

**Spain**: 1221 Brickell Ave, tel: 358-1992.

**Surinam**: 7235 N.W. 19th St, tel: 593-2163.

**Togo**: 200 S. Biscayne Blvd, tel: 371-4286.

**Uruguay**: 25 S.E. 2nd Ave, tel: 358-9350.

**Venezuela**: 1101 Brickell Ave, tel: 577-3834.

# Practical Tips

## Business Hours

Most offices and business are open Monday through Friday from 9am–5 or 5.30pm with never any closing hours for lunch. Banks are usually open from 9am–3pm Monday through Friday with some having Saturday hours of 9am–noon. Most large shopping centers are open from 10am–9.30pm Monday through Saturday and from noon–6pm on Sunday.

## Tipping

Gratuities are usually not included on most restaurant bills and the suggested rate is 15 to 20 percent. Porters are readily available at the airport; tipping is expected and $1–1.50 per suitcase is customary. Wheel chairs and attendants are also available.

## Religious Services

There are services available for dozens of different Christian denominations, inter-denominational, Unitarian, African, non-denominational, Jewish and New Age religions. Christian services are usually held on Saturday nights and Sunday mornings.

### Catholic

**St Frances De Sales**, 600 Lenox Ave, Miami Beach, tel: 672-0093.

**St Hugh**, 3460 Royal Rd, Coconut Grove, tel: 444-8363.

**St Agnes**, 100 Harbor Dr., Key Biscayne, tel: 361-2351.

### United Church of Christ

**Plymouth Congregational Church**, 3400 Devon Rd, Coconut Grove, tel: 444-6521.

**Coral Gables Congregational Church**, 3010 DeSoto Blvd, Coral Gables, tel: 448-7421.

**Church-By-The-Sea**, 501 96th St, Bal Harbour, tel: 866-0321.

### Baptist

**First Baptist Church of Miami Beach**, 2816 Sheridan Ave, Miami Beach, tel: 538-3507.

### Christian Science

**First Church of Christ Science**, 410 Andalusia Ave, Coral Gables, tel: 443-1427.

**Second Church of Christ Science**, 3840 Main Hwy, Coconut Grove, tel: 446-6933.

### Islamic

**Ismailia Cultural Center**, 2045 N.E. 151st St, N. Miami Beach, tel: 944-1710.

### Jehovah's Witness

**J. W. Kingdom Hall**, 910 Lincoln Rd Mall, Miami Beach, tel: 532-8588.

**J. W. Kingdom Hall**, 3161 S.W. 21st Terr., Coral Gables, tel: 446-9850.

## Synagogues

**All People's Synagogues**, 7455 Collins Ave, Miami Beach, tel: 861-5554.

**Beth Torah Congregation**, 1051 N. Miami Beach Blvd, N. Miami Beach, tel: 947-7528.

**Beth David Congregation**, 2625 S.W. 3rd Ave, Miami, tel: 854-3911.

**Hillel Jewish Center of the University of Miami**, 1100 Stanford Dr., Coral Gables, tel: 665-6948.

## Media

### Newspapers

The *Miami Herald* is Florida's most respected daily paper. It offers sound coverage on local, state and Latin American news. A Spanish language supplement, *El Nuevo*, is included in the *Herald* when bought in Spanish-speaking neighborhoods. Its Friday edition offers a useful what-to-do weekend tabloid and on Sunday there is an extensive classified section.

*New Times*, a free alternative press weekly, delivers an offbeat view of the city. Its calendar of events rivals the *Miami Herald's* and its personal ads let visitors know what's hot and happening in the city. *Miami Today*, a free weekly tabloid, caters to the Miami business community and the *Miami Review* covers the city's legal matters.

*Diario Las Americas* is a Spanish-language daily whose coverage emphasizes Cuban/Central American news and politically leans toward the right. *Miami Times* is a weekly that covers the area's black community. Pick up the *Jewish Journal* for information on the best Kosher restaurants, Hebrew classes and the latest synagogue news.

### Radio

AM frequencies in Miami tend to carry more talk shows and commercials. FM stations offer a wider range of programs and higher quality stereo sound. Some local favorites:

#### AM

560-WQAM: oldies
610-WIOD: news, talk
640-WLVJ: religious
670-WWFE: Spanish news, music
790-WNWS: news, talk
830-WRFM: Spanish, gospel

940-WINZ: news, talk
980-WWNN: self help
1170-WAVS: Caribbean
1210-WCMQ: Spanish, contemporary
1340-WLQY: international
1380-WLVS: religious
1420-WDBF: big band
1470-WRBD: blues
1600-WPOM: soul

## FM

88.9-WDNA: public radio
90.3-WAFG: religious
90.5-WVUM: universal Miami
91.3-WLRN: public radio
92.3-WCMQ: Spanish contemporary
93.1-WTMI: classical
93.9-WLVE: contemporary
94.9-WZTA: rock
98.3-WRTV: Spanish contemporary
99.1-WEDR: blues
99.9-WKIS: country
101.5-WLYF: easy listening
102.7-WMVJ: oldies
105.9-WAXY: contemporary
107.5-WQBA: Spanish contemporary

## Television

A weekly television guide is published on Sunday in the Miami Herald. Cable television stations are abundant, including many that are available at area hotels and motels. The national network channels are: 2 (WPBT-PBS), 4 (WTVJ-NBC), 6 (WCIX-CBS), 10 (WPLG-ABC). There are 15 other Miami area channels including several Spanish-language stations.

## Postal Services

Information on Miami's postal facilities can be found by telephoning 599-0166. Post offices in Dade County are open 8.30am–5pm Monday through Friday, with most also open on Saturday 8.30am–noon. At all branches, overnight and express mail services are available, along with a general delivery service that allows out-of-towners to receive mail and parcels.

## Post Offices

**Airport Mail Facility**, Miami International Airport, Miami, tel: 871-3327.
**Biscayne Branch**, Two S. Biscayne Blvd, Miami, tel: 372-9473.
**Coconut Grove Branch**, 3195 Grand Ave, Coconut Grove, tel: 443-0030.
**Coral Gables Branch**, 251 Valencia Ave, Coral Gables, tel: 445-8841.

**Key Biscayne Branch**, 59 Harbor Dr., Key Biscayne, tel: 361-1399.
**Miami Beach Branch**, 1300 Washington Ave, Miami Beach, tel: 531-3763.
**North Miami Beach Branch**, 16400 W. Dixie Hwy, tel: 895-3002.

## Phone & faxes

The area code prefix for the Miami area is 305. To ask an operator for a Miami area number telephone 411. To ask for a number outside of Miami but in the 305 area code, telephone 1-305-555-1212. For long-distance or international assistance dial 0. Toll-free numbers for various businesses and services are indicated by the prefix 800. The toll-free information number is (800) 555-1212.

Public phones are located in gas stations, restaurants, hotels, sidewalk booths and numerous public places.

### Fax/Telex/Telegrams

Dozens of businesses offering communication services are listed in the telephone directory. Many are open 24 hours a day.
**Telex & Fax Services**, tel: 223-3333.
**Kinkos**, tel: 662-6717.
**Western Union**, tel: (800) 325-6000.

## Emergencies
### Security and Crime

A rash of crimes committed against tourists in the early 1990s forced the Florida community to come up with effective safeguards to protect visitors from unwanted and dangerous attacks. One of the most important is that car rental agencies are now removing the special license plates which formerly earmarked hired cars, and replacing them with standard-issue plates, the sort used by residents. According to police, one of the tricks muggers have employed in the past is to bump a moving vehicle from behind, especially a car which is carrying tourists. When the bemused driver gets out to investigate, he or she is robbed at gunpoint.

Don't fall prey to this tactic: if you get bumped, proceed to the nearest well-lit and crowded spot, such as a gas station or convenience store, before stopping. Other tips: always park your car in a well-lit area, never in a shady back corner of a parking lot.

When you first arrive in Miami, plot your route from your point of arrival to your hotel in advance, with the aid of a map. (A spate of attacks in the city occured because jet-lagged tourists disembarked from longhaul flights, missed the highway signs for Miami Beach, and, only a couple of wrong turns later, found themselves in a violent part of town.) Better still, arrange to pick up your rented car from an agency near your hotel on the morning after you arrive rather than attempt to negotiate unfamiliar routes when very tired. Many car rental agencies will deliver to your hotel at no (or only a small extra) charge. Be sure to keep your car doors locked and windows closed while driving.

While in the street, use common sense and act like a New Yorker. In other words, don't carry around large sums of money or expensive video/camera equipment, don't make eye contact with unwelcome strangers, and don't travel alone at night.

To reach the **police in an emergency** telephone 911. No money is needed in pay phones for this number.

For police non-emergencies telephone 595-6263.

For lost property information telephone 471-2900. There is a lost and found office at the Miami International Airport, tel: 876-7377. It is open seven days a week 8am–6pm.

## Medical Services

There are several walk-in medical and dental care offices located throughout the Miami area. These are listed in the telephone directory under "Clinics." For dentist referrals, tel: 667 3647. A 24-hour pharmacy can be found by calling Walgreens Pharmacy, tel: 893-6860.

### HOSPITALS

**Coral Gables Hospital**, 3100 Douglas Rd, Coral Gables, tel: 445-8461.
**Humana Hospital**, 20900 Biscayne Blvd, Miami, tel: 932-0250.
**Jackson Memorial Hospital**, 1611 N.W. 12th Ave, tel: 325-7429.
**Mercy Hospital**, 3663 S. Miami Ave, Coconut Grove, tel: 854-4400.
**South Shore Hospital and Medical Center**, 630 Alton Rd, Miami Beach, tel: 672-2100.

## CLINICS

**Around the Clock Medical Services**, 3097 N.E. 163rd St, N. Miami Beach, tel: 940-9000.

**Today's Woman Medical Center**, 1320 S. Dixie Hwy, Coral Gables, tel: 665-4357.

**Health Crisis Network**, 1351 N.W. 20th St, Miami, tel: 324-5148.

**Miami Beach Medical Center**, 1218 Washington Ave, Miami Beach, tel: 532-4122.

# Getting Around

## Orientation

Except for the Art Deco District, Miami is not a walking city. That is, the areas of interest are so far apart that motorized transportation is usually required to travel from one to another. One suggestion is to take a local trolley tour to get acquainted, and then go back on your own to places of interest. Good detailed maps are available at most bookstores, news-stands and gas stations. Hitchhiking is illegal.

## From the Airport

### Taxis

The Miami International Airport is just 8 miles from downtown. **Taxis** are available outside the terminal.

### TAXICABS

**Metro Taxicab**, tel: 888-8888.
**Society Cab**, tel: 757-5523.
**Tropical Taxicab**, tel: 945-1025.
**Yellow Cab**, tel: 444-4444.

### Limousines

**Limousine service** by the hour or day is available.
**Ambassador Limousine**, tel: 931-3111.
**American H VIP Limousine**, tel: 666-5466.
**Limousines of South Florida**, tel: 940-5252.

## Other

There is a van service called **Super-Shuttle** that operates from the airport and can accommodate up to 11 passengers at a time. It operates 24 hours a day, seven days a week. Fares are lower than taxi rates. For information telephone 871-2000.

**Public buses** are available from the airport, but the system is a bit confusing to new arrivals. Connections to other parts of the city can be time-consuming.

**By car** (*see "Private Transportation"*).

## Public Transportation

The **Metrobus** system that operates throughout Dade County services 200,000 riders a day on 65 routes. The fare is $1 a person. Hours of operation depend on the route. For information telephone 638-6700, 6am–11pm. For maps of the system telephone 654-6587 or write to 3300 N.W. 32nd Ave, Miami, FL 33142.

## Metrorail

Miami's above-the-ground train system, offers a modern 21-mile ride from South Miami to Hialeah in the north, with spectacular views along the way. The fare is $1 and exact change in quarters is required. Hours of operation: 6am–9pm weekdays and 6.30am–6.30pm weekends, with special hours to accommodate festivals and special events.

### METRORAIL STATIONS

**Dadeland South**, 910 Dadeland Blvd.
**Dadeland North**, 8300 S. Dixie Hwy.
**South Miami**, 5949 Sunset Dr.
**University**, 5000 Ponce DeLeon Blvd.
**Douglas Road**, 3100 S.W. 37th Ave.
**Coconut Grove**, 2780 S.W. 27th Ave.
**Vozcaya**, 3201 S.W. 1st Ave.
**Brickell**, 1001 S.W. 1st Ave.
**Government Center**, 111 N.W. 1st St.
**Overtown**, 100 N.W. 11th St.
**Culmer**, 701 N.W. 11th St.
**Civic Center**, 1501 N.W. 12th Ave.
**Santa Clara**, 2050 N.W. 12th Ave.

## Metromover

The Disney-like electric train that locals call the "People Mover," connects with Metrorail at Government Center Station and loops around a 26-block area of downtown Miami. Its fun ride offers dramatic – at times breathtaking – views of the city's bustling center. The system operates: 6am–9pm weekdays and 8.30am–6.30pm weekends. The low fare is a good deal.

### METROMOVER STATIONS

**Government Center**, 111 N.W. 1st St.
**Miami Avenue**, S.W. 1st St.
**Fort Dallas Park**, S. Miami Ave, between 2nd and 3rd St S.E.
**World Trade Center**, S.E. 3rd St, between 1st and 2nd Ave.
**Bayfront Park**, Biscayne Blvd, between 3rd and 4th St.
**First Street**, N.E. 2nd Ave, between 1st and 2nd St.
**College**, N.E. 2nd Ave, located between 3rd and 4th St.
**Edcom**, N.E. 5th St and 2nd Ave.
**State Plaza**, N. Miami Ave and 5th St.

## Private Transportation

### By Car

**Rental cars** can be picked up at the airport, but it is advisable to have the car delivered to your hotel the next day (*see "Security and Crime"*). Cars are relatively inexpensive and a desirable way to see the city. A small day tax is added to all car rentals in Florida. Models range from modest economy cars to luxury convertibles. Some company choices are:

**Alamo**
US (800) 327-9633
International +1-305-522 0000
**Avis**
US (800) 331-1212
International +1-918-664 4600
**Budget**
US (800) 527-0700
International +1-214-404 7600
**Dollar**
US (800) 800-4000
International +1-813-877 5507
**Hertz**
US (800) 654-3131
International +1-405-749 4424
**National**
US (800) 227-7368
International +1-612-830 2345

## Bicycle/Scooter Rental

For information on bicycle or scooter rentals contact:

**Dade Cycle**, 3216 Grand Ave, Coconut Grove, tel: 443-6075.
**Miami Beach Bicycle Center**, 923 W. 39th St, Miami Beach, tel: 531-4161.
**Mangrove Bicycle Rentals**, 260 Crandon Park Blvd, Key Biscayne, tel: 361-5555.

# Where to Stay

## Hotels

Accommodation in Miami ranges from chi-chi romantic hotel suites to the standard major chain hotel rooms, with hundreds of choices to choose from. Prices range from $60 to $300 a night and discounts are given for weekly rates. Reservations should be made in advance. Rates vary from the high-season in winter to the off-season of May–June and September–October. Hotels add an additional 5 percent on top of the 6.5 percent state sales tax on all rooms rented in Dade County, and an additional 2 percent tax on all food and beverages sold.

There is no official rating system of area hotels. The following hotels have been categorized as follows: expensive – above $150; moderate – $75–150; inexpensive – under $75.

**The Alexander**, 5225 Collins Ave, Miami Beach, tel: 865-6500, (800) 327-6121, fax: 864-8525. An all-suite hotel with both one- and two-bedroom mini apartments, the Alexander offers luxury accommodations amid beautiful oceanfront surroundings. Expensive.
**Avalon Hotel**, 700 Ocean Dr., Miami Beach, tel: 538-0133, fax: 534-0258. Classic art deco in traditional 1930s style with a fine restaurant and full services. Moderate.
**Chateau By-the-Sea**, 19115 Collins Ave, Sunny Isles/Miami Beach, tel: 931-8800, fax: 931-6194. Good quality rooms with a tropical Swiss Chalet decor and wonderful swimming pool. Inexpensive.

**Casa Grande**, 834 Ocean Dr., Miami Beach, tel: 672-7003, fax: 673-3669. Tropically decorated suites with mahogany beds, original art, and full kitchens. Expensive.
**Delano Hotel**, 1685 Collins Ave, Miami Beach, tel: 672-2000, fax: 532-0099. Along with being one of Madonna's favorite hangouts, the sleek Delano has a loyal, hip New York clientele, and is one of the trendiest spots on the beach. Expensive.
**Desert Inn**, 17201 Collins Ave, Sunny Isles/Miami Beach, tel: 947-0621, fax: 944-7050. A sprawling, family-oriented hotel with pool, tennis courts, and oceanfront patio bar. Inexpensive.
**Driftwood Inn**, 17121 Collins Ave, Sunny Isles/Miami Beach, tel: 944-5141, fax: 945-0762. Oceanfront budget efficiency rooms with laundry facilities and pool. Inexpensive.
**Essex House**, 1001 Collins Ave, Miami Beach, tel: 534-2700, fax: 532-3827. A sleek, deco hotel with porthole windows, a sophisticated piano bar, and teddy bears on the pillows. Moderate
**Hampton Inn**, 2800 SW 28th Terrace, Coconut Grove, tel: 448-2800, fax: 442-8655. A modern and pleasant hotel with fitness center and free breakfasts within walking distance of Coconut Grove's entertainment district. Moderate.
**Kent Hotel**, 1131 Collins Ave, Miami Beach, tel: 531-6771, fax: 531-0720. Nothing fancy, but comfortable and practical with complimentary patio breakfasts. Inexpensive
**Marseilles Deco Beach Hotel**, 1741 Collins Ave, Miami Beach, tel: 538-5711, fax: 673-1006. A well managed, well located and well priced hotel with small kitchens in most rooms. Inexpensive.
**Paradise Inn**, 8520 Harding Ave, Miami Beach, tel: 865-6216, fax: 865-9028. Situated one block from the ocean with modest but well-kept rooms. Inexpensive.
**Park Central**, 640 Ocean Dr., Miami Beach, tel: 538-1611, fax: 534-7520. An architectural deco masterpiece with excellent service and a fine Italian restaurant. Moderate.
**Park Washington**, 1020 Washington Ave, Miami Beach, tel: 532-1930, fax: 672-6706. A modest but pleasant low-priced hotel with original 1930s furnishings. Inexpensive.

**The Waterside**, 2360 Collins Ave, Miami Beach, tel: 538-1951, fax: 531-3217. Popular with European tourists with simple rooms and a friendly atmosphere. Inexpensive.
**Bay Harbor Inn**, 9660 E. Bay Harbor Dr., Bay Harbor, tel: 868-4141. A pleasant surprise in this northern community's land of big, brooding hotels. Inexpensive.
**Cavalier Hotel**, 1320 Ocean Dr., South Miami Beach, tel: 531-2135, fax: 531-5543. One of the best-run Art Deco hotels on the beach. Moderate.
**Everglades**, 244 Biscayne Blvd, downtown Miami, tel: 379-5461, fax: 577-8445. Convenient downtown hotel across from Bayside Marketplace. Inexpensive.
**Fontainebleau Hilton Resort and Spa**, 4441 Collins Ave, Miami Beach, tel: 538-2000, fax: 534-7821. One of Miami Beach's most popular large hotels. Expensive.
**Grand Bay Hotel**, 2669 Bayshore Dr., Coconut Grove, tel: 858-9600, fax: 859-2026. Features luxurious rooms and views. Expensive.
**Hotel Cardozo**, 1300 Ocean Dr., South Miami Beach, tel: 531-2135, fax: 531-5543. One of the first hotels on the block to be restored to classic Art Deco. Moderate.
**Hotel Mia**, Miami International Airport, tel: 871-4100, fax: 871-0800. Located right at the airport for those too tired to search around upon arrival. Moderate.
**Hotel Place St Michel**, 162 Alcazar Ave, Coral Gables, tel: 444-1666, fax: 529-0074. Classic small hotel in the middle of the Coral Gables business district. Moderate.
**Hyatt Regency**, 400 S.E. 2nd Ave, downtown Miami, tel: 358-1234, fax: 358-0529. On the north bank of the Miami River, the Hyatt is a popular and well-run downtown hotel. Expensive.
**Mayfair House**, 3000 Florida Ave, Coconut Grove, tel: 441-0000, fax: 446-0147. A posh European-style luxury hotel located in the sophisticated Mayfair shopping center. Expensive.
**Miami River Inn**, 118 S.W. South River Dr., Little Havana, tel: 325-0045, fax: 325-9227. Recently restored classic inn located right on the Miami River. Moderate.
**Omni International Hotel**, 1601 Biscayne Blvd, downtown Miami, tel: 374-0000, fax: 374-0020. A modern

highrise hotel with a large shopping center nearby. Moderate.

**Sonesta Beach Hotel & Tennis Club**, 350 Ocean Dr., Key Biscayne, tel: 361-2021, fax: 361-3096. This plush beachfront resort has a collection of museum-quality modern art decorating the property. Expensive.

**Turnberry Isle Yacht & Country Club**, 19735 Turnberry Way, N. Miami Beach, tel: 932-6200, fax: 933-6554. A 300-acre bayfront site with golf, tennis and lots of beautiful people to watch. Expensive.

## Condominium & House Rentals

There are many real estate companies in the Miami area that specialize in renting condominium apartments and homes to tourists. Lengths of stay can be from one week to one year and accommodation ranges from studio apartments to waterfront estates. Most come fully equipped with furnishings and cookware; some even come with maid service. Almost all require security deposits.

For information try the following:

**Century 21**, tel: 235-2621 or 264-6000.

**Keyes**, tel: 443-7423.

**Alexander Realty**, tel: 672-1500.

**Coconut Grove Real Estate**, tel: 448-4123.

**Renters Paradise**, tel: 865-0200.

## Youth Hostels

The Miami Beach International Youth Hostel at 1423 Washington Ave, in the heart of the historic Art Deco District, is a bargain at around $15 a night for a dormitory-style room. It is affiliated with and regulated by the American Youth Hostels system, tel: 534-2988.

## Campgrounds

**South KOA**, 20675 S.W. 162nd Ave, tel: 233-5300. Campsites for tents are about $25 and RV hook-ups are about $35 per night.

**Larry and Penny Thompson Park**, operated by the Dade County Parks and Recreation Dept, 12451 S.W. 184th St, tel: 232-1049. Offers campsites for four people starting at about $15.

# Eating Out

## What to Eat

Most people agree that Miami tastes good. Along with fresh seafood, ethnic flavors are everywhere, with a heavy accent on the garlic. There are hundreds of sophisticated restaurants and hole-in-the-wall cafes that can satisfy any culinary desire. Prices range from a filling $6 dinner at a Cuban cafeteria to a $100 "fine dining experience." The free weekly newspaper "New Times" produces the best listing of local restaurants in town. Almost all restaurants accept credit cards and traveler's checks, and have designated smoking/non-smoking sections.

## Where to Eat

A general price guide for the following restaurants: $ Inexpensive, dinner for two with wine less than $40. $$ Moderate, dinner for two with wine $40-80. $$$ Expensive, dinner for two with wine above $80.

### Inexpensive

**Arnie and Richie's**, 525 41st St, Miami Beach, tel: 531-7691. Overstuffed pastrami sandwiches, tart coleslaw, smoked whitefish, and every deli delight imaginable. $

**Au Natural Gourmet Pizza**, 1427 Alton Rd, Miami Beach, tel: 531-0666. Nontraditional but delicious pizza such as chicken Mexicana and pizza pesto. $

**Bagel Emporium**, 1238 S. Dixie Highway, Coral Gables, tel: 666-9519. A classic New York-style deli with roasted chicken, stuffed cabbage, braised brisket, and bagels, bagels, bagels. $

**Biscayne Mile Cafeteria**, 147 Miracle Mile, Coral Gables, tel: 444-9005. Simple, Southern cooking served help-your-self cafeteria style. $

**Bimini Grill**, 620 N.E. 78th St, Miami, tel: 758-9154. Very casual canal-front cafe specializing in Bahamian dishes like conch fritters and Bimini bread. $

**Charlotte's Chinese Kitchen**, 1403 Washington Ave, Miami Beach, tel: 672-8338. Light and tasty Hong Kong and Szechuan specialties with great egg rolls. $

**Chez Moy**, 1 N.W. 54th St, Little Haiti, tel: 756-7540. Classic Haitian cooking in a family atmosphere. $

**Cisco's Cafe**, 5911 N.W. 36th St, Miami Beach, tel: 871-2764. Buttery guacamole, burritos, chimichangas, and fajitas amid roaring fireplaces. $

**Fudrrucker's**, 3444 Main Highway, Coconut Grove, tel:442-8164. Informal atmosphere overlooking a lively street, huge make-it-yourself hamburgers and real french fries. $

**Islands**, 2345 Douglas Rd, Coral Gables, tel: 444-0344. Spicy West Indian cuisine with tasty curried goat. $

**La Esquina de Tejas**, 101 S.W. 12th Ave, Little Havana, tel: 545-5341. Casual, noisy atmosphere with inexpensive home-style Cuban cooking. $

**Lulu's**, 1033 Washington Ave, Miami Beach, tel: 532-6147. A funky neighborhood hole-in-the-wall with chicken fried steak and mashed potatoes smothered in gravy. $

**The Palace**, 1200 Ocean Dr., Miami Beach, tel: 531-9077. Soups, salads, sandwiches, and general light and healthy fare. $

**Puerto Sagua**, 700 Collins Ave, Miami Beach, tel: 673-1115. Large and loud but comfortable and good. Abundant choices of Cuban dishes served in enormous portions. $

**Joe's Seafood**, 400 N.W. North River Dr., Little Havana, tel: 374-5637. Friendly fish-house on the Miami River with several resident cats. Fresh fish can be chosen from the ice and prepared to order. $

**Granny Feelgood's**, 48 East Flagler St, downtown Miami, tel: 358-6233. Homemade vegetarian and natural foods. $

**Hy-Vong**, 3458 S.W. 8th St, Little Havana, tel: 446-3674. A small and often crowded spot, but well worth the wait for authentic Vietnamese specialties. $

**Unicorn Village**, 3565 N.E. 207th St N. Miami Beach, tel: 983-8829. A sprawling, waterfront eatery with gourmet vegetarian specialties. $

**Vakhos**, 1915 Ponce de Leon Blvd, Coral Gables, tel: 444-8444. Enormous helpings of salads, souvlaki, and stuffed eggplant in a Greek family environment. $

**World Resources**, 719 Lincoln Rd, Miami Beach, tel: 534-9095. A combination Thai restaurant and funky art gallery with excellent pad Thai. $

---

## Moderate

**Caffe Abbracci**, 318 Aragon Ave, Coral Gables, tel: 441-0700. Features refined Italian specialties such as snails and polenta, marinated veal chops, and Campari sorbet. $$

**Cafe Kolibri**, 6901 Red Rd, South Miami, tel: 665-2421. Mediterranean, Middle Eastern and vegetarian specialties amid a sleek setting. $$

**Chart House**, 51 Chart House Dr., Coconut Grove, tel: 856-9741. Friendly service in an elegant marina setting with great grilled seafood and an enormous salad bar. $$

**Christine Lee's**, 18401 Collins Ave, Miami Beach, tel: 931-7700. Delicious Canton, Szechwan and Mandarin dishes. $$

**Darbar**, 276 Alhambra Circle, Coral Gables, tel: 448-9691. Authentic Indian specialties – lamb and basmati rice, stewed lentils, and hot currys. $$

**El Inka**, 1756 S.W. 8th St, Little Havana, tel: 854-0243. Peruvian cuisine with four kinds of ceviche, marinated beef hearts and fried sea bass. $$

**Embers**, 1661 Meridian Ave, Miami Beach, tel: 538-0997. A 1940s eatery recently revived with New American cuisine and some old-fashioned classics. $$

**Il Tulipano**, 11052 Biscayne Blvd, N. Miami Beach, tel: 893-4811. A virtual pasta paradise with an extensive wine list. $$

**John Martin's**, 253 Miracle Mile, Coral Gables, tel: 445-3777. An old-fashioned Irish emporium with steaks, stews, and poached salmon. $$

**Las Puertas**, 148 Giralda Ave, Coral Gables, tel: 442-0708. Mexican cuisine as art – enchiladas with scallops and duck fajitas, all done in nouvelle style. $$

**Los Ranchos**, 401 Biscayne Blvd, downtown Miami, tel: 375-0666. Tender, juicy steaks served with a variety of garlic and pepper sauces. $$

**Mandarin Garden**, 3268 Grand Ave, Coconut Grove, tel: 446-9999. A neighborhood favorite for years with spicy sesame chicken, hot and sour soup, and gingery dumplings. $$

**Nimo Restaurant**, 100 Collins Ave, Miami Beach, tel: 532-4550. A splashy and ornate place with first rate nouvelle cuisine such as salmon wrapped around alfalfa sprouts. $$

**Norma's on the Beach**, 646 Lincoln Rd, Miami Beach, tel: 532-2809. Fine Caribbean cuisine with a French flair in a Jamaican setting. $$

**Oggi Cafe**, 1740 79th Street Causeway, Miami Beach, tel: 866-1238. Gourmet fetuccine, tortelloni, ravioli and every pasta dish imaginable. $$

**Rincon Argentino**, 3650 Coral Way, Miami, tel: 444-2494. Argentinian and Uruguayan specialties – parrillada, chorise steak, and ensalada rusa. $$

**Sakura**, 440 S. Dixie Highway, Coral Gables, tel: 665-7020. Friendly sushi bar with great Japanese entrees. $$

**Thai Orchid**, 9565 S.W. 72nd St, Miami, tel: 279-8583. Excellent Thai and vegetarian cuisine in a room full of fresh orchids. $$

**Tony's New Tokyo Cuisine**, 1208 Washington Ave, Miami Beach, tel: 673-9368. A fashion conscious setting with excellent teriyaki beef, sushi, and miso soup. $$

**Rusty Pellican**, 3201 Rickenbacker Causeway, Key Biscayne, tel: 361-3818. Good Florida seafood with one of the most beautiful waterfront views in town. $$

---

## Expensive

**A Manno**, 1440 Ocean Dr., Miami Beach, tel: 531-6266. The state of California comes to the city of Miami with citrus cured salmon, honey marinated tuna, and mango mousse. $$$

**Chef Allen's**, 19088 N.E. 29th Ave, N. Miami, tel: 935-2900. An award-winning New World eatery with such innovative creations as Caribbean antipasto, jerk calamari, and swordfish sprinkled with sun-dried fruit. $$$

**The Forge**, 432 41st St, Miami Beach, tel: 538-8533. Grand and a bit gaudy, but a local institution with five-pound lobsters and succulent steaks. $$$

**Mark's Place**, 2286 N.E. 123rd St, N. Miami, tel: 893-6888. Considered one of the finest restaurants in the US, this upscale spot has put Miami on the food map with its grilled rabbit, pheasant with truffles and gourmet desserts. $$$

**Dominique's**, 5225 Collins Ave, Miami Beach, tel: 865-6500. Elegant fine dining with a few rarities like grilled rattlesnake, alligator, and braised oxtail. $$$

**Grand Cafe**, 2669 Bayshore Dr., Coconut Grove, tel: 858-9600. Classic French cuisine with a tropical flair – soft-shell crabs over buckwheat linguini and foie gras with ginger. $$$

**Charade**, 2900 Ponce de Leon Blvd, Coral Gables, tel: 448-6077. A combination Swiss/French eatery with romantic piano music and an Old World look. $$$

**Christy's**, 3101 Ponce de Leon Blvd, Coral Gables, tel: 446-1400. American classics with an emphasis on massive cuts of beef and an upwardly mobile clientele. $$$

**La Bussola**, 270 Giralda Ave, Coral Gables, tel: 445-8783. Formal and well-polished with fine Northern Italian cuisine. $$$

**Le Pavillon**, 100 Chopin Plaza, downtown Miami, tel: 577-1000. Dark green marble and lots of elegant leather sofas with classic Americana cuisine. $$$

**Norman's**, 21 Almeria Ave, Coral Gables, tel: 446-6767. Award-winning chef and cookbook author Norman Van Aiken showcases his exquisite New World cuisine. $$$

**Pacific Time**, 915 Lincoln Rd, Miami Beach, tel: 534-5979. Elegant, Pacific Rim style with tropical tastes including tempura catfish and Chinese duck with plum sauce. $$$

**Yuca**, 177 Giralda Ave, Coral Gables, tel: 444-4448. Trendy, new wave Cuban cooking with guava-basted ribs, coconut-curry rice, and plantains stuffed with beef. $$$

---

## Drinking Notes

Miami has a rum-soaked, good-time reputation that is in fact warranted. Bars and clubs are scattered throughout the area. The legal drinking age is 21, and identification is required if there are any doubts. Alcoholic beverages, including beer, cannot be sold before 1pm on Sundays in some areas. Closing time for bars varies between midnight and 6am.

# Attractions

## Greater Miami

Those tiring of Miami's sun, sea and lush natural scenery can take trips to the area's points of interest.

**Ancient Spanish Monastery**, 16711 W. Dixie Hwy, N. Miami Beach, tel: 945-1461. First erected in Segovia, Spain, in the year 1141, the monastery was moved to America and reassembled in Miami in 1954. Open: Monday–Saturday 10am–5pm, Sunday noon–5pm.

**The Barnacle**, 3485 Main Hwy, Coconut Grove, tel: 448-9445. This rustic residence of Miami pioneer Commodore Ralph Munroe sits undisturbed amid the jungle of high rises and boutiques that is today's Coconut Grove. A walk around the grounds and through the house is one of the few glimpses of the past Miami has to offer. Tours Thursday–Monday at 10.30am, 1pm and 2.30pm.

**Charles Deering Estate**, 16701 S.E. 72nd Ave, Miami, tel: 235-1668. A 360-acre historic bayfront estate turned public park. Open: Saturday and Sunday 9am–5pm.

**Coral Castle**, 28655 S. Dixie Hwy, tel: 248-6344. An eccentric man from Latvia hand-carved this structure out of 1,000 tons of coral as a tribute to his fiancée who jilted him hours before their wedding. Open: daily 9am–9pm.

**Coral Gables House**, 907 Coral Way, tel: 442-6593. This classic coral rock home with a red tile roof is the house that gave the city its name. Open: Sunday and Wednesday 1–4pm.

**Fairchild Tropical Gardens**, 10901 Old Cutler Rd, Coral Gables, tel: 667-1651. The nation's largest tropical botanical garden full of rare and exotic plants. Open: daily 9.30am–4.30pm.

**Joe Robbie Stadium**, 2269 N.W. 199th St, N. Miami, tel: 623-6471. Home of the Miami Dolphins, the stadium offers guided tours for diehard football fans. Opening hours vary depending on games.

**Metrozoo**, 12400 S.W. 152nd St, S. Miami, tel: 251-0403. The largest cageless zoo in the country that features rare Bengal tigers and Australian koala bears. Open: daily 9.30am–5.30pm.

**Miami Seaquarium**, 400 Rickenbacker Cswy, Key Biscayne, tel: 361-5705. Stars are TV's Flipper and Lolita the killer whale. Open: daily 9.30am–6.30pm.

**Miccosukee Indian Village**, 35 miles west of Miami on US 41, tel: 223-8388. Native Indians educate visitors about their heritage and crafts. Open: daily 9am–5.30pm.

**Monkey Jungle**, 14805 S.W. 216th St, Kendall, tel: 235-1611. Monkeys roam free as the humans are caged inside walkways. Open: daily 9.30am–5pm.

**Orchid Jungle**, 26715 S.W. 157th Ave, Homestead, tel: 247-4824. A natural hammock that cultivates extraordinary orchids from around the world. Open: daily 8.30am–5.30pm, closed: Christmas.

**Parrot Jungle**, 11000 S.W. 57 Ave, tel: 666-7834. A garden of tropical flowers and trees where thousands of exotic birds fly free and perform circus-like shows. Open: daily 9.30am–6pm.

**Venetian Pool**, 2701 DeSoto Blvd, Coral Gables, tel: 460-5356. A Venetian-style freshwater lagoon carved out of coral rock with waterfalls and a sandy beach.

**Vizcaya Museum and Gardens**, 3252 S. Miami Ave, Coconut Grove, tel: 250-9133. An Italian Renaissance palace full of European antiques surrounded by formal gardens. Open: Monday–Friday 11am–7.30pm, Saturday and Sunday 10am–4.30pm.

## Surrounding Area

The cities and towns that surround the Greater Miami area have their own eclectic collection of attractions worth visiting.

**Bonnet House**, 900 N. Birch Rd, tel: 563-5393. This whimsical private residence of the Bartlett family sits secluded amid the craziness of Ft Lauderdale's beach. Open: Sunday only May–November. Call in advance for viewing appointment.

**Museum of Art**, 1 E. Las Olas Blvd, tel: 763-6464. A permanent collection of 19th- and 20th-century American and European art. Open: Tuesday 11am–9pm, Wednesday–Saturday 10am–5pm, Sunday noon–5pm.

**Stranahan House**, Las Olas Blvd at the New River Tunnel, tel: 524-4736. Fully restored house built in 1901 by the city's first citizen, Frank Stranahan. Open: Wednesday, Friday and Saturday 10am–4pm.

**Morikami Japanese Park and Museum of Culture**, 4000 Morikami Park Rd, Delray Beach, tel: 407-495-0233. A 180-acre preserve created as a tribute to the Japanese colony that lived here in the early 1900s. Open: Tuesday–Sunday 10am–5pm.

**Henry Flagler Museum**, Coconut Row, Palm Beach, tel: 407-833-6870. Housed in Whitehall, the 1901 mansion of the man who made Palm Beach famous, the museum is a fine example of the opulent Palm Beach lifestyle. Open: Tuesday–Saturday 10am–5pm, Sunday noon–5pm.

**Norton Gallery**, 1451 S. Olive Ave, W. Palm Beach, tel: 407-832-5194. An impressive collection of classic and modern art. Open: Tuesday–Saturday 10am–5pm, Sunday 1–5pm.

## Tours

**All Florida Adventure Tours**, tel: 270-0219. Custom outdoor, nature, city, and historical tours.

**American Sightseeing Tours**, tel: 688-7700. City, Art Deco, cultural, and Everglades tours.

**Deco Tours South Beach**, tel: 531-4465. Art Deco, historic, and cultural tours.

**Art Deco District Tours**, 1224 Ocean Dr., Miami Beach, tel: 672-2014. A walking tour conducted by the Miami Design Preservation League offered on Saturday mornings. It highlights the architecture of this historic district.

**Historical Museum of Southern Florida**, 101 W. Flagler St, tel: 375-1492. With the assistance of historian Paul George, the museum offers walking tours of several Miami neighborhoods. Times vary. Call the museum for information.

**Biscayne Helicopters**, Tamiami Airport, tel: 252-3883. Aerial tours of downtown Miami, Coral Gables and Key Biscayne.

**Tropical Balloons**, 4790 S.W. 72nd Ave, tel: 666-6645. Hot-air balloon tours of the upper Keys and Miami area.

**Island Queen**, 400 S.E. 2nd Ave, tel: 379-5119. This 90-passenger boat departs from the downtown Hyatt Regency Hotel for a tour of Miami's millionaire's row. Daily departures at 10.30am, 1.30pm and 3.30pm.

## Activities for Children

Several of Miami's attractions are ideally suited for children, such as the **Miami Seaquarium**, **Monkey Jungle**, **Metrozoo**, **Miami Museum of Science and Space Transit Planetarium**, and the **Miami Youth Museum**.

Others, such as the **Miami City Ballet**, **New World Symphony** and **Florida Philharmonic Orchestra**, offer special performances geared just for children. And every March the **Dade County Youth Fair** features amusement rides, educational exhibits and concerts for children on fairgrounds a few miles west of the city.

## Culture
### Museums

**Historical Museum of Southern Florida**, 101 W. Flagler St, downtown Miami, tel: 375-1492. Well-organized and colorful exhibits on Florida and Miami history. Open: Monday–Saturday 10am–5pm except Thursday 10am–9pm, Sunday noon–5pm.

**Miami Museum of Science and Space Transit Planetarium**, 3280 S. Miami Ave, Coconut Grove, tel: 854-4247. Over 150 exhibits help visitors explore the mysteries of science. Open: daily 10am–6pm.

**Weeks Air Museum**, 14710 S.W. 128th St, Tamiami Airport, Kendall, tel: 233-5197. A display of aircraft that ranges from the beginning of flight to the end of the World War II era. Open: Wednesday–Sunday 10am–5pm.

**Gold Coast Railroad Museum**, 12400 S.W. 152nd St, Miami, tel: 253-0063. A large collection of old historic railroad cars and memorabilia. Open: Saturday–Sunday 10am–3pm, Monday–Friday 10am–5pm.

**Miami Youth Museum**, 5701 Sunset Dr, tel: 661-2787. Hands-on cultural exhibits for kids. Open: Saturday–Sunday noon–5pm, Monday–Friday 10am–5pm.

**American Police Hall of Fame and Museum**, 3801 Biscayne Blvd, tel: 573-0070. Only in Miami would you find a museum dedicated to authentic police memorabilia – electric chairs, shackles, cuffs and guns galore. Open: daily 10am–5.30pm.

### Art Galleries and Museums

**Center for the Fine Arts**, 101 W. Flagler St, tel: 374-1700. Major exhibits from around the world located on the downtown cultural plaza. Open: Tuesday, Wednesday, Friday and Saturday 10am–5pm.

**Bass Museum of Art**, 2121 Park Ave, Miami Beach, tel: 763-7530. Renaissance, Rococo and Modern art. Open: Tuesday–Saturday 10am–5pm.

**Lowe Art Museum**, 1301 Stanford Dr., University of Miami, Coral Gables, tel: 284-3536. A permanent collection of Renaissance and Baroque art with several visiting collections during the year. Open: Tuesday–Friday noon–5pm, Saturday 10am–5pm, Sunday noon–5pm.

**North Miami Center of Contemporary Art**, 12340 N.E. 8th Ave, N. Miami, tel: 893-6211. Rotating exhibits of contemporary Florida artworks. Open: Monday–Friday 10am–4pm, Saturday 1–4pm.

**South Florida Art Center**, 924 Lincoln Rd, Miami Beach, tel: 674-8278. A center for emerging and established area artists. Hours vary, call for relevant information.

**Bacardi Art Gallery**, 2100 Biscayne Blvd, tel: 573-8511. Works by local and international artists. Hours vary, call for information.

**The Wolfsonian**, 1001 Washington Ave, Miami Beach, tel: 531-6287. An unusually impressive collection of propaganda, decorative, design, and architectural arts from the late 19th and 20th centuries with rotating exhibits. Open: Tuesday–Friday 10am–6pm, Saturday–Sunday 12–6pm.

### Music and Dance

**Florida Philharmonic Orchestra**, 836 Biscayne Blvd, tel: (800) 226-1812. South Florida's major symphony orchestra performs classical music and popular concerts from October–May.

**New World Symphony**, 541 Lincoln Rd, Miami Beach, tel: 673-3330. An advanced training orchestra that presents gifted young musicians performing innovative concerts. October–May.

**Greater Miami Opera**, 1200 Coral Way, Coral Gables, tel: 854-7890. Miami's fine opera company that features artists from around the world. November–May.

**Miami Chamber Symphony**, University of Miami campus, Coral Gables, tel: 662-6600. Chamber orchestra that performs October–May.

**Miami City Ballet Company**, 905 Lincoln Rd, Miami Beach, tel: 532-4880. Under the direction of Ballanchine-trained former dancer Edward Villella, the Miami City Ballet has emerged as a provocative, world-class company. October–May.

**Ballet Flamenco La Rosa**, 1008 Lincoln Rd, Miami Beach, tel: 672-0552. A professional flamenco/ballet troupe.

### Theaters

Ticketmaster is the main ticket outlet in Dade County. For a small service charge, tickets can be purchased with credit cards, telephone 358-5885. For upcoming concert/theater information telephone 372-1442.

There are several small and university-related repertory companies scattered around the area with performance schedules listed in the weekend section of the local newspapers. There is no specific theater district in Miami.

**Coconut Grove Playhouse**, 3500 Main Hwy, Coconut Grove, tel: 442-4000. Live performances in a Spanish Rococo theater built in the 1920s. October–June.

**Dade County Auditorium**, 2901 W. Flagler St, Miami, tel: 545-3395. A 2,500-seat auditorium that hosts the Greater Miami Opera and stages ballet and concert productions.

**Gusman Center for the Performing Arts**, 174 E. Flagler St, downtown Miami, tel: 372-0925. Built in 1926, an ornate palace interior that hosts various theater, dance and concert productions.

**Jackie Gleason Theater of the Performing Arts**, 1700 Washington Ave, Miami Beach, tel: 673-8300. Known locally as TOPA, the theater features major Broadway productions from September–May.

**Minorca Playhouse**, 232 Minorca Ave, Coral Gables, tel: 446-1116. Home to several theater companies including the Florida Shakespeare Festival and the Hispanic Theatre Festival. September–June.

**Colony Theatre**, 1040 Lincoln Rd, Miami Beach, tel: 674-1026. Dance, music and live theater productions in the Art Deco District.

## Cinema

In addition to many large chain theater complexes, there are a few independent movie houses in the area. Generally, afternoon matinees are less expensive than evening shows. Complete time schedules are listed daily in local newspapers.

**Astor Art Cinema**, 4120 Laguna Dr., Coral Gables, tel: 443-6777. Foreign and art films.

**Bakery VII**, 5701 Sunset Rd, S. Miami, tel: 662-4841. First-run films.

**Beaumont**, University of Miami campus, Coral Gables, tel: 663-3446. Foreign/art films for movie buffs.

**Byron-Carlyle**, 500 71st St, Miami Beach, tel: 866-9623. First-run films.

**Cinema 10 at Miracle Center**, 3301 Coral Way, tel: 442-2299. First-run films.

**Cobb's Mayfair**, 3390 Mary St, Coconut Grove, tel: 447-9969.

**CocoWalk**, 3015 Grand Ave, Coconut Grove, tel: 448-6641. First-run films.

**Omni 10**, 1601 Biscayne Blvd, downtown Miami, tel: 358-2304. First-run films.

**Miracle IV**, 280 Miracle Mile, Coral Gables, tel: 443-5201. First-run films.

**AMC Marina 8**, 18741 Biscayne Blvd, N. Miami, tel: 931-2872. First-run films.

## Nightlife
### Nightclubs and Discos

**Amnesia**, 136 Collins Ave, Miami Beach, tel: 531-5535. Over 30,000 sq. ft of marble dance floor with five bars, disc jockeys, and a hip, young crowd.

**Bash**, 655 Washington Ave, Miami Beach, tel: 538-2274. A European dance club with a bohemian flair that attracts models, actors, film-makers, and beautiful on-lookers.

**Baja Beach Club**, 3015 Grand Ave, Coconut Grove, tel: 445-0278. A high-energy disco/bar with wet tee shirt contests and an emphasis on the body beautiful.

**Centro Vasco**, 2235 S.W. 8th St, Little Havana, tel: 643-9606. Classic but cool live Cuban music during the weekend.

**Doc Dammers Saloon**, 180 Aragon Ave, Coral Gables, tel: 441-2600. Sophisticated and elegant piano bar and live jazz.

**1800 Club**, 1800 N. Bayshore Dr., downtown Miami, tel: 372-1093. This is a popular drinking spot for local journalists, lawyers, and urban professionals with an eat-drink-and-be-merry atmosphere.

**Hungry Sailor**, 364 Grand Ave, Coconut Grove, tel: 444-9359. Elbow room only when live reggae bands play on weekends.

**Les Violins**, 1751 Biscayne Blvd, downtown Miami, tel: 371-8668. A plush supper club reminiscent of Havana in the 1950s with glamorous, feather-clad show-girls.

**MoJazz Cafe**, 928 71st St, Miami Beach, tel: 865-2636. Classic and smooth live jazz from Thursday through till Sunday in a casual but sophisticated setting.

**Warsaw Ballroom**, 1450 Collins Ave, Miami Beach, tel: 531-4555. A funky and often wild gay dance club that has become a local institution with occasional amateur strip contests.

## Cabaret

**Les Violins**, 1751 Biscayne Blvd, downtown Miami, tel: 371-8668. Live stage performances full of sequins and feathers.

# Festivals
### General

Annual festivals occur all year round in warm-weather Miami. Specific dates change yearly but months usually remain constant.

#### JANUARY
Orange Bowl Festival, Art Deco Weekend, Taste of the Grove Food and Music Festival, Key Biscayne Art Festival.

#### FEBRUARY
Miami Film Festival, Coconut Grove Arts Festival, Grand Prix of Miami, Miami International Boat Show.

#### MARCH
Carnaval Miami/Calle Ocho Festival, Lipton International Tennis Tournament, Italian Renaissance Festival, Dade County Youth Fair.

#### MAY
Coconut Grove Bed Race, Arabian Knights Festival, Greater Miami Billfish Tournament.

#### JUNE
Miami/Bahamas Goombay Festival.

#### JULY
Everglades Music and Crafts Festival.

#### AUGUST
Miami Reggae Festival

#### SEPTEMBER
Festival Miami

#### OCTOBER
Columbus Day Regatta.

#### NOVEMBER
Miami Book Fair, South Miami Art Fair, Banyan Arts and Crafts Fair.

#### DECEMBER
King Mango Strut Festival, King Orange Jamboree Parade.

# Shopping

## Shopping Areas

There are several shopping areas in Greater Miami that range from exclusive indoor malls specializing in designer clothing to outdoor, waterfront marketplaces. Most are open seven days a week and offer as much entertainment as they do things to buy. Many South Americans make regular trips to Miami just to shop.

**Bakery Center**, 5715 Sunset Dr., South Miami, tel: 662-4155. A modernistic shopping mall on Sunset Drive in South Miami which itself is full of boutiques and art galleries.

**Bal Harbour Shops**, 9700 Collins Ave, Bal Harbour, tel: 866-0311. Elegant shopping with designer shops in abundance.

**Bayside Marketplace**, 401 Biscayne Blvd, tel: 577-3344. A festive waterfront arcade designed after the historic Quincy Market in Boston. Dozens of restaurants and shops, boat rides and live entertainment.

**Cauley Square**, 22400 Old Dixie Hwy, tel: 258-3543. South of Kendall, this hodgepodge creation is full of authentic antique and craft shops.

**CocoWalk**, 3015 Grand Ave, Coconut Grove, tel: 444-0777. Major retailers along with specialty boutiques and outdoor cafes.

**Dadeland Mall**, 7535 Kendall Dr, tel: 665-6226. A homogenized American shopping mall with large chain stores like Saks Fifth Avenue and Lord & Taylor.

**Downtown Miami**, the neighborhood of Flagler Street and South Miami Avenue bustles with shopping traffic Monday through Saturday. It is the area to find the best buys on electron-ics and jewelry with lots of haggling done in Spanish.

**Española Way**, an east/west street in South Miami Beach between 14th and 15th Streets, Española is a colorful few blocks of vintage clothing stores and unusual antique shops.

**The Falls**, 8888 S.W. 136th St, tel: 255-4570. An upscale shopping center built around beautiful (manmade) waterfalls.

**Mayfair Shops in the Grove**, 3390 Mary St, tel: 448-1700. An architectural beauty with plenty of high-fashion Gucci in the heart of Coconut Grove which itself is full of fun shops.

**Miami Design District**, N.W. 36th to 41st Streets between N.E. 2nd Ave and N. Miami Ave. Eighty five show-rooms that cater to interior decorators.

Large purchases can usually be shipped home on major airlines with a small, additional shipping fee. Should any problems arise in purchasing or shipping, contact the Greater Miami Chamber of Commerce, 1601 Biscayne Blvd, tel: 539-3063; or the Dade County Consumer Services Department, 140 W. Flagler St, tel: 375-1250.

## Clothing Sizes

| Men | | Women | |
|-----|-----|-------|-----|
| **Suits** | | **Suits/Dresses** | |
| US | Metric | US | Metric |
| 34 | 44 | 8 | 36 |
| 36 | 46 | 10 | 38 |
| 38 | 48 | 12 | 40 |
| 40 | 50 | 14 | 42 |
| 42 | 52 | 16 | 44 |

| **Shirts** | | **Blouses/Sweaters** | |
|-----|-----|-------|-----|
| US | Metric | US | Metric |
| 14 | 36 | 32 | 40 |
| 14.5 | 37 | 34 | 42 |
| 15 | 38 | 36 | 44 |
| 15.5 | 39 | 38 | 46 |
| 16 | 40 | 40 | 48 |
| 16.5 | 41 | 42 | 50 |

| **Shoes** | | **Shoes** | |
|-----|-----|-------|-----|
| US | Metric | US | Metric |
| 7 | 39 | 5 | 35 |
| 7.5 | 40 | 5.5 | 35 |
| 8 | 41 | 6 | 36 |
| 8.5 | 42 | 6.5 | 37 |
| 9 | 43 | 7 | 38 |
| 9.5 | 43 | 7.5 | 38 |
| 10 | 44 | 8 | 39 |
| 10.5 | 44 | 8.5 | 39 |

# Sports & Leisure

## Participant Sports

With year-round perfect weather, Miami is definitely an outdoor sports city. Among the choices many are:

### Tennis

Besides the hundreds of courts located at area hotels and homes, Greater Miami has over 25 public tennis parks listed in the directory. Or call the Metro-Dade County Parks and Recreation Dept, tel: 579-2676. Most public courts charge non-residents an hourly fee. For general information, call the Florida Tennis Association, tel: 652-2866.

#### PUBLIC TENNIS COURTS

**Flamingo Tennis**, 1000 12th St, Miami Beach, tel: 673-7761.

**Haulover**, 10800 Collins Ave, Miami Beach, tel: 940-6719.

**Henderson**, 911 N.W. 2nd St, Miami, tel: 325-8359.

**Judge Arthur Snyder Center**, 16851 W. Dixie Hwy, N. Miami Beach, tel: 948-2947.

**Kirk Munroe**, 3101 Florida Ave, Coconut Grove, tel: 442-0381.

**Miami Shores Tennis Center**, 9617 Park Dr, Miami Shores, tel: 758-8122.

**Salvadore Park Tennis Center**, 1120 Andalusia Ave, Coral Gables, tel: 442-6562.

**Sans Souci Tennis Center**, 1795 Sans Souci Blvd, N. Miami, tel: 893-7130.

### Golf

Since early Miami was designed to woo tourists from the northeast, golf courses in the area are abundant. Both 9 and 18-hole courses are open all year round. Green fees range from $8 to $40 and reservations are suggested at most. For general information on public courses call Metro-Dade County Parks and Recreation Dept, tel: 579-2968.

## GOLF COURSES

**Bayshore Golf Course**, 2301 Alton Rd, Miami Beach, tel: 673-7705.
**Briar Bay Golf Club**, 9373 S.W. 134th St, tel: 235-6667.
**Country Club of Miami**, 6801 N.W. 104th St, Hialea, tel: 821-0111.
**Doral Park Silver**, 4825 N.W. 104th Ave, tel: 594-0954.
**Fountainebleau Country Club**, 9603 Fountainebleau Blvd, tel: 221-5181.
**Granada Gold Course**, 2001 Granada Blvd, Coral Gables, tel: 442-6484.
**Greynolds Park Golf Course**, 17530 W. Doxoe Hwy, tel: 949-1741.
**Haulover**, 10800 Collins Ave, Miami Beach, tel: 940-6719.
**Key Biscayne Golf Course**, 6700 Crandon Blvd, Key Biscayne, tel: 361-9129.
**Miami Springs Golf Club**, 650 Curtiss Pkwy, Miami Springs, tel: 888-2377.
**Normandy Shores Golf Course**, 2401 Biarritz Dr., Miami Beach, tel: 673-7712.
**Par Three Course**, 2795 Prairie Ave, Miami Beach, tel: 673-7112.
**Palmetto**, 9300 Coral Reef Dr., Miami, tel: 238-2922.

## Bicycling

There are about 100 miles of flat, paved bicycle paths throughout Dade County with dozens of bicycle rental shops listed in the telephone directory. For information call the Bicycle/Pedestrian Program of Dade County, tel: 375-4507.

## Windsurfing

Calm waters and constant breezes make this a Miami favorite. Matheson Hammock Park offers rentals and quiet waters for lessons. Several rental shops are located along the Rickenbacker Causeway heading over to Key Biscayne, including **Sailboards Miami**, tel: 361-7245.

## Scuba Diving

The Miami area offers a generous range of diving sites on both natural and artificial reefs. The Metro-Dade County Artificial Reef Program, established in 1981, has constructed over 15 artificial reefs off Miami's coasts that have increased the habitat available for native marine life. For information on the program, contact the Department of Environmental Resources, tel: 375-3376.

For information on **scuba lessons** or **rental of equipment** contact:
**Miami Aqualung**, 8410 Flagler St, Miami, tel: 225-3483.
**The Diving Locker**, 223 Sunny Isles Blvd, N. Miami, tel: 947-6025.
**Underwater Unlimited**, 4633 Le Jeune Rd, Coral Gables, tel: 445-7837.

## Boating

Officials say there are over 40,000 registered boats in the Miami area, many of which can be rented. From one-paddle canoes to crew-equipped yachts with every possible sailboat configuration in between, Miami can provide a rental to suit everyone's needs. Facilities are available at:
**Action Bay Boat Rentals**, 100 Sunny Isles Blvd, N. Miami, tel: 945-2628.
**Adventurers Yacht and Sailing Club**, 2480 S. Bayshore Dr., Coconut Grove, tel: 854-3330.
**American Bahamas Charters**, 3265 Virginia St, Coconut Grove, tel: 443-8310.
**Beach Boat Rentals**, 2380 Collins Ave, Miami Beach, tel: 534-4307.
**Cigarette Power Boat Charters**, 555 N.E. 15th St, Miami, tel: 373-7723.
**Club Nautico**, 2560 S. Bayshore Dr., Coconut Grove, tel: 858-6258.
**Delta Boat Rentals**, 4441 Collins Ave, Miami Beach, tel: 532-2006.
**Easy Sailing**, 3360 Pan America Dr., Coconut Grove, tel: 858-4001.

## Fishing

From bridges, boats, piers and the surf, fishing is a common diversion in Miami. While not as good as it was 20 years ago, deep-sea fishing is, nevertheless, still big business in the area. Boats are available from the MacArthur Causeway, Haulover Marina, Watson Island, Bayside Marketplace, Collins Avenue on Miami Beach and many area marinas.

Most provide bait, tackle and someone to remove your catch from the hook. The boats are available for half or full-day trips. Common catches include pompano, snapper, grouper and an occasional shark. Bring a sun hat. Freshwater fishing is available in the Everglades, but a license is required.

## FISHING PIERS

**Haulover Pier**, 10501 Collins Ave, N. Miami Beach. Open: 24 hours. Entrance fee. Tel: 947-6767.

**Holiday Inn-Newport Beach Pier**, 16701 Collins Ave, N. Miami Beach. Open: 24 hours. Entrance fee. Tel: 949-1300.
**Sunshine Pier**, Government Cut, Miami Beach. Open: 24 hours. Free.

## DEEP-SEA FISHING

**Abracadabra Charters**, 4000 Crandon Park Blvd, Key Biscayne, tel: 361-5625.
**Blue Sea II**, 1020 MacArthur Causeway, Miami Beach, tel: 358-3416.
**Good Time IV**, 10800 Collins Ave, Haulover Marina, tel: 945-0281.
**Reel Time Sport Fishing**, 2560 S. Bayshore Dr., Coconut Grove, tel: 856-5605.

## Swimming

Although many hotels in Miami have their own swimming pools and most people prefer the ocean anyway, there are several olympic-size public pools throughout the area for those who worry about sharks. Entrance fees vary, but hours are usually from 9am to 6pm. Swimming lessons and exercise classes are often available.

## SWIMMING POOLS

**Flamingo Park Pool**, 1200 Jefferson Ave, Miami Beach, tel: 673-7750.
**Jose Marti Pool**, 351 S.W. 4th St, Little Havana, tel: 575-5265.
**Miami Shores Pool**, 10000 Biscayne Blvd, Miami Shores, tel: 758-8105.
**Normandy Isle Park Pool**, 7030 Trouville Esplanade, Miami Beach, tel: 993-2021.
**Venetian Pool**, 2701 DeSoto Blvd, Coral Gables, tel: 460-5356.

## BEACHES

In Miami they say life is a beach. All public beaches have lifeguards on duty during daylight hours. They are also free of entrance fees but most charge parking fees for vehicles.
**Bill Baggs/Cape Florida**, 1200 S. Crandon Blvd, Key Biscayne, tel: 361-5811.
**Crandon Park**, 4000 Crandon Park Blvd, Key Biscayne, tel: 361-5421.
**46th Street Beach**, 42nd to 59th St, Miami Beach.
**Haulover Beach Park**, 10800 Collins Ave, Miami Beach, tel: 947-3525.
**Lummus Park Beach**, 6th to 14th Street, Miami Beach.

### Jet- and Water-Skiing

Although restricted to certain areas in the Miami vicinity, both jet-skiing and water-skiing are year-round sports. For information on rental of equipment contact:
**Greater Miami Water Ski Club**, 1800 N.W. 94th Ave, Miami, tel: 592-9130.
**Tony's Jet Ski Rentals**, 3501 Rickenbacker Cswy, Key Biscayne, tel: 361-8280.
**Club Nautico**, 3621 Crandon Blvd, Key Biscayne, tel: 361-9217.

## Spectator Sports
### Football

The Miami Dolphins play home games at the Joe Robbie Stadium in north Dade County at 2269 N.W. 199th St. On game days public transportation is available. For ticket information telephone 620-2578. For information on transportation, tel: 638-6700.

The University of Miami Hurricanes play their home games at the Orange Bowl, 1501 N.W. 3rd St. For information, tel: 284-2655.

### Basketball

The Miami Heat is Miami's national Basketball Association team. Home game season usually runs November–May. Games are played at the Miami Arena, 721 N.W. 1st Ave. For information, tel: 530-4400 or 577-4328.

### Soccer

Miami Freedom is Miami's team in the American Soccer League. Their season runs from April–August and matches are usually played at Milander Stadium in Hialeah. For details, tel: 858-7477.

### Jai-Alai

Originating in the Basque region of Spain, Jai-Alai is considered the world's fastest game as players try to catch the *pelotas* (Jai-Alai balls) that can travel at 170 mph. Games are played in a court called a *fronton*. The Miami Jai-Alai Fronton is located at 3500 N.W. 37th Ave and its season runs November–September. For information, tel: 633-6400.

### Cricket

Over 25 teams belong to the South Florida Cricket Association which plays on Sunday mornings at various parks

in the Miami area. Most players are from the Commonwealth Caribbean. Game times and places are listed in the Friday sports section of the *Miami Herald*. For information, tel: 620-0275.

### Horse Racing

Florida's largest thoroughbred race track is Miami's Calder Race Course. Since the track is glass-enclosed and air-conditioned, Calder offers both a winter and summer season but months vary each year, so check in advance. It is located at 21001 N.W. 27th Ave, N. Miami Beach. For information, tel: 625-1311.

Hialeah Park is Florida's most beautiful race track with a racing season that runs from March to May. It is located at 2100 E. 4th Ave, Hialeah. For information, tel: 885-8000.

### Dog Racing

Along with the horses, Miamians love to go to the dogs and watch greyhounds chase a mechanical rabbit to the finish line. Biscayne Kennel Club is located at 320 N.W. 115th St, Miami Shores. For season information telephone 754-3484. Flagler Greyhound Track is at 401 N.W. 38th Ct, tel: 649-3000.

### Auto Racing

The Miami Grand Prix, held around the end of February, is when the city of Homestead is transformed into a noisy, European raceway. For information, tel: 230-5200.

## Armchair Travel
### Movies

The following movies were either set in or filmed in Miami:
**Absence of Malice**
**Deep Throat**
**Drop Zone**
**The Mean Season**
**Miami Rhapsody**
**The Perez Family**
**Scarface**
**The Specialist**
**True Lies**
**Up Close**
**Personal**

# Further Reading
## General

*Miami – City of the Future* by T. D. Allman (Atlantic Monthly Press 1987).
*Deco Delights* by Barbara Baer Capitman (E.P. Dutton 1988).
*Tropical Deco: The Architecture and Design of Old Miami Beach* by Laura Cerwinske (Rizzoli 1981).
*Historical Sketches and Sidelights of Miami, Florida* by Isidor Cohen (Harvard University Press 1905).
*Season of Innocence* by Deborah A. Coulombe and Herbert L. Hiller (Pickering Press 1988).
*Miami* by Joan Didion (Simon and Schuster 1987).
*The Everglades: River of Grass* by Marjory Stoneman Douglas (Pickering Press, 1990).
*The Lives of Vizcaya* by Kathryn Chapman Harwood (Banyon Books 1985).
*From Wilderness to Metropolis* by Historical Preservation Division of Metropolitan Dade County (Franklin Press 1985).
*Mostly Sunny Days*, edited by Bob Kearney (Miami Herald Pub. 1986).
*Miami: The Capital of Latin America* by Barry B. Levine (Wilson Quarterly, Winter 1985).
*Miami, USA* by Helen Muir (Pickering Press 1990).
*The Commodore's Story* by Ralph M. Munroe and Vincent Gilpen (Ives Washburn 1930).
*Miami – The Magic City* by Arva Moore Parks (Continental Heritage Press, 1981).
*Lemon City* by Thelma Peters (Banyon Books 1976).
*Billion Dollar Sandbar* by Polly Redford (Dutton 1970).
*Going to Miami* by David Reiff (Little, Brown 1987).
*Up for Grabs* by John Rothchild (Viking 1985).
*Eat at Joe's, The Joe's Stone Crab Restaurant Cookbook* by Jo Ann Bass and Richard Sax (Clarkson Potter 1993).
*The Perez Family* by Christine Bell (Norton 1980).
*Miami* by Pat Booth (Crown 1992).
*The Corpse had a Familiar Face* by

Edna Buchanan (Random House 1987).

*Miami, it's Murder* by Edna Buchanan (Random House 1994).

*Miami Purity* by Vicki Hendricks (Alfred A. Knopf 1995).

*Double Whammy* by Carl Hiaasen (Putnam 1987).

*Tourist Season* by Carl Hiaasen (Putnam 1986).

*Miami Beach: A History* by Howard Kleinberg (Centennial Press 1994).

*Frost in Florida* by Helen Muir (Valiant Press 1995).

*Miami: In Our Own Words* (Miami Herald Publishing Co. 1995).

*My Love Affair With Miami Beach* by Richard Nagler (Simon & Schuster 1991).

*A Guide to the Architecture of Miami Beach* by Arlene R. Olson (Dade Heritage Trust 1978).

*Miami Spice* by Steve Raichlen (Workman 1993).

*The Exile: Cuba in the Heart of Miami* by David Reiff (Simon & Schuster 1993).

*Raw Deal* by Les Standiford (HarperCollins 1994)

*South Beach* by Bill Wissler (Arcade, 1995).

## Other Insight Guides

The 190 books in the *Insight Guides* series cover every continent and include 40 titles devoted to the United States, from Alaska to Florida, from Seattle to New Orleans. Destinations in this particular region include:

*Insight Guide: Florida.* An expert team of local writers and photographers combine incisive text and vivid photojournalism to seek out all the information and spectacular scenery contained in America's Sunshine State.

*Insight Guide: Bermuda* shows the essence of this complex culture, part-British, part-American, while at the same time sophisticated and sporty.

## Other Insight Titles

*Insight Guides* have two newer series for visitors in a hurry. *Insight Pocket Guides* act as a "substitute host" to a destination and present a selection of full-day, morning or afternoon itineraries. They also include a large, fold-out map. *Insight Compact Guides* are miniature travel encyclopedias, carry-along guidebooks for on-the-spot reference.

*Insight Pocket Guide: Miami.* A local host introduces you to the sights, sounds and sensuous charm of cosmopolitan Miami.

*Insight Pocket Guide: Florida.* The perfect guide for short-stay travelers which maps out the state's attractions in a series of easy to follow itineraries.

*Insight Pocket Guide: Florida Keys.* Detailed maps, ravishing photographs and colorful prose highlight all the essential sights of these tropical islands.

*Insight Pocket Guide: Bermuda.* All the charms and comforts contained in this diminutive ocean gem are explored in a series of locally written itineraries that are as elegant as the island itself.

No vacation in America's No.1 sunshine state would be complete without this essential reference guide. *Insight Compact Guide: Florida* is crammed full of facts and figures which explain the history, culture and features of the state in an easy-to-follow style.

# Index

A
B
C
D
E
F
.
H
I
J
a
b
c
d
e
f
g
i
j
k
l